Where in the Hell is Sourdough, Alaska?

Tales of Mischief, Males, and Mayhem

Josef Chmielowski

with a foreword by Evan E. Swensen

PO Box 221974 Anchorage, Alaska 99522-1974

ISBN 1-888125-79-9

Library of Congress Catalog Card Number: 2001087784

Manufactured in the United States of America.

Acknowledgments

I thank the true sourdoughs from Sourdough (all of my family) for providing me with good times, great memories, and interesting experiences to make this book a reality.

I am grateful to Susie Snyder for her patience and support while I struggled with my early writing career; Mike and Linda Snyder for allowing me to use their computer (even when it was inconvenient for them); Allyson Bourke for her insightful comments; Marcy White, Kathleen Carr, Marian Sloan, Richard Krzeczkowski, and Cecilia Chmielowski for editorial comments; Ray Chmielowski, Laura Larson, and Hal Gage (Gage Photographic) for cover art and graphic design; and Jessie Carr for her logistical support and helping me edit and print my original manuscript.

Finally, I am indebted to my editor, Marthy Johnson—who transformed my work into a finished product.

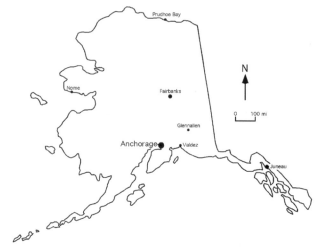

Copper River Basin

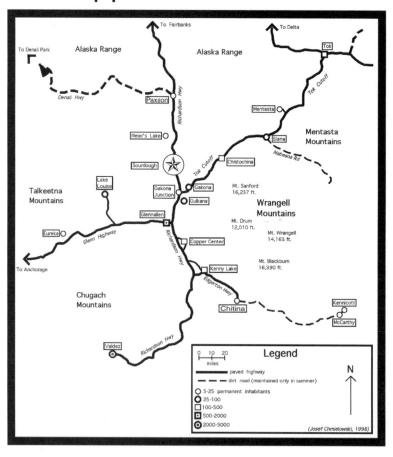

Ode to an Outhouse

Ever go to the outhouse at 50 below?
Try and concentrate, ya still can't go?
Meditate, relax, it's going well,
Thighs are freezing, it's cold as hell!
Finally here, it's on the way,
Don't stop now, you hope and pray.
Hold your breath and clench your teeth,
Your butt cheeks sting, there's no relief.
Almost done, you here it drop,
Hits the mound with a muffled flop.
Roll that tissue, roll and roll,
To return alive, your only goal.
Time is of essence, you must be quick,
If you're not, you'll freeze your...Bic-
Lighter, the only light that's here,
Can't see your zipper, too unclear.
Catch your manhood, it kinda hurts,
"Holy Shit!" out loud you blurt.
Hit the door, and run outside,
You're almost ice, you almost died!
Though it seemed like hours, it's hard to tell;
You endured only 30 seconds in that frozen hell.

Josef Chmielowski
Winter, 1991

Table of Contents

Foreword

Where in the Hell is Sourdough, Alaska? Represents almost any boy's outdoor fantasies and every mother's worst nightmare. Cecilia Chmielowski, Josef's mom, puts Aunt Polly to shame. Her five sons, while growing up on a homestead at Sourdough, Alaska, had the imaginative personality of Tom Sawyer and the disposition for trouble of Huck Finn. Given their preponderance for mischief, it is Alaska's good fortune that these five rapscallions were raised far away from civilization and any "Beckys" in the neighborhood.

No matter where boys grow up, trouble seems to find them. But every time the Chmielowski Clan went looking for it, they found it—even if it meant plaguing each other with their latest pranks.

Yet, the five brothers, you will find as you rollick through these pages, came by their nature naturally. The boys cannot take one hundred percent ownership of all the devious pranks they played, because Mom and Dad Chmielowski were not entirely innocent themselves. In many cases, the antics of their boys were the parent's just rewards.

When I finished reading the last page, I felt like I had just got off a Disneyland ride. I could not sit the book down until it was finished and I was glad it was over—but I wanted more. I wanted the story from Mom and Dad's point of view. I wondered how Cecilia Chmielowski kept her sanity and why she left Philadelphia, what Bubz Chmielowski thought about his homestead and his offspring, and if Josef's big brothers were really the bullies he remembers them being. But mostly, I wondered how in the world did the Chmielowskis survive all those wild Alaska adventures?

Evan E. Swensen

Prologue

There are essentially two reasons why I am writing this collection of short stories. The first, and most important, is so that my brothers and I will never forget the good old days. I want to write down everything I can remember about our childhood so that fifty years from now we can sit around a table and talk about the time we did this and the time we did that. All five of us seem to be plagued with tremendous memory loss and to forget these historical events would be a shame. Furthermore, my ultimate goal is to grow old and BS all day just like Uncle Joe, Uncle Ray, and Dad. The three of them can pick comfortable chairs and tell the same story again and again. Although we have heard all their stories a hundred times, they are always worth hearing again. I wish that I could write down my father's and uncle's childhood stories, but those tales are foggy and forgotten. My childhood will not be forgotten.

The second reason I am writing about my childhood experiences is for my mental health. As I travel this wonderful country, I realize that most people are ignorant of rural living and that they are grossly misinformed about Alaska. I want to write a collection of short stories describing how true Alaskans live. Not how the city slickers in Anchorage and Fairbanks live, or how Natives live, but how true homesteaders live. Wherever I travel, people ask the same questions: "Is it dark all the time? Is it always cold up there? Are you an Eskimo? Do you see polar bears and whales? Are there trees up there? Where in the hell *is* Sourdough, Alaska?" Now, instead of spending hours answering these exasperating questions, I will smile, hand them a copy of my short stories and be on my way.

I am not attempting to write a sensational book about "the last frontier," but instead, chronicle the day-to-day life of a rural Alaskan family. I believe there is more valuable and accurate information contained in the comedy, monotony, and subtle details of our home lives than in any stereotypical Alaskan adventure novel. I have endeavored to write a book based on truth, not fiction or exaggerations. Thus, I have made a conscious effort to record the thoughts of children who grew up in isolation; to edit them would be unfair to the reader, writer, history, and the family.

I am not sorry if the reader is offended. If you do not like the material, put down the book. If you disagree with the ideas and lifestyle portrayed here, travel back in time and visit our home in the woods. I sincerely believe that you will not find a happier family, albeit quite odd, in the past or present.

These stories are all true and have been retold as accurately as possible. Many of them are solely from my point of view, and my brothers and parents may disagree on little details, but this is how they happened. This is the *true* history of a *true* Alaskan family.

To my family: "I never found a companion so companionable as solitude." Henry David Thoreau

1991: The only existing photo of our entire family. Rear, from left to right: Steve, Ray, Mom, Dad, and Jon. Front, from left to right: Karl and Joe.

Family History

My grandfather on my father's side came from Poland when he was young, and my grandfather on my mother's side came from Germany when he was young also. I never met either of them because they both died well before I was born. Likewise, I never had the opportunity to meet my grandmothers. They both died when I was in elementary school and our family did not have enough money to visit them in the Lower 48.

My father was born in 1930 (see timeline, Appendix C) and was officially named Florian Frances Chmielowski. However, as a child he despised this feminine name and therefore most people called him Bubz. He grew up in Mahanoy City, which was a small coal-mining town in northern Pennsylvania. He had seven siblings, from oldest to youngest: John, Emily, Josie, Ed, Joe, (Bubz), Ray, and Lenny. Dad always talked about Mahanoy City and said how nice a town it was to grow up in.

In 1942, when he was twelve, the family moved to Philadelphia. Dad never liked Philadelphia and to make matters worse he attended Ben Franklin High School, which was in the heart of downtown Philly. Here he was one of only a few white students and among many black children felt like "a snowball in a coal bin." He quit high school in the tenth grade.

After working for a year as a storeroom clerk in downtown Philly, my father joined the army in 1947. He became an enlisted soldier whose MOS (military occupational specialty) was forward observation for the field artillery. He went to boot camp at Fort Dix, New Jersey and later in his career was stationed in Hackensack, New Jersey, and Boston, Massachusetts. He was also stationed in Korea toward the tail end of the Korean War (his brothers John and Ed were in World War II and Joe was in the thick of the Korean War).

In 1950 Dad was stationed in Alaska and became interested in the territory (it was not a state yet). Later, he was honorably discharged from the army and in 1960 convinced Joe and Lenny to drive to Alaska from Philadelphia. When the three of them arrived in Alaska and were driving on the Richardson Highway, they pulled over to relieve themselves. While Dad was thus engaged, he noticed a pristine lake with beautiful trees and decided that it was a perfect spot to build a cabin. They built their dream cabin and spent the next couple of years hunting, trapping, fishing, and cutting firewood to survive. While living this harsh subsistence lifestyle, they managed to support themselves and fall 100 percent in love with Alaska.

1946: Dad at sixteen years of age living in downtown Philadelphia. Shortly after this photo was taken he forged his mother's signature and joined the army.

My mother's given name was Cecilia Brenda Niehaus and her story was quite different. She was born in 1939 in Philadelphia and was raised in a relatively well-to-do German household. Like any respectable 1950s German parents, her mother and father were very strict and expected a lot from her. My mom had an older sister, Bobby, who eventually became a nun, and two younger brothers, Eric and Barney. I know little about Mom's early life, except that it bordered on martial law and was miserable.

After graduating from high school, Mom hoped to attend college. However, though she was a top honors student at an all-girl Catholic school, her father said, "No." He did not say no because of personal financial concerns, but instead, he absolutely forbade her to attend college even if she paid for it herself. He firmly believed that "college was no place for girls" and denied an intelligent student the same educational opportunity that he proudly extended to Eric and Barney.

My mom was extremely determined and worked hard to save her money. Upon seeing her noteworthy progress, her father compromised and allowed her to attend night school. Of course, he did not help her financially and after five years of night school and active discouragement by her dad, she quit.

Although Mom was old enough to be on her own, her parents would not let her leave the house until she was legally an adult (at this time in Pennsylvania it was age twenty-one). As a result, they forced her by law to stay home, pay rent, and chip in for food and other expenses. Worse yet, when she attended night school, she received spankings if she brought home B's on her report cards.

1960: After an honorable discharge from the Army, Dad and his two brothers drove from Philadelphia to Alaska and began building a cabin off the Richardson Highway.

Finally, when she managed to save up enough money to buy her dream car, her father forbade the purchase and forced her to buy a different car that better suited his tastes. After growing up in this household and being treated like a child well into her early adulthood, Mom could not wait to leave home. The day she turned twenty-one years old she left the house for good and that was that. Not long after moving out, she remembered having dated (three times) a nice guy named Bubz Chmielowski. She then decided to take a chance and wrote to him in Alaska stating that she wanted to move there and marry him. She did exactly that.

After growing up on the East Coast and spending much of their young lives there, both Mom and Dad had had enough of society. They could not "take that crap" anymore and were forced to go to the farthest ends of the earth to attain happiness. Although life was rough in those early years, they each found what they were looking for, and lived happily ever after (almost).

When Mom arrived in Alaska, she saw the quaint little log cabin that my father and two uncles had built and was thunderstruck with love. She thought that she was going to have a cozy home similar to the original cabin on the lake. She was gravely mistaken though, especially when my Dad explained the situation. "I've peeled enough logs for a thousand years," he said, "so instead of building a log cabin, we'll just build a house out of lumber."

"Not a bad idea," thought Mom, but when she beheld the source of the lumber her heart sank into her stomach.

1959: Mom at age nineteen while living in Philadelphia. This photo proves beyond a shadow of a doubt that she was a sassy city girl who made a bold change in her life by moving to the middle of nowhere, Alaska.

In an old state road commission's gravel pit stood a dilapidated wooden supply shack. It had scrappy black tarpaper covering its gray boards, and boasted four small windows. Upon entering the questionable structure, much to Mom's horror she spied a large hole in the middle of the floor. It was circular in shape, more than two feet around, and had been gnawed out by an unknown but very hungry creature.

"Porcupines," Dad explained nonchalantly. But Dad's explanation fell on deaf ears as Mom stood and cried.

Mom had come from a horrible childhood and a much-disliked society to a far-off land expecting a new and perfect life. However, this was not to be. She simply exchanged confinement for freedom bordering on banishment and traded the evils associated with her father's money for unending labor and poverty. She knew that she could not return to the Lower 48, but she also knew that if she stayed in Alaska, she would never have money or any of the conveniences of a large city. Mom was torn to pieces.

Every last person who has had the honor of meeting my father agrees that he is "honest, sincere, easygoing, good-humored, well tempered, and very loving." Mom must have shared these same viewpoints because she stayed and married Dad. She decided that my father's good qualities outweighed the harshness of Alaska, and that her wildest Alaskan nightmares paled in comparison to the indignities of her childhood in Philadelphia. So Mom remained in Alaska and my parents built a small house out of secondhand lumber—not logs. The house is one mile south of the original cabin.

The construction shack that Mom despised was disassembled one board at a time and reassembled in our yard exactly as it had been in the gravel pit. Every last board was used, and every nail was hammered straight and re-used. Mom and Dad cut down all the trees in the yard by hand and built their house (Mom performed most of the manual labor while pregnant). They scrounged the sides of the road for loose pieces of lumber that occasionally fell off trucks and used these materials for construction as well. Finally, they insulated the house and before long it was finished. Although not remarkable, the house was built with their own hands, and best of all they didn't owe a dime on it (or on the property). Furthermore, it was sturdy and in a rustic sense rather cozy.

In 1963, they had their first child, Steve, and a year later they had Ray. One week after Ray's birth, the 1964 Alaska earthquake hit. According to the United States Geological Survey, its magnitude was 9.2 and it lasted approximately four to five minutes. Anchorage incurred a lot of damage, Valdez and Seward were washed away and much of the state was hit hard. Not Mom and Dad's house, though. It shook and swayed, bent and twisted, rolled and careened, squeaked and squawked, but never gave in. The construction-shack-turned-house braved this cataclysmic event with little effect and came out in better shape than when it started.

After this historic event, in 1968 Mom, Steve and Ray flew to Philadelphia to attend my grandfather's funeral. I'm not sure why my mother went, considering how her father had treated her, but she went. Prior to the funeral, her family had nearly severed communications with her not only because she'd moved to Alaska, but most of all because she married my father, who had no money and was Polish.

After returning from Philadelphia she gave birth to Karl. Being pre-occupied with two young children and a newborn, Mom lost all communication with her family except with her brother Barney who had homesteaded adjacent to our land and was at this time in the army. Unlike Mom's family though, Dad's seemed to follow in his footsteps and in later years his brother Ray, sister Josie, and nephew George moved to Alaska. The Chmielowski Clan spread through the state like a deadly cancer.

In 1972 my parents had a fourth son named Jon, and in 1973 they had their fifth son whose name was Joe. He was an accident. They had always hoped for at least one girl and kept trying unsuccessfully throughout the years. After Jon, they decided that they could only have boys and officially gave up. That is when I came along. I was a surprise to them, and continued to surprise them throughout my entire childhood. I cannot say that I always surprised them in a positive manner, but I can say that I surprised them often.

My parents had everything. They had land on a small lake in the deep wilderness of Alaska, a sturdy home, five strong boys, and a lot of love. What money or material item could be better than this, I cannot say. I am sure that many visitors considered our family to be rednecks, hicks, eight balls or even white trash, but we were happy and that was all that mattered to us.

We had freedom in the woods, could do as we chose, answered to no one, and were surrounded by nature. Dad had successfully fulfilled his idea of an isolated paradise, and Mom found in our family what had always been missing in hers.

Home Life

I was born and raised, along with my four brothers, in the Alaskan bush. I grew up thirty-six miles north of Glennallen (population approximately 900) in the middle of nowhere, or as my Aunt Ruth used to say, "the boonies." Our nearest neighbors to the north, not counting Uncle Joe's cabin, was a family that owned Meier's Lake Lodge about twenty-six miles away. Our nearest neighbors to the south were the Lausens, Sourdough Lodge, Danny Draper, Stan, and the Pedersen family (2, 2^1/$_2$, 3, 7 and 8 miles away respectively).

1999: The original cabin as it appears today. Nearly forty years ago the three brothers made a deal: the last one married got to keep the cabin. That is how the original homestead fell into Uncle Joe's hands.

As far as we were concerned, there was no east or west. What I mean is that there were no roads or civilization in either direction, only miles and miles of forests, swamps, hills, creeks, rivers, and mountains. If I had climbed the tallest tree in our area and looked around in a fifty-mile radius, I would not have seen any houses or signs of mankind, save those already mentioned. My aunt was right, we lived in the boonies.

Glennallen was the town nearest to us and is located in the Copper River Basin (possibly the last unorganized area in the United States; i.e., no town, city, county, or borough governments). It is spread out over more than twenty miles and boasts two restaurants, a few gas stations, a couple of gift shops and a high school. The high school had about ninety students total, some of whom commuted more than sixty miles (my brothers and I commuted thirty-six miles one way).

About twelve miles north of Glennallen, on the Richardson Highway, was a small Native village named Gulkana (see Alaska map).

1999: A view (looking north) of the Richardson Highway in front of our home. A short fifteen-minute walk in this direction leads to Uncle Joe's (the original cabin), while a forty-five-minute walk south leads to Sourdough.

There were no businesses here and only a small collection of modest houses standing next to one another. Finally, about three miles north of Gulkana was Gakona. This town consisted of a post office, the Gakona Lodge, and an elementary school (a two-room school house my brothers and I attended). We lived twenty-three miles north of Gakona.

Everyone who lived near us in these hamlets, and nearly all the people across the state of Alaska, have "normal" houses with all, or nearly all the modern conveniences. However, our house was not modern. We did not have electricity, running water, a telephone, or plumbing. In the wilderness of Alaska, we lived a spartan lifestyle.

I must reiterate the fact that my family and home life were out of the ordinary (save for the Pedersen family) and that most of Alaska is not so outdated. I hope to make it clear to the reader, especially if he or she has never been to Alaska, that in Anchorage, Fairbanks, and most of the other towns (large or small), they have all conveniences found in the Lower 48.

Now then, with the understanding that our house was unusual (even compared to the houses of the Gulkana Native village), I will attempt to describe in some detail our living conditions.

We never owned a telephone and still do not. The telephone lines ended about twenty miles south of our home and started thirty-

1991: The original Sourdough Lodge, built in 1903. During my childhood, the old log buildings were owned and operated by Bud, Ella, and Ray Lausen. Before the lodge burned down in 1994, it was the oldest operating lodge in the state of Alaska. photo by Rollie Ostermick

five miles north of us. For years the nearest telephone was in Gakona, but while I was in high school, Sourdough Lodge purchased a radiophone. They charged customers $1.00 per local call and required the use of a calling card. These high charges resulted from the fact that the lodge had to pay a fee of $300 per month for basic phone service. Not only was the sound quality poor, but the perpetually noisy bar made it very unpleasant to use the phone. Worse than that, sometimes the drunken owner would listen in on customers' conversations from his personal phone in the back. At any rate, Sourdough Lodge (the oldest lodge in operation in Alaska) burned down a few years ago and took its telephone to the grave. So, as in the old days, the nearest telephone is in Gakona.

Those few individuals who wished to communicate with my family had to use a service called "The Caribou Clatters." This was an answering service provided by KCAM, the local AM Christian radio station. Someone would call from a telephone and leave a message on KCAM's answering machine. The person trying to contact us would say who the message was to, and who it was from. Then, KCAM would have a brief ten-minute radio show in the morning, afternoon, and evening during which the announcer read all the messages. One message might have sounded like this: "To Cecilia and Bubz Chmielowski, from Boss Hogg. I am leaving Anchorage on Thursday and will be home for dinner. I'll see you soon. Love, Boss." Many times, those of us who had to rely on this message service would use code names. That way, the locals and especially the gossip-hungry citizens of Glennallen, could not pry into our private business even though our transactions were public. When we received a message, if need be, we would drive twenty-six miles to Gakona and make a return phone call. As a result, we did not enjoy using phones and even grew to dislike them (except when my brothers and I were in high school and we could not call girls).

We had no constant electricity. The power lines ended with the telephone lines and hence we were without juice. However, Dad, being the crafty old sourdough that he was, rigged up an ancient army generator for occasional power. Later on, after the pipeline years, we bought a large new generator. Still later, we replaced this generator with an even newer one. Although these generators provided some electricity, they were used sparingly (about once every other day for three hours) because they required a lot of fuel and maintenance. They were used chiefly for powering the washing machine and for the freezer in the summer. Eventually we acquired a television and Dad would watch the news and one or two other programs at night when the generator was running.

Even with the generator, we had no electric lights (we used kerosene and propane lights), no electric heat (a wood stove), no electric range (a propane stove), no air conditioning (it can get up to 95 degrees in the summer) and no kitchen or bathroom appliances. Because we had no electricity we used an icebox instead of a refrigerator (see Appendix A, icebox, and Appendix B, ice shed). We slid a big ice block into our antique icebox, which kept all our perishables cool throughout the summer. We even used to have a propane freezer. In addition, Mom had a propane dryer, and an old

21

wringer washer that would occasionally grind her hands (and even caught her breast once). Owning a home without electricity really bothered my Mom (as it would most people), but my brothers and I, who never had it—we never missed it.

We had no running water. As a result, we had no plumbing and no indoor bathroom. When we wanted to urinate or whiz, we took a walk down the "pissing path" or into the woods. We then picked a spot that looked interesting and commenced pissing. When we needed to defecate (crap, pinch a loaf, pitch a load, or heave), we went to the dreaded outhouse. This contraption was cold in the winter, and smelled vile in the summer. Thus, the woods and the outhouse were our bathrooms (see property map and sheds, Appendix B).

When we wanted to bathe, we had an old tin bathtub much like that used by cowboys. It was not long enough to stretch out in, had soldered patches near the butt area, and could be filled up only about an inch. The reason it could be filled only an inch is that we had to work very hard to get the water. We would pack the water by hand, heat it up in kettles on the propane stove, and then pour it into the tub. After washing we picked up the tub itself and poured the dirty water into a plastic bucket whose contents we then poured into the woods. It was a lot of work for one pathetic sponge bath and thus we bathed only once per week.

One summer Dad rigged up a shower. I must say, it was unlike any other shower I have ever encountered. He called it the "Polak shower" and it consisted of a rectangular skeletal frame made of scrap wood with no roof or walls. Over the gaping hole where the roof should have been, he hung a black plastic hose, and using the pump from the washer, pumped cold water straight from the lake onto the victim inside. The poor soul who thought he would receive a pleasant shower was instead pelted with shrimp, larvae, assorted bugs and weeds, and doused with ice water. All of these misfortunes befell the innocent person while mosquitoes poured in through the false walls and freely drank of their warm blood. We eagerly chose the tin tub over the shower and hence, Dad's contraption quickly fell into disuse.

When it was time to do dishes or get drinking water, we had to pack it all by hand. In the winter, we chopped an icehole through a foot of ice, strained the water (for bugs and weeds) and carried the water in buckets up a short bank, across our yard and into the house. Although we covered the icehole with Styrofoam and snow when finished with our work (this kept the ice about one inch thick no matter how low the temperature dipped), chopping it open every other day for water was no picnic.

22

In the summer, Dad rigged up a hand pump so that we could pump the water directly from the lake (see things in the yard, Appendix B). He took one end of a hose and attached it to a plastic Clorox bottle in the lake so that it did not sink to the bottom and get clogged by bugs and weeds. Then he took the other end of the plastic hose and attached it to an old, green, cast-iron pump near our porch. When operated, a small stream trickled from the mouth of the pump, passed through a metal screen set on top of our bucket (to filter out any random bugs or vegetation), and finally into the buckets themselves. Then we packed the 5-gallon buckets into the house and filled our water cooler and copper boiler.

The water cooler consisted of a tall, green plastic garbage can set inside a wooden box constructed by Dad. Around the garbage can was a black plastic garbage bag to catch any leaks, ice, or dripping water from the buckets when we emptied them into the cooler. About once a week, when the water was

1991: Dad (age 61) chopping open the icehole to get water for drinking, washing, and bathing.

low and green with algae, we took this old water and put it into the copper boiler. This was an antique copper container with an 18-gallon capacity that sat on top of our wood stove. By this method, we had hot water when we needed it.

To do dishes, Mom took the two kettles of warm water off the wood stove and heated them on the propane stove. She'd pour some hot water from the kettles, and some cold water from the water cooler into our copper-lined sink (see house map and furniture descriptions, Appendix A). Next, she brought all the dishes from outside (which were sitting on a spool table adjacent to the house, and which the animals, birds, and rain had already pre-cleaned), and washed them by hand. Afterwards, she let the dirty water drain into a bucket and Dad or one of us boys would empty it in the forest. This is how our family made do without running water or plumbing.

For heat we had a wood stove. Every year in the summer, Dad and some of us boys would go into the forest and cut down a lot of trees. However, we always cut down the dead ones because they

1974: Karl looks on as I take a bath in our copper-lined kitchen sink.

were lighter, burned better, and did not have to season as long as live, sappy trees. I think that our family did the forest a great service by removing the dead trees, which blocked out light, posed a fire hazard, and contained the destructive spruce bark beetle.

We stacked all our logs in piles in the forest, and in the winter hauled them back on a sled pulled by a snowmachine. Then we stacked them in a monstrous but orderly pile in front of the house. Finally, in the spring and summer we cut them into lengths of two feet and restacked them yet again in smaller piles. These short logs could be fed easily to our wood stove. The stove produced a dry warmth that cannot be duplicated by electric radiators, oil stoves, or any modern heating methods. It gave our house a characteristic smell of smoke and spruce, and warmed us even when temperatures plummeted to fifty-five below.

Our family owned a blue 1967 Chevrolet pickup truck and a tan 1970 Ford Maverick. Both vehicles were incredible eyesores and worked only when the mood struck them. Later on, when I was in high school, Mom bought an eight-year-old Chevette car, which turned out to be even worse than either the truck or the Maverick. All our cars were pieces of crap, held together by duct tape, wire, glue, and any other contraption that Dad could jury-rig. To make a long story short, they were fit only for the dump and not for a family. All the kids in Glen-

Dad standing in front of the porch. Fang's doghouse is visible (left) as is the solid iron wheelbarrow we used to haul wood from the log pile to the house.

nallen, and any average sixteen-year-old living in the Lower 48 owned better cars than the Chmielowski Clan.

Other things were out of the ordinary at our home as well. We vacuumed only once a week or every second week with the electric vacuum. In between cleanings we would "nit-pick," which was a monotonous chore. My brothers and I crawled on our hands and knees and picked up pieces of wood, lint, pebbles, and dirt. Later, we had a nonelectric push vacuum that had a rotating brush and Dad called this device "the jigger-jigger." It was primitive and simply pushed dirt from one side of the house to the other, occasionally picking up some bits of material by luck.

We had nowhere to put our garbage and had to burn all our paper, wood, and plastic in a 55-gallon barrel drum. We then hauled the ashes deep into the forest and discarded them. There was no dumpster, trash pickup, or recycling. Furthermore, we put all our organics in a pile (which we affectionately referred to as "the slop

pile") at the end of the pissing path (see property map in Appendix B). The birds, rabbits, foxes, and dogs would take care of them and our family, as well as nature's creatures, benefited from this symbiotic relationship.

We did not have fresh milk, vegetables, or fruits. For milk, we mixed powdered Milkman with our lake water. The resulting combination tasted nothing like real milk. Worse yet, sometimes shrimp and other bugs would be incorporated into the mix by accident and would disenchant the milk drinker. The first time I ever had real milk was at David Dawson's house and I must have drunk the whole dang gallon. After that, we always referred to store-bought milk as "Dawson milk."

Every day we burned our garbage in the trashbarrel out front of our house. We used the poker (left) to stir the ashes and the iron pan (foreground) to catch old motor oil from our vehicles.

Our family had one salad while I was growing up, and none of the males in the family tried it. We could purchase vegetables only in Glennallen, at high prices and in very poor condition. Occasionally we got apples and oranges, but they were also in sorry shape and never lasted long in our home.

For food we had a lot of moose and caribou. A moose lasted my seven-member family the whole winter and a caribou lasted about half as long. We made steaks, hamburgers, and sausages out of the wild animals. They were "good eatin'" and enabled our family to minimize long trips to Park's Place (Glennallen's only grocery store). Although it was quite a bit further, Mom and Dad would drive all the way into Anchorage (250 miles one way) to stock up on groceries twice a year. This allowed my parents to obtain a variety of food that was not offered in Glennallen, and also to save money by buying in bulk.

We had no neighbors closer than two miles away and hence, no one came over to visit, no one called us, and no one complained about our odd lifestyle. We enjoyed not having any neighbors and choosing to do whatever we damn well pleased. We loved the fact that we could run outside and piss in the front yard, swim naked, and legally fire assault rifles on our lawn. Our family would not have had it any other way (except when the brothers were teenagers and their desire for female companionship knew no bounds).

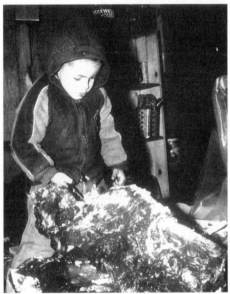

1976: Here I am "helping" cut up a moose. We made steaks, hamburgers, and sausages and one moose would last my seven-member family the whole winter.

Although there are hundreds of other little quirks about our house and family, I cannot detail them all here. As I write more about my childhood and life, they will be brought to light. I wish to reiterate once more that all the things I have described pertain only to the Chmielowski household and are copyrighted by it alone. Most other Alaskans do not live in this manner, but instead, have all or nearly all the modern conveniences of the Lower 48.

Our house is an anomaly and was designed that way specifically by Dad and Mom in order to simplify our lives and avoid the burdens of financial debt. To our family, it did not matter if society frowned on our odd ways because we were not part of society and proud of it. We were individuals who lived our lives simply and did not compare ourselves to "the Joneses."

Living in this remote environment and being such independent individuals, the Chmielowski Clan never heard the beat of the drum. As a matter of fact, if the winds of society had blown just right and we had heard a drum, we undoubtedly would have heard a different drummer.

A view of our home from the bank of the lake. Left to right: the blue truck, porch, kitchen, living room, middle room, and back bedroom (see house map, Appendix A).

Bubz

Dad's real name was Florian Frances Chmie-lowski, but when he was a kid the name was too feminine for his liking. As a result, his family and friends called him Bubzy, which is Polish for "little spook." Apparently he was so skinny and moved so quickly, that he resembled a shadow. That was then, and this is now.

As far back as I can recall, Dad always had a big stomach. His stomach was not a beer belly, a bowlful of jelly, or a deposition of any fatty substance whatsoever. Instead, it was like a great big basketball attached at his midsection. His stomach was as hard as a rock, and as spherical as it was large.

As for the rest of Dad's physical features—he closely resembled Popeye the sailor. His forearms, upper arms, and calves were disproportionately large and muscular, while his thighs were relatively skinny and his butt nonexistent. There was not a single spot on Dad that wiggled or could be considered cellulite.

Dad stood five feet, six inches, had no neck (thanks to his Polish heritage), and did not have a single hair on his entire body. I'm not simply indicating that his head was completely bald, but literally mean that he had no hair on his body. He had no eyebrows, sparse eyelashes, and no arm or leg hair. He lost all his hair in the 1960s after he returned from Korea, and believes that the government was using some sort of chemical over there during the war (all other members of my father's family have a thick head of hair to this day, not to mention an overabundance of leg, arm, and back hair as well).

Due to Dad's complete baldness, short muscular stature, and huge stomach, he struck quite an imposing figure. But instead of being as rough on the inside as he was on the outside, Dad loved the quiet surroundings and peace that nature offered. In fact, he loved the woods so much that he lived as far away from mankind as possible and since moving to Alaska in 1960, has only left the state once. He left Alaska in February of 1996 for the first time in thirty-six years when Steve, Karl, Uncle Joe, and Uncle Ray took him to Las Vegas. This little excursion was quite overwhelming and fully guarantees that he will never set foot outside the state again.

Although Dad wanted nothing to do with cities and people, he did have to occasionally make the dreaded five-hour trip to Anchorage (due to a major catastrophe or emergency). During these monumental excursions, Mom always drove and Dad slept. Although, one time he did offer to drive near Eureka Lodge, but only went about fifteen miles while cussing the whole time. Then his back and neck hurt too badly, and Mom drove the rest of the trip.

1991: Dad takes a short break from winter work by preparing his twelve o'clock lunch.

While heading toward any sort of civilization, no matter how large or small, Dad cussed incessantly and complained about the number of people and how bad he hated "suburbia." It was understandable that Dad loathed going to the city of Anchorage, or that he disliked the farming community of Palmer, but he even despised the small town of Glennallen. "Oh God, I have to go to town this week. That god-forsaken town," he would moan.

Those not accustomed to my father's theatrics would swear that he was driving to the abyss in order to have tea with Satan. Of course, that was not the case, and he was most likely driving to Glennallen to fill oil drums or simply pick up a car part at NAPA. Poor Dad, he hated the "big town of Glennallen" with its horrendous traffic (not one traffic light in the whole town or within a 150-mile radius), and multitudes of people (about 900 total). I really believe that he would have rather had tea with Satan than leave his secure home.

Although Dad did not like towns, cities, or large numbers of people, he was a very likable person. He was easy to talk to, easier to get along with, and always willing to help someone, no matter how badly the situation inconvenienced him. In addition, Dad always smiled, laughed a lot, and made many jokes. Those who occasionally visited our home (usually my friends from school who stayed the night) always thought he was the greatest dad.

Even the Natives down at Gulkana Village liked Dad because he had been up in the country for so long that they considered him to be a Native at heart. Of course, maybe they liked him a lot because he gave a beaver tail (gourmet food for some Natives) to the Gene Clan, and because he gave our old stationwagon to a village Native for next to nothing. Though the car was originally supposed to be sold for $100 and a .22 rifle, the old Native never gave us the rifle. This sour deal didn't bother Dad and he harbored no grudges. As a matter of fact, he let the deal rest because he figured the old guy needed the car and rifle more than our family did.

Dad's heart was big, but his reputation for colorful language was certainly bigger. I can proudly and with confidence say, that I knew of no other man who could turn the air blue with cuss words like Dad. He could shame a plumber, run rings around a trucker, and make a Hells Angel's biker sound like an innocent child.

For instance, on a typical morning when he was cooking punchkies (a Polish breakfast, which consists of deep-fried bread dough) he often spewed forth interesting strings of seldom-used vocabulary words in very creative ways. These peculiar phrases did not indicate that he was necessarily angry, but could have meant any number of things. Perhaps some grease splattered on his arm, or perhaps he dribbled some batter on the counter, or perhaps he was overly excited that a batch turned out particularly well.

You see, Bubz did not cuss just because he was angry. He cussed if a number of things occurred: general excitement, thought, dinner preparation, car mechanicking, snowblowing, roof shoveling, water packing, pretty much any chore, going to town, listening to news on the radio (many sparks here), normal conversation, happiness, or because his mouth was open. Dad knew how to cuss, he loved it, and he meant no harm by it. He never curbed his language for Mom or any of us, and definitely not for any visitors. Cussing was just part of Dad's vocabulary, part of his being, part of his soul, and there was nothing he or anyone could do about it except laugh and enjoy the show.

Thus, although a very happy man, Dad cussed nonstop and everyone accepted his eccentric behavior with good humor. The five of us brothers often joked that if a priest came to visit, Dad would smile sincerely, shake the holy man's hand and exclaim (not in these *exact* words, mind you), "Goshdarn, you old son-of-a-gun, how the heck ya doin'?"

The five brothers and even Mom used to make fun of Dad's cussing and repertoire of odd expressions. He said quite often, "I hear engines," which meant that he thought a visitor was pulling up the driveway. Sometimes we looked up and saw Josie pulling in the drive, but just as often we looked up and didn't see a dang thing. He'd then say, "You don't hear them?"

"Uhhh, not really Dad," we'd reply.

Poor Dad, he was just hard of hearing. In his defense, though, one time he said, "I hear engines. Jon, who's coming?" Jon (who was about nine years old) stood on the couch and looked out the window.

He then said matter-of-factly, "An airplane's comin'."

Dad responded with a good-natured, "You're full of bull. Now who's comin'?"

"An airplane," Jon repeated.

Sure enough, when Dad looked out the window a Cessna airplane was taxiing up our little driveway. It turned out that a female pilot ran out of gas and had to make an emergency landing on the Richardson Highway (technically the longest airstrip in the world because the entire length of the highway is considered an official emergency runway). Dad asked no questions, filled up her tank, gave her coffee and she was on her way.

Oh yeah, Dad also "heard engines" three separate times when we had a fire on our property. If it were not for him "hearing noises," we would have lost all we owned. Perhaps his hearing wasn't so bad after all.

We teased him about his odd expressions and poor hearing, but Dad was never truly angry except the one time when Ray sassed him. In this isolated incident, Dad used a log instead of a wooden spoon to discipline Ray. However, for the most part, Dad was calm and left all the nagging and yelling to Mom.

I think the secret to Dad's inner peace was that every morning he woke up at four-thirty, drank coffee (while stirring it up to a hundred times: clink, clink, clink ...), listened to the staticky radio, and then at 6 a.m. played the "Good morning, good morning, good morning, it's time to rise and shine ..." song at maximum volume. This grating song always woke us up for school and inevitably put us in a foul mood. To top the morning off, as we left the house to catch the schoolbus Dad would say in an angelic voice (he called it his TV father's voice), "Don't forget your books, hats, gloves, coat, lunches, shoes, socks, underwear, jigger-jiggers etcetera ..." He ran through the same list every morning for all five of us boys until the day I graduated from high school in 1991.

When Mom and us boys went to school during the winter months, Dad stayed home and worked (he worked construction only in the summer due to the weather). No one really knows what he did all day, but when we came home and asked, he'd give us his verbal chore list.

"I jigger-jiggered (vacuumed with the nonelectric push vacuum cleaner) today, I washed dishes, I chopped wood, I got water, I burned trash, and I shoveled all of the paths. Don't tell me about a long day."

We never did give Dad any lip about his long day, but on one occasion I got to thinking about his work at home. Granted, the chores he listed sounded like a lot of work, but an able-bodied man should be able to complete them before noon (especially when this able-bodied man got up at four-thirty every day). Which led my four brothers and me to believe that he undoubtedly napped, listened to the radio and relaxed a good deal.

I never played baseball, camped, or hiked with Dad. I never did any of those things that kids on TV always did with their dads. My father was too old for that and was "stove-in" from too much trapping and ditch digging. You see, growing up in the Depression with little food, going into the army, and spending a good chunk of your life hunting and fishing in Alaska does a number on a guy. Dad's back ached, his hip hurt, his knees were out of whack, his shoulders ratcheted like a socket wrench, his neck popped, and his feet sometimes refused to move. Hence, I never shared those Hallmark moments with him.

Instead, Dad sometimes took us fishing (illegally, I might add) down by the pipeline bridge on the Gulkana River. Other times he shot guns with us on the platform by the lake, took us to Sourdough Lodge, or shot fireworks with us in the yard and gravel pit. For the most part, the five of us boys just BS'ed with Dad, and spent quality time with him as we did our daily chores.

My favorite chore was wood-gettin', and I wish I could do it a thousand more times with Dad. From going into the forest and cutting the dead trees, to hauling them in on the snowmachine and stacking them in rows, wood-gettin' was always hard work but fun because Dad was there.

The Grim Reaper

Dad was not only a hermit, but a dang good one. He took his job very seriously and avoided civilization at all costs. He considered going to Anchorage on a par with going straight to hell, and he had similar feelings concerning the small town of Glennallen. Try as he might to avoid these seething pits of humanity, at times it was absolutely necessary that he travel into their depths.

On the occasions when Dad was literally forced to "go to town," he fired up the blue 1967 Chevrolet pickup. Although the gear shift pattern was backwards (thanks to Karl in high school auto shop) and the gas mileage was terrible, Dad considered it far more comfortable to drive in than our tan, rusted-out 1970 Ford Maverick. He often pointed out the fact that the truck had nice bench seats (although squirrels had made a meal of them) and that the car had low bucket seats which hurt his legs, knees, back, neck, and nearly twoscore of his other body parts.

Thus, it was on one of those rare days that Dad had to go to Glennallen and pick up an important item (in this case, a special part to fix the generator), that a great adventure occurred.

Watching Dad mope around the house with a nervous air about him caused Jon and me to feel sorry for him and we offered to ride with him. Dad took us up on the offer and the knowledge that we would be with him on this miserable journey visibly relaxed him. The three of us then hopped in the truck and in a few minutes Dad was intently grinding gears and cussing as we backed out of the driveway.

As usual, he nearly took out a few spruce trees and was only saved by my quick reactions. "Dad! Spruce tree! Get left!" I yelled repeatedly. After several minutes of chaos, Dad safely navigated down our 100-foot, perfectly straight driveway. Then, after lingering in the middle of the Richardson Highway for a few moments, (while he vigorously ground the gears and cussed more), he eventually found the right gear and we were off to the big city of Glennallen.

Dad's desire to reach our destination was reflected in the speed at which we traveled. What I mean is, because Dad disliked traveling to Glennallen (especially when he had to drive himself rather than ride as a passenger), he took his time in order to avoid his ultimate misery. As a result, driving towards town Dad averaged between thirty-five and forty-five miles per hour, but upon leaving, this was not the case at all.

After arriving in town and spending fifteen minutes there successfully conducting our business at NAPA Auto Parts (which is nearly a forty-mile drive, one way), Dad said, "Let's get out of this town! It's making me nervous!"

Without hesitating any longer, the three of us jumped in the truck and headed for home. After leaving the outskirts of town, Dad took full advantage of the wide smooth highway and soon the old blue truck closely resembled a sleek blue rocket. Trees whipped by and so did the miles as we drove at unthinkable speeds.

On one occasion my fears were confirmed when I looked at the speedometer and was horrified to find that he had actually broken the speed limit. The needle was at fifty-eight and climbing. There was no stopping Dad; he was driving like an escaped convict heading to the Mexican border.

As we clipped along at high velocities, I became distinctly aware that I wasn't wearing my safety belt. "Wait, there are no safety belts in this truck," I nervously thought to myself. "Ah, we'll be all right though." I looked at Jon for reassurance. But Jon was looking out the side window and seemed more than a little agitated, which set me even further on edge.

I turned to Dad to say something, but a look of grim determination was etched on his face, and I knew there was no reasoning with the man. Feeling a wave of hopelessness and despair settle over me, I looked out the front window and saw a car in our lane. "Oh God! He's gonna try to pass it!" was all that flashed through my mind (Dad was not good at passing cars because he usually went so slow that everyone passed him).

Sure enough, Dad hesitated a mere three or four minutes before getting up the nerve to pass the slow-moving car. As he punched the accelerator and switched lanes, our speed gradually increased (and I do not use "gradually" frivolously). It seemed like we spent an eternity in the on-coming lane as we crept past and slowly overtook the car in the right lane. Just then, Jon and I looked up and our eyes locked on the horizon. There, in the distance, about a half mile down the long straight stretch approached a truck.

"Dad, there's a truck coming, you might wanna slow down," I calmly suggested. But my plea fell on deaf ears as he pressed the accelerator to the floor. Unfortunately, our speed didn't increase as he pushed on the gas pedal and apparently our blue truck was taxed beyond its limits. However, instead of Dad letting off on the gas and safely pulling behind the slow car, he kept going and soon we were abreast of it.

"I hope we get by soon," I thought as I kept my eye on the approaching vehicle in our lane.

Well, we didn't get by as soon as I would have liked. Everything moved in slow motion as the truck approached us. The car Dad was trying to pass actually speeded up and neither Dad nor the truck slowed down.

"It's a good day to die," I thought to myself as I gazed steadily at the oncoming truck.

Just then, I swear to God I saw the Grim Reaper himself. He had jumped onto our hood and was holding on with a death-like grip. He was slowly clawing his way towards our window, smiling wickedly with the knowledge that the three of us were an easy harvest. Jon and I looked at him and were sweating bullets as he raised his scythe.

At the last possible second, the oncoming truck moved to our left, Dad squeezed in close to the car on our right, and the three vehicles passed one another safely on the two-lane road. The Grim Reaper looked both shocked and disappointed, and immediately leapt off our hood and into the trees in search of other victims.

Jon and I sat ramrod straight and didn't utter a word as Dad completed passing the car. In fact, Jon and I didn't say anything for the next twenty miles. We only shifted silently in our seats trying to relax our anal orifices (which had contracted to such an extent that a stout blacksmith could not have driven a toothpick into them with a heavy hammer).

"Jon, did you see him?" I asked at length.

"Yeah, the Grim Reaper was a-knockin' on the window!"

"Dad, how come you didn't slow down?" I asked.

"'Cause I couldn't! That guy approaching should have!" he replied vehemently.

"No, how come *you* didn't slow down?" Jon repeated.

"'Cause I had to get out of that dang town! It was killin' me, boys!"

Thus, Dad proved to Jon and me that he was indeed the grandfather of all hermits and that he would rather face death himself than the sprawling metropolis of Glennallen, Alaska.

Dad is Home

When construction on the pipeline began in the early 1970s, it made economic sense for my dad to work as a laborer rather than hunt and trap. As a result, when the laborers' union annually hired locals, Dad left home for work. He usually left in late spring or early summer and worked until the weather shut down the construction season (mid-September to October). Dad went anywhere the union sent him to work, but for the most part he stayed in the interior of Alaska (Livengood, Coldfoot, Delta, Glennallen, Paxon, etcetera). He worked long, hard hours during the short work seasons and like other Alaskan laborers, was gone all summer.

1967: Ray shown in front of the Bingedy-Bangedy school bus. Mom, Dad, Steve, and Ray lived in this deluxe dwelling during Dad's summer work seasons in the mid-late 1960s.

Being a laborer meant that Dad traveled to far places, worked hard, and consequently worked up an enormous appetite. His appetite was similar to his fellow laborers' who all ate like horses. Apparently, the State and the pipeline camps fed them very well because they were happy and always managed to retain their large bellies throughout the hectic work season.

The laborers ate dinner at a cafeteria set up by their employer and at the end of the day my Dad would collect all the leftover junk food. He collected the cookies, brownies, fudge, and other extras that would otherwise have been thrown in the garbage. He didn't garner the treats for himself, but instead for his five hungry boys at home.

Dad occasionally came home for a day or two in the summer. On one such occasion, we were going about our daily chores when we looked out of our living room window and saw a yellow state truck pulling up the driveway. An unknown chauffeur was driving while Dad relaxed in the passenger seat. We (Karl, Jon, and I) ran out of the house and yelled, "Dad's home, Dad's home!" Then we waited expectantly to see what he brought us.

Dad reached in the back of the truck and pulled out his duffel bag, which contained all his work clothes, rain gear, and his construction helmet. Then, he leaned down again and pulled out three large black trash bags. The trash bags contained the good stuff and we each grabbed one and ran into the house to open it. The sheer quantity of junk food contained in the bags left us dumbfounded and awestruck. We didn't remain paralyzed for long, and immediately commenced ingesting the sugar-laden treats.

Each bag contained staggering quantities of cookies. There were chocolate chips, peanut butters, and a lot of sugar cookies. Most of the cookies were not whole, but broken into small bits and pieces. Some of the larger chunks were a good find, but they tended to be well-rounded and worn by Dad's long trip.

In general, the brownies fared much better than the cookies because brownies are tough and not apt to disintegrate during jostling truck rides. However, it must be noted that brownies were considered a gamble. On the one hand, they were sometimes soft and delicious. On the other hand, they could be hard as a rock. Regardless of their strength or texture, we ate them quickly and without hesitation.

Fudge was rarer but we considered it by far the best dessert. It tasted good whether it was hard or soft but usually it did not go stale as quickly as the cookies and brownies. The only time I didn't eat fudge is when I found nuts in it. I despised nuts and although my soul cried out for chocolate, I abstained because of my hatred of nuts. Only in desperate cases would I pick out, cut out, or suck out the fudge from in between the nuts.

In addition to cookies, brownies, and fudge, the black bags contained many other types of junk food including weird breads, unidentifiable chunks, assorted candies, firm doughnuts, stale things, soft whatchamacallits, and unsorted crumbs. We ate these food items dead last (in the above order). Nothing was too stale, too mushy, or too odd to discard, and we consumed all the junk food by bedtime.

Although our family dearly missed Dad during the summer months, the knowledge that he loved and thought of us often made his absence bearable. His love for us was expressed in his work and the many sacrifices he made for our family. His frequent thoughts of us were reflected in the bulging trash bags of treasure he always collected for us.

Mother Hubbard

Like most children, I considered my mom eccentric, and as I grew up and met my friends' mothers, I realized that Mom was not only eccentric, but was by far the weirdest mother of them all. It was not her physical features, though; she did not look odd. Instead, she was pleasantly plump, had short, curly, poodle-like hair (characteristic of women who grew up in the '50s), and she smoked. I think what made Mom different from other mothers was the taxing company she kept.

Mom lived secluded in the woods with Dad and the five of us boys with no female companionship. Though she visited other families every now and again (visitors rarely came to our home), she was for the most part locked up with six males for 365 days of the year. As a result of this brutal torture, her feminine powers drained quickly away and were replaced by a very warped sense of humor (perhaps perpetual cabin fever) and stern demeanor.

Without friends to visit or places to go, Mom didn't leave her rocking chair if she could avoid the inconvenience. Ever since she'd bought her rocking chair, it was as if some little fairy had superglued her butt to it. From her rocking chair, Mom read books, watched TV, visited, talked, smoked, and commanded like it was a throne.

I often found Mom engrossed in a book, with her feet curled up beneath her and reading intently. Upon noticing my presence, she'd peer over her reading glasses and fix me with a mesmeric stare. Then with a cigarette dangling in the corner of her mouth (which waved like a wand every time she uttered a syllable), she'd say something to the effect of, "Joe, since you're going outside, take the ground meat to the meat shed."

Always looking for an argument as a child, I would rebut with something like, "But I'm going to the pissing path and that's nowhere near the meat shed!"

"Take it out anyway," would be her final, inevitable, motherly reply.

Which of course prompted me to counter with, "Why?"

Mom, being an old veteran at these games, came back with conviction and finality. "Because."

Her logic usually worked on us as children, but Mom also had to convince Dad to do chores. "Bubz, since you're going outside, take out the dishwater," Mom once commanded.

"But I'm going to the generator shed."

"But this way you'll have to make only one trip instead of two," she answered.

Dad muttered something incomprehensible under his breath as he hauled out the dirty dishwater. I know that Dad was probably thinking the same thing that always ran through my mind, "If Mom spent half the effort doing the chores that she so painstakingly avoided, she would have already been done with them yesterday."

The only thing that Mom hated more than unearthing herself from her rocker, was going outside. Thus, Dad and the children would get assigned a myriad of outside

After the Civil War, photos reveal that stress aged Abe Lincoln well beyond his years. This particular photo demonstrates that a similar calamity befell Mom after doing years of combat with her five energetic sons.

chores without any thought to their locale or how they were to be completed. I think Mom justified her actions and appeased her conscience by using some twisted logic akin to this: "All outside chores occur outside. No matter if they are five feet or one mile from the house, they are still outside. Furthermore, I know that all the men do outside chores, and I know that I will not go outside. Therefore, Dad and the boys should do outside chores regardless of their inconvenience and the distances traveled because these chores are outside."

Sometimes we would try to fight or argue (Dad included), but we inevitably lost against Mom's devious and calculating mind.

"Jon, take the frying pan to the spool table," she once said.

On this particular day Jon was less than happy and replied, "But Mom, I'm going to make popcorn. I'm not even going outside!"

At this point Mom's voice changed to a drill-sergeant-like tone (which was actually quite a common occurrence) and she hollered, "You little so and so, don't disobey me! I brought you into this world, I changed your messy diapers, and now you're my slave. Why do you think I had five children? I had them so I could have a bunch of little slaves!" Of course, she meant this as a joke, but Jon and the rest of us always took her quite seriously and sprang into action no matter how miserable the chore.

Mom called the shots from her rocking chair. If she wasn't yelling like a jail warden, or cussing like a trooper (or any good Chmielowski, for that matter), she was probably stressing or worrying about something beyond her control.

Once, I came in from outside when it was thirty below zero and slammed the door shut to keep the house warm. She then visibly jumped and exclaimed, "Jon ... Karl ... Ray, I mean Joe. You know who I mean. Don't slam the door!" She spoke these words in a quivering, stressed-out, pathetic, old-lady voice and not her usual lion tamer's voice.

Later on, she sat in her rocking chair and didn't say a word for over half the day. She just held her head in her hands. "Mom, what's the matter?" Karl asked.

"Nothing," she replied in that same weak, quavering voice exhibited earlier.

"C'mon, what is it?"

"Ohhhh, it's the Chevette, boys. The dang thing has my stomach in knots! I can't eat, I can't sleep, and I can't stop thinking about it!" At this point, Karl and I were not sure if she was referring to a recent car repair or if she was concerned about the half-inch skiff of snow that had settled on the ground overnight (any amount of snow worried Mom because the Chevette's small engine would pack with snow and die).

In this case and many others similar to it, Mom was easily stressed out. Worse than that, when she worked herself into these conditions, the effects were far reaching. First, her physical health went downhill (once she got Bell's Palsy and her eye dropped), and then she lashed out at us. In her drill sergeant's voice, coupled with that of an auctioneer, she'd yell, "Boys! Vacuum the house, get water, get ice, start generator, burn trash, fix car, do dishes, do this, do that, get this, get that, feed bird, clean turtle ... now get crackin'!" This lengthy command was expelled in a single breath, with no pauses between syllables or sentences.

To retaliate when she worked herself up like this, we all chanted in unison, "Oh, poor Mother Hubbard. Poor, poor Mom. Lost in the woods. Poor, poor Mom. Lost innnnn the wooooods." This little ditty always pissed Mom off, which made us infinitely happy. Afterwards, we went about our chores gaily and whistled our favorite work song in very low tones, "Poor, poor Mom ..."

Though Mom was usually tired, stressed, beat, bushed, winding-down, listening to news, unwinding, plagued with headaches, reading, rocking, etcetera, sometimes she found time for a joke. Like the time Jon and I went to a Halloween party at Gakona School.

She thought it would be funny to dress us up like girls—wigs, makeup, dresses and all. Jon and I were quite miserable during the party, and when all the kids paraded their costumes, Mom made us go too. Of course, no one knew that we were in drag, and I think the audience thought, "Who are those two ugly little girls, and why are they marching in the school contest without costumes?" But these worries didn't cross Mom's mind (watching from the corner of our two-room schoolhouse at a safe distance). She had had her fun and joke, and continued to talk about it for years, much to our chagrin.

Another time when Mom was a teacher in Glennallen High School (a bilingual teacher's aide), she threatened to whip a kid with a cold noodle because he wasn't doing his homework. The high schooler (a Native) knew Mom and just smiled because he thought she was joking. The next day, while he was diligently studying, she whipped him on the back of the head with a real, wet, cold noodle. "That was for yesterday," she stated simply. Although the student was confused, he was not shocked because everyone knew that Mrs. Chim had a warped sense of humor.

In addition to possessing an eccentric funny bone, Mom was the master of guilt trips. She was the queen of guilt herself, and could get her boys (slaves) to do whatever she desired. "Mom, can I stay the night at Cameron's house?" I once asked.

"Joe, I can't believe that you'd want to leave your poor old mother here all alone. I haven't seen you all week. You've been at school and wrestling for months. When am I going to see my son? Why, just yesterday you were five years old and you used to sit in my lap. Now though, you're almost out of the house. I'm not going to have you for much longer. Why don't you stay here? I miss you so much, son."

This was her crafty answer, and it almost convinced me to stay home. However, after considerable experience with Mom, and possessing a quick wit myself, I tried to find a weak spot in her armor.

"Mom, I've been here fifteen years and I'll be here another three. You'll see me plenty. Also, Dad will be here. And besides, when I leave the house, I'll always come home and visit," I stated logically and confidently.

She then replied with a very blunt, "No. No means no." And thus, her "poor me" façade crumbled and the issue was settled.

Mom often used her guilt tactics to persuade me to play cards. "I'm so bored, Joe. None of the other boys or your father likes to play cards. You're good at them—why don't you treat your poor old mother to a game or two?" she'd say smoothly.

She liked 500 rummy, but her true passion was playing a card game called "Spite Malice." Perhaps the title of this game reflected Mom's intent best because she'd sit in her chair calmly smoking cigarettes and continually pound the crap out of me until I was a gibbering idiot.

One day, Mom convinced me to play and I foolheartedly accepted her plea. In no time the air was blue with smoke (while Dad and my brothers nearly choked to death and dodged outside to conveniently look for chores), and she repeatedly flipped and snapped cards without mercy. I sat restless and watched her score point after point, which made me feel useless and enraged. She didn't stop, however, but actually increased her rhythm of snapping the cards, which subtly rubbed in the fact that I was losing badly.

After nearly half an hour of not scoring a single point and watching her casually trash my ego, I was burning up inside and went crazy. Thus, at the ripe age of nine, I lost my senses and threw my cards all over the table and floor. At that moment, on that day, I took a stand and vowed never to play Spite Malice with Mom again. I kept my word.

The only thought that brought me comfort after this intense confrontation (and during all the designated chores and relentless guilt trips throughout my childhood) was the simple and well-known fact that Mom hated mosquitoes, but boy they loved her.

Whereas Dad and the rest of us went outside and braved thousands of mosquitoes every day, Mom nearly "went off her rocker" when a single bloodthirsty insect entered the house. The men didn't mind them, though, because there were so many, and they were so large that there was no use fighting them and we accepted the fact that we were just part of the food chain.

We used to joke that we didn't need to go hiking out back, when we could get a free fly-in from the mosquitoes. "Bring it on into this lake, guys. Just a little lower," we imagined saying to a swarm of mosquitoes carrying us bodily. But Mom could never joke with us and took her mosquito eradication duties very seriously. She hung bug strips in the house, lit a smoke-producing material ("Pic") near the door, and if one mosquito entered the house, she spent all afternoon lying in wait for it. Of course, the mosquito often waited until night when she fell asleep. Then it would draw out her blood, awaken her with its itch, and send her into a tizzy. All of this commotion would undoubtedly awaken Dad, at which point he'd roll over and moan sleepily, "Poor, poor Mom. Lost in the woods …"

Cakes

Dad always said he would eat rocks if he could, and none of us ever doubted him. In fact, he was never known to have turned down food or complain what type of dish was served or how. Dad truly loved food and was convinced that there was nothing in the world so bad that he couldn't eat it and enjoy it as well. His conviction and our belief in him held true over the years until one summer afternoon.

While occupied with our usual daily chores we were startled to see a large recreational vehicle pulling up our narrow driveway. We

Our friends from Japan showed up one day in a motorhome and enjoyed a Chmielowski cookout. In return, they prepared an interesting treat for us.

were even more surprised when our Japanese friends (who actually live in Japan) hopped out and greeted us excitedly. In almost no time they had taken over our yard, house, and surrounding area like a colony of ants. Their faces were sparkling as they inspected the lake, took pictures of our home and probed the family with questions concerning our lives and Alaska. It was good to see them and as usual my Dad decided that they needed food immediately upon arrival. As a result, our family set about our outdoor fireplace (see things in the yard, Appendix B) and started an excellent Chmielowski cookout.

Our friends were truly pleased and had sampled our cooking during past visits. Hamburgers and hot dogs were our main entree but they knew we would eventually give them their favorite dish, salmon cakes. To show their appreciation of our hospitality they ran to their camper, clambered around a bit, and finally emerged with some rice and other ingredients. They then explained that they would make us a special treat, rice cakes.

As soon as Dad and us boys heard the magic word "cakes" our stomachs growled and saliva glands activated. We all figured they would taste like rice pudding mixed with a classic white cake, or something close to this anyway. We milled about the kitchen and hovered near their work area in anticipation of the palatable delight.

After a short time the Japanese and my Mom finished with a flourish and a platter of greenish cubes. Our numerous friends gathered around, took one cake themselves, and distributed one cube to each family member. They then occupied themselves by chatting and consuming the little cakes eagerly. I took a bite not so eagerly, and decided to take a long walk outside. Apparently my four brothers and father had similar notions and we left like a horde of rabid elephants.

The cakes were horrible and there were no two ways about it. They were composed of a tasteless, airy rice kernel base, and overlaid by some sort of raw seaweed. Hence, their greenish luster. Worse than that, the spices and general texture of the things would cause even the hardiest vulture to shy away. To top it off, they swelled up and filled the oral cavity and throat like some sort of industrial foaming agent. They were inconsumable and a course of action had to be taken quickly.

I casually sauntered to the lakeshore and pretended to be looking for frogs. When none of our friends (although it was hard to call them friends after this cruel trick) were watching, I flung the abominable cake into the "hungry weeds" of our lake. I was careful not to let it fall near a frog or other friendly being, for fear of poisoning it.

While occupied, I was unaware of how Steve, Ray, and Jon unloaded their burdens, but I am sure it was in a similarly clever manner. When I returned from my grave duty I noticed that Karl and Dad were not as fortunate as I, and each held his cursed cake while entertaining a friend.

I stood next to Karl near the fireplace and reveled in the knowledge that this cake was killing him. As a matter of fact, it made me feel so good I smiled openly and the male Japanese friend Karl was talking to thought I found their conversation pleasing. On the contrary, I found Karl's incalculable suffering delightful and cherished the moment.

My perfect world came to a crash when the man turned away to put down his soda, and Karl suddenly flung the once-bitten cake into the campfire. Without noticing, the man placed his can onto the bench, resumed his position and commenced conversing with Karl. "Dang! How could he not have seen that pathetic move?!" I thought as the green cake sizzled near our feet. "And how come he doesn't notice that miserable treat cooking and the foul odor accompanying the smoke?" I continued to muse. No matter, now that Karl was no longer squirming I decided to see how Dad fared.

Dad was in a similar situation as Karl, holding a once-bitten green cake and conversing with a tourist. "This should be interesting," I thought as I sidled up alongside Dad. They chatted about this and that and Dad looked around nervously all the while. Then, with a quickness that would shame a wolverine, my Dad threw the cake on top of the porch roof. He did this at the exact instant his partner turned to look at something near the lake. Once again, the man did not notice, or appear to notice, and immediately he resumed conversing with Dad.

How that man did not see Dad throw the cake, or question the fact that his hands were now empty is beyond me. However, Dad's luck was good that day and when a camp robber (Alaskan gray jay) landed on the roof and snatched up the cake, the man missed that too! What are the odds of not seeing a rather large bird flying around the yard with a rice cake in its beak? Especially one that was as proud as an eagle with its kill?

Before long, I began to notice that the trees were alive with activity and camp robbers were feasting on abundant green cakes. I guess that is where Steve's, Ray's, and Jon's cakes ended up. Although I must admit, after a halfhearted peck or two, even the birds rejected the evil tidbits. Had I not tried one myself, I would never have comprehended such a foul and vile thing in my life, and now I felt bad, witnessing the birds' agony.

I eventually returned to the house when I was 100 percent sure there were no leftovers and was shocked to find Mom looking quite queasy.

"Oh God, don't tell me!" I thought as I looked in horror upon her countenance. "She couldn't escape! She was forced to stay in the house keeping the women company and had to consume the most repulsive treat in existence!"

My heart and my sympathy went out to Mom. She had done what none of us could do. She alone had eaten the same cake that my father and all five of us boys had vehemently rejected. It was then that I realized how strong my mother was and that although my father might eat rocks, he would never, ever, in all his life, eat a green rice cake.

Our family never once took a vacation, but Mom was able to take countless mental vacations by reading hundreds of books in her rocking chair. In my opinion, Mom is the only woman who could have withstood so many hardships for so long with nearly perfect stoicism.

The Zoo Wagon

Mom and Dad were always broke and as a result the Chmielowski Clan never had what could be called a luxurious car, or even a decent car, for that matter. I would even go so far as to say that the cars our family owned were

The infamous Chmielowski Clan. Rear, from left to right: Mom, Karl, Ray, and Dad. Front, left to right: Joe and Jon (Steve not pictured).

downright pathetic. They were consistently outdated by twenty years, well rusted, and broke down once a month. Heck, our vehicles were in such poor condition that even the Natives from Gulkana Village could have beaten us in a drag race. It wasn't Mom and Dad's fault though, because what little money they did have went straight to food and fuel and not to extravagant things such as a properly functioning vehicle.

The first automobile my parents owned was a '52 Chevy pickup truck, which ran surprisingly well and was very sturdy. But, as the years wore on, the truck wore out and they were forced to purchase a Ford Falcon and later a white station wagon. Both of these cars went down the tubes one way or another and around the time I was born they purchased a huge Ford station wagon. It was one of those '70s station wagons that was about twenty-five feet long and resembled the Bismarck battleship. The boys called the station wagon "The Lugger" because of its behemothic nature (big and slow) and also because it could lug a bunch of kids and groceries.

The Lugger had a maroon paint job, was extremely wide, and sported four doors (each of which were a full four feet in length). Furthermore, it had a V-8 engine that could power a commuter airliner and on its roof it had a chrome luggage rack. To top it all off, Mom got the bright idea to put permanent stickers spelling "ZOO WAGON" in six-inch capital block letters on the back of the rack. That way, whenever we drove down the road, everyone behind us could read "ZOO WAGON" and sympathize with Mom's plight of having to deal with five young boys.

Wherever we went, the Chmielowski Clan moved as a unit. We were like a squad-sized element in the army, and virtually inseparable. When we went to Glennallen in the Zoo Wagon, all seven of us piled in with military precision. We each knew our assigned seats and they were thus: Mom drove, Dad slept (in the passenger seat), Steve, Ray, and Karl sat in the back seat (with Karl on the hump), and Jon and I were relegated to the very back storage area. After packing ourselves into the car like sardines, we always sat stone-faced and silent as Mom backed out of the driveway and headed to Glennallen. Of course, we were all excited to go to the big town, but we never wanted to talk loudly or yell, because we dared not invoke Mom's wrath (which usually included hitting us with a Halloween devil's prod from Ray's childhood costume—she did this while driving). So we always stoically contained our excitement and hunkered down for a long, miserable ride while KCAM blared on the radio.

Inside the Zoo Wagon the upholstery was a tan vinyl (nice and sweaty during the summer, and cold as a witch's tit during the winter) and so too was the carpet. The whole inside of the wagon reeked of stale cigarettes and coffee, and to make matters worse Mom always lit up a cigarette once on the road (just in case the smell ever decided to subside). Dad had his job down pat and would pull up the head rest, lean back and begin snoring within three minutes. Steve often sat smiling and watching trees go by, while Karl constantly perturbed Jon and me. Ray sat with his head against the window because he was always pissed off at something and dreaded going to Glennallen. He despised going to Glennallen with the family because he was afraid people would see him with the Clan. Ray would rather have had bamboo slivers driven under his fingernails than to be seen with us.

Jon and I sat in the back of the wagon because we were the smallest. The storage area where we sat had a tan metal floor that was slippery and cold. Our only other option was opening two hatch doors (by pulling on a couple of metal rings in the floor) that exposed two small tan vinyl seats that faced one another. Inevitably, after being tossed around in the storage area for a few miles we opted for these plush seats because they were the lesser of two evils. But the hidden seats were not without their problems and were very cold (being so far from the heater in front) and our feet would quickly turn numb. We were always miserable in those seats (the word icebox comes to mind).

Jon and I only occasionally spoke because we were inevitably sick and felt that at any given moment we would hurl. The reason for our queasiness was that the Zoo Wagon drove like a ship and because of this, it swayed like a ship. To make matters worse, the Richardson Highway in Alaska is famous for its infinite frost heaves, bumps, cracks, swells, potholes, rough spots, turns, bends, heaves, turns, bends, heaves, turns, bends ... Needless to say, Jon and I were always carsick and never in a good mood. To add to the nausea, the exhaust system funneled gas fumes right under our seats and into our local air space. As a result, we spent the entire ride gagging on carbon monoxide, gas fumes, Mom's cigarette smoke, and the smell of stale coffee.

The exhaust, gas, smoke, and coffee were not the worst of our problems. Nope, there was one more problem that made our situation utterly unbearable: Jon's stomach. Jon had a weaker stomach than I and he puked on nearly every road trip. Typically, I sat facing him for a while and we'd chat somewhat. Then, he ceased talking altogether and sat rigid and watched the trees go by. Next, he turned slightly pale, then a shade of red, and finally he began breathing like a woman giving birth.

"Pppwwwaaa, pppwwwaaa, pppwwwaa ..." he wheezed loudly.

"Mom! Open the back window! He's gonna puke!" I yelled. Mom reached down with her right hand and flicked a switch. The huge electric window in the back went down smoothly and fresh air rushed in to our rescue. Almost. With the rush of the fresh air came more exhaust fumes and more of Mom's cigarette smoke (drawn from the front of the car by the vacuum). We then got very cold and our breathing conditions were much worse.

"I'm gonna pull over!" Mom announced.

Dad always started from his sleep at this point and inquired, "What on God's green earth is going on?" As if something new and unforeseen was happening.

Then the peanut gallery in the second row complained in unison, "How come we're pulling over?"

"Dang it! He's not gonna puke. Dang Jonny Cakes. Dang Yukey Lodge," Ray mumbled. Yukey Lodge (a takeoff on the original Pukey Lodge) was Jon's nickname because of his uncanny ability to puke while in the car or at any convenient lodge we could locate along the road. Mom slowed down the Lugger, pulled over and the situation was neutralized. There were times, though, when she put on the brakes too fast and the Lugger lurched to a stop too quickly. During these special occasions the jolt put Jon over the edge and he puked.

"Aaarrrrr, arrrrrrrr, aaakkk … cough, cough, slurp, aaarrr!" he'd sputter. I would scramble out of the seats and try my best to avoid his spew. Sometimes he got my leg, sometimes he didn't. Sometimes the smell from his puke caused a chain reaction and one or more of us would hurl. Sometimes he got his head out the back window in time and sometimes it was a false alarm. One thing was for sure, though, he always managed to puke on the tan vinyl seats, and under them on the black rubber mats on the floor. Thus, after years and years of Jon riding in the back of the Zoo Wagon, the rear storage area (and to a lesser extent, the entire car) acquired a strong hurl-whiff that could have made a skunk sick (luckily, skunks don't live in Alaska so they were spared). Thus, even if there was one time in our lives when we weren't carsick from the frost heaves, Mom's smoke, the exhaust or coffee fumes, we were always sick thanks to Jon and his amazing stomach.

On each trip, after Jon puked we spent the remainder of the ride in silence looking out the back window longingly. We imagined the fresh air in our lungs and our despair continually grew. The only thing interesting (other than watching the trees go by and looking for animals) was when someone approached us from the rear. The vehicle always approached at a speed of fifty to sixty miles per hour and then slowed down suddenly when it came upon us (usually maxed out at forty-five). The motorist would look perturbed or annoyed or usually both and then attempt to pass us. However, because the road was so curvy and bumpy it often took the angered motorist about five to ten miles to find a safe opportunity. When he or she did find an opportune moment, no time was spent hesitating and the vehicle passed up the Zoo Wagon in a blur. We were always embarrassed when cars "got stuck behind us" and we slithered and slunk down into the seats as much as possible. Cars got stuck behind the Zoo Wagon quite often and as a matter of fact, it usually happened about five times on the way to Glennallen.

When we finally reached Glennallen and the ordeal was over, we were, without a doubt, very happy (except Ray, of course). We invaded Park's Place en masse, the Cracker Barrel, the Hobby Shop, and if we were really lucky the Tasty Freeze. We moved as an orderly mob to and from the Zoo Wagon and the store of interest. At the end of the day we were worn out and went through the whole trip again. The bumps, heaves, smells, and yes, even the puking. This horrific nightmare was repeated each and every time we made the one-hour trip to Glennallen. I dare not attempt to detail the six-hour voyage through the rugged Chugach Mountains to Anchorage.

Eventually we sold the Zoo Wagon to an old Native who thought it was a real gem. He figured he could probably haul ten or twelve of his cronies in it with little effort. We sold it to him for a hundred-dollar bill and a promised .22 caliber rifle. We got the hundred bucks, but we never did see the gun. We didn't complain, though; on the contrary, we gladly let it slide. After all, now that poor guy had to deal with the infamous Zoo Wagon.

Stevo-Revo

I don't remember much about my brother Steve (whom the family nicknamed Stevo-Revo for unknown reasons). He was eleven years older than I and graduated from high school when I was in second grade. Granted, Ray graduated the same year as Steve, but I remember Ray vividly and Steve only vaguely. My memory is biased because Ray was cruel and twisted, whereas Steve was "Mr. Sensitivity" and extremely nice. As the years rolled by, I didn't remember the pleasant things in my early life, only the pain and torture. Hence, I remember little of Steve and much of Ray.

Steve was born first and was followed by his brother Ray a year later. As a child, Steve was always thoughtful, sensitive, kind, caring, nice, sincere, honest, hard-working, and the son every mother dreams of.

However, Steve was such a nice guy his easygoing character actually worked against him. He was too nice. Growing up, Ray walked all over Steve and perpetually coaxed him into doing less than honorable things. Over the years many others manipulated Steve as well. Steve was a pushover when someone needed his help and he considered all people as honest as himself.

In Steve's early childhood, he grew up with Ray in virtual isolation. Occasionally Uncle Joe, Uncle Lenny, or the Sipary family (our Eskimo friends) visited, but for the most part Steve and Ray were alone in the forest with only Mom and Dad to interact with.

To demonstrate how isolated they were: Steve and Ray believed in Santa until the ripe age of twelve. Furthermore, while attending Gakona Elementary School they fought other students over Santa's existence. When their classmates claimed that Santa Claus was not real, Steve and Ray beat the crap out of them on the spot—they wouldn't have anyone bad-mouthing good old Saint Nick.

Later that evening, Mom and Dad told their sons the truth about Santa. This news nearly killed them both, but the impact was greatest on Steve because of his sensitive nature. His face fell and his lip quivered as he spoke, "So, there's no Easter Bunny, or Patrick [the elf who lived in our attic] either?"

As Steve grew up, he had a weight problem in elementary school and ballooned up around the age of ten, at which point he tipped the scales at 200 pounds. His life was miserable.

All the other kids made fun of his weight and he felt very self-conscious. In addition to his weight problem, his easygoing nature made him a perfect target for the malicious little brats of Gakona School. After enduring a few years of this relentless torture he went on a crash diet and became very trim. He never gained weight again and throughout high school and even afterwards has always been in great physical shape.

Although Steve was nice to the point of making the Pope himself uneasy, he had his dark moments as well. The earliest example of his ornery tendencies was the grass fire. When Steve and Ray were very young, Steve convinced Ray to go by the drainage ditch of our lake and start little pieces of paper on fire. They sat near the lake's bank igniting small scraps of paper and throwing them into the water. After a bit, one landed in the grass and caught the long, brown straw on fire. A raging inferno started.

They both knew they couldn't tell Mom and Dad (a sure spanking for starting a fire), but they couldn't let the house and forest burn down either. As a result, Steve took balls in hand, did the right thing, and told Dad about the raging blaze.

Of course, good old Dad put out the fire and both Steve and Ray got their butts whipped. While Ray was howling and crying, Uncle Joe happened to pull up our driveway and said, "Why Ray-Ray cry-cry? Heh, heh, heh ..." At which point Ray ran over to Uncle Joe and bit his shin bone. To this day Ray has not forgiven his older brother Steve for getting them both in trouble or for getting Ray's butt peppered.

Another occasion when Steve was less than an angel was when he was behind the hobby shop and decided to break the windows out of Kupper's shed. He simply picked up a large steel pole and smashed out several panes of glass. While Steve was thus engaged, Ray happened to come along and within seconds Steve convinced Ray to do the same.

Ray smashed a couple of windows himself and was having a grand time. The sound of breaking glass caught Dad's ear so he decided to check things out. Perhaps a burglar or hitchhiker had broken into the shed. As he rounded the corner, though, he spotted neither hitchhiker nor thief. Instead, he witnessed Ray diligently breaking the expensive windows out of his new outbuilding (while Steve stood by casually surveying the destruction). Thus, he gave both culprits a sound butt whippin', and once again Ray was chagrined for being duped by his "naïve" older brother.

Grant it, Steve may have inadvertently caused Ray some occasional pain (via Dad's trusty wooden spoon), but he never suggested trouble-some activities with malicious intent. Steve did not plot cruel tricks or think evil things. He was a simple person and only once did he ever intentionally harm someone. That someone was Ray.

On this certain day, Ray teased Steve too much about his weight. Steve (approximately 200 pounds) picked Ray up bodily (approxi-mately 90 pounds), and threw him a full five feet into the bed of Dad's blue truck. Getting physically thrown not only got Ray's attention, but gave him a few bruises as well. After this particular incident, Ray still teased Steve, but he was always careful not to push him past his limits.

Another interesting event occurred while Steve and Ray (the two are inextricably linked like salt and pepper) were wood gettin' across the lake. They were cutting down the dead spruce trees and bringing them to the bank of the lake. They then loaded the logs into our small aluminum boat and rowed them across the lake to our home. Of course, Ray was not doing a lick of work, just sitting idle in the boat while Steve loaded it entirely himself.

All Ray had to do to make Steve work was simply talk to him and keep his mind occupied. As Ray kept talking, Steve kept loading and after several minutes Ray's chatter turned to yelling.

It soon became apparent that neither of them was paying any at-tention to the wood and Steve overloaded the boat. The laden craft sank with Ray in it and all the logs floated to the top of the water. Dad witnessed this comical event and made both of them fish every log out of the lake so that he wouldn't run over them with his snow-machine in the winter. As usual, Ray was pissed at Steve for getting him in trouble. This time Ray did not get a blistering, instead he got entirely soaked.

When Steve was in high school, he fell in love with Deanna Daw-son. She was pretty, intelligent, nice, honest, and just as sensitive as Steve was. Her only flaw (if it could be considered one) was her age. Deanna was five years younger than Steve.

The generation gap seriously inhibited their relationship, but while it lasted, Steve and Deanna were inseparable and perfectly made for each other. The definition of "true love" could have easily been based on this couple. Steve was serious about Deanna (as in marriage), but she was too young to consider it. Thus, their relationship went sour and the two lovers went their separate ways.

After this severe blow, Steve began to go downhill quickly. Though still in high school, he seemed to be desperately searching for someone to fill the void left by Deanna. I don't remember Steve ever dating another girl again. Deanna was his first and last girlfriend in high school.

Steve remained sensitive after their breakup but he became very distracted. He still retained his best qualities, but he certainly lost the "thoughtful" part of himself. Nothing seemed to matter to him except his ex-lover.

Though distracted by Deanna's loss, Steve's love for his brothers never wavered. Whereas Ray would rap us soundly on the skull with his knuckles, Steve would make us grilled cheese for lunch. Instead of laughing at us for wiping out on our old green bicycles or tying fishing line between trees to knock us off our bikes (Ray's and Karl's favorite trick), Steve would pick us up and pamper us when we were little. Steve even changed Jon's and my diapers when we were babies. Ray would have just let us sit and die in the same situation. Steve loved all his younger brothers and took great pains to take care of us.

Most of what I have related about Steve has been hearsay from my older brothers and parents. As for me personally, I don't remember much about Steve. I don't remember every time he did my brothers and me a favor. I don't remember every time he did all the household chores, or every time he took care of the family when Dad was away. I don't remember because I was young and because it's hard for me to remember his praiseworthy deeds amongst the many atrocities committed by Ray and Karl. However, though my memories of Steve are dreamlike and disjointed, they are nonetheless always pleasant and bring back a sense of happiness and security.

1982: Hamburger (aka Ray) and Revo (aka Steve) prepare for their high school graduation. Revo, right, seems sincerely happy on this momentous occasion, while Ray, left, appears to be mentally concocting a new torture for his younger brothers.

The Pit and the Posse

What would you think if you rounded a corner on a deserted highway, and saw five young boys armed to the teeth with rifles, pulling a red wagon full of toys, followed by two very large black dogs? I'm sure the average person

During warm summer months the five of us would skinny-dip in our lake. Steve and Ray are in the background; Karl is in the innertube; Jon is climbing onto the dock and I am preparing to play in our tin tub we borrowed from inside the house.

(or common tourist) would most likely be astonished, if not petrified and would also most likely try to quickly maneuver past the motley crew. Although this sounds like an odd and rare situation, it actually occurred quite often near our home on the Richardson Highway.

On hot summer days when we grew bored of swimming in our lake and playing around the house, we filled our red metal wagon with Tonka trucks and King Size toys. Then we each collected our personal .22 rifles and a box of bullets. Finally, we roused the dogs and the whole entourage moved en masse down the road to the gravel pit.

Mom and Dad were not concerned that we each carried a firearm because they were the ones who'd given them to us. At the ripe age of five, each of the brothers learned gun safety and the proper way to handle and fire a rifle. This was not only hunting training, but training as a defense against persons of dubious character. Because we lived thirty-six miles from Glennallen and we didn't have a phone, our family was on its own. As is typical in most of rural Alaska, the police could be depended on *not* to help.

My first encounter with a gun was when I found a loaded .38 pistol under the Maverick seat. I was four years old at the time, and Mom and Dad had parked outside Eureka Lodge on the way to Anchorage. They went in to use the restroom and I was left in the car. Out of curiosity I crawled on the floor and spotted the pistol. I picked it up, looked at it, but did not fool with it. I remembered Dad always told us, "Never touch the trigger or hammer and treat each gun as if it's loaded." With this in mind, I investigated the chrome-plated, snub-nosed revolver, but I did not endanger myself. Furthermore, I kept it in my lap because in my opinion, Mom and Dad must have lost it under the seat and would be very happy that I found it.

When Mom and Dad returned from the restroom they were alarmed at seeing their four-year-old boy with a pistol in his lap. I told them casually, "I didn't touch the trigger," and they praised me for this. The next year I was taught all about guns, their purpose, and how to safely handle them. In addition, that year I received my first .22 rifle from Dad. Its nickname was "old hair trigger."

As a result of my early experiences, I shouldered old hair trigger like a weary veteran and mingled inside the house with my four armed brothers. Mom and Dad were as unconcerned as if we'd been playing Hot Wheels. After all, they had taught us caution, respect, and responsibility with firearms.

Once assembled outside, we closely resembled a cross between The Little Rascals and the Jesse James gang. We milled around outside the porch, checking and rechecking our rifles as the hot sun beat down on our bald white heads. We double-checked that certain toys were not forgotten and double-knotted our shoelaces in anticipation of the long journey. Finally, after a good forty minutes of preparation, the unit was ready to roll.

Steve led the pack because he was the oldest. Ray stood abreast of him and Karl stood behind Ray. Jon and I were the smallest, so we brought up the rear. Steve pulled the heavy wagon because he was strong and because Ray was too embarrassed to pull it. He was always afraid a car would drive by and someone would laugh at him. I firmly believe that his fears were unfounded because it is highly unlikely that anyone would have the nerve to laugh at five bald boys with guns.

Steve told us to "walk on the white line" and "go on the gravel berm when cars come." In addition, he told Jon and me to insure that Boy and Fang stayed off the road or else they would get hit. Though we were a large, well-equipped gang, we were also very orderly.

As we progressed down the paved but narrow Richardson Highway, we talked, laughed, threw rocks, and shot things. We had contests to see who could shoot a certain limb off a certain tree, or who could nail the milepost sign from a hundred yards away. Sometimes Karl and Ray put a small flower in their rifle barrels. Then they held their rifles straight up, warned the others to stand back, and fired. Petals and shreds of vegetation rained down on us. We were easily entertained.

While walking down the highway we would pass a trail on our left that led to an old, abandoned trapper's cabin near Sourdough Creek. Further down, we passed the milepost sign (it looked like a saltshaker's lid) which was also on our left. Still further yet, we passed a big swamp on our right where an old bar had once been. Eventually, we reached the gravel pit on the east side of the highway and at this point we cut in on an old dirt road.

We moved like an army squad (and had enough fire power to shame most) to our first stop. This area was a small intermittent pond that swelled during rains and evaporated during hot droughts. If we were lucky, the water would be deep and we could start our day of fun. We scoured the dirt road and surrounding area for bottles and cans discarded by tourists and collected them in a big pile. Then we threw them all into the water and watched them float. Next, everyone locked and loaded their rifles and the games began.

At this point, our little band looked and sounded like George Washington's army. Hundreds of shots, sprays of water and shouts of joy and anguish filled the air as each of the boys attempted to outshoot the other. Of course, we all shot from the same side of the pond and towards a dirt embankment to insure that no one was hurt in the melee.

Bottles were a rare treat and exploded on impact. All the boys sought out these targets first and there was much rivalry over them. "Yaaa! I got the green bottle!" someone would yell. "Who cares? I sank two beer cans!" someone else boasted.

Whereas bottles went down with a single shot, some cans could withstand fifteen direct hits before sinking. So, although not as much fun to shoot as bottles, cans signified greater marksmanship and they too were worth bragging about. "I sank a Budweiser can with only one shot! I hit it low below the water line and it sank like a rock!" Karl often bragged as he attempted to hide his grief over missing the bottles.

I usually did the worst in shooting contests because I could barely hold my rifle, and when I aimed I was wiggly. Jon wasn't much better than I, but he was able to get around this handicap because his rifle was a semi-automatic 10-22. True, he wasn't accurate, but the odds of hitting something were on his side as he unloaded twenty-five rounds in twenty-five seconds.

After exhausting our targets and ammo, or if the pond was dry, we rumbled down the dirt road until we came to the sandpiles. Here we unloaded the "Red Swanson" wagon (so named because our wagon had a "Vote for Red Swanson" campaign sticker on its side) and distributed trucks and toys to everyone. Of course, Steve, Ray, and Karl got the biggest and best trucks, while Jon and I were left with only the dregs. The situation was even worse if we brought the old GI Joe dolls, because Steve, Ray, and Karl each had one, but Jon and I didn't. Regardless, we all spread out, claimed a portion of the sandpiles and began a long day of work.

Steve made the best roads for his trucks. They were wide, flat, and perfectly detailed. Ray would make roads for a bit, but usually resorted to blasting tunnels with firecrackers. Karl tried to imitate Steve but quickly lost interest and assisted Ray with the explosives. Jon and I played together and felt depressed because our pathetic roads did not compare with our older brothers'. Furthermore, because there were never enough firecrackers (and mostly because Ray and Karl were stingy), we could not be part of the demolition team.

As a result, Jon and I usually moved to a distant area and made sand castles. There we were left in peace (although sometimes Ray and Karl would throw firecrackers at us when they were tired of blasting tunnels), and did not have to compete with Steve's perfectly constructed roads.

Jon and I made huge sandcastles and we stood with pride upon completing them. On occasion, our magnificent structures attracted Ray and Karl to our area like flies to a salmon carcass. They infiltrated our work zone, set up their explosives and destroyed our mighty castles. As if this was not enough, when they rebuilt them out of pity for us, they created such perfect structures that it was a mockery of our original work. Jon and I were dejected and moped around the gravel pit like refugees.

At the end of the day, around four-thirty p.m., Steve would give the word and we prepared to go home. Supper was always at 5 p.m. sharp and to be late or miss it would be unthinkable. We collected our toys, guns, and dogs and assembled to do a security check. After everything was accounted for and Steve deemed us ready, we headed home.

Inevitably, after less than five minutes of walking, I complained, "Steve, I have to empty my shoes!" The posse came to a grinding halt, waited impatiently, and rustled and shuffled with exasperation. I put down my rifle, untied my shoes, took them off, beat them, and then turned them over. Rocks, pebbles, and a cup of sand came pouring out of each shoe. Then I tied my shoes, retrieved my rifle and felt much better. The gang lurched back into motion and continued along the dirt road like a swarm of angry wasps. We traveled a short distance until Jon whined, "Steve, I got sand in my shoes!" Thus, it took Steve's unending patience and many more minutes before we arrived at home.

When we came to the highway, we obeyed all Steve's rules and walked on the side of the road. Occasionally, tourists from the Lower 48 would drive by looking for Alaskan wildlife but instead they spotted five sand-encrusted, bald-headed, well-armed boys with a wagonload of toys and two black dogs. They gaped at us in awe as they drove slowly by in their huge Winnebago campers. We stared right back at them thinking how foolish they looked staring at us.

Heck, we always wondered what they were staring at. In our opinion, there was nothing out of the ordinary about a gang of armed children walking down a nearly deserted highway in 1978. However, when reflecting on those childhood days, it's a wonder that we were never accidentally run over by a spooked tourist or arrested for looking like outlaws. But we didn't know any better; we were just happy kids passing away long summer days in Alaska.

Hamburger

Ray was a tortured soul. He had perpetual migraine headaches, three younger brothers, and a short fuse. It's no surprise that he was always pissed off.

Furthermore, Ray was like an old grizzly bear that had been shot five times with a high-powered rifle. Sure, he kept going. But he growled a lot, scowled even more, and took his pain out on Karl, Jon, and me. To make a long story short, Ray was not a happy camper. I can't even remember one single time during my childhood when he truly smiled. The only time he wore anything that remotely resembled a smile was when he thumped us. However, though he enjoyed watching our anguish, I don't think he really smiled. Instead, he wore an inverted frown.

Ray's nickname was Hamburger (or Burg for short), after the McDonald's character Hamburglar who consumed massive quantities of food. Although Ray was a big eater, he was lean and muscular, and wrestled a couple of years in high school. He was a "lean, mean, fighting machine" which was great for his ego, but bad for his little brothers. I truly believed that he kept in such good physical shape in order to torture us with maximum efficiency and minimal effort.

For the most part, Ray spent his adolescent years on top of his red bunk bed, in a dim room, listening to his J.C. Penney's tape player through monstrously large, '70s headphones. In addition, he always had a pillow covering his face to keep out unwanted light and noises. On a typical day, I would creep toward him and ask an innocent question such as, "Ray, can you take us to the gravel pit?" His usual response was, "Shut up, I have a headache. Get out of here!" That was always my cue to exit quickly before he gave me a good thumping.

Ray used to delight in making Jon and me miserable. It was truly the only light in his life. For instance, on some occasions Jon and I played in the back bedroom and Ray intentionally walked near us.

Instantly we'd grow quiet, our hearts sagged and every muscle in our bodies tensed as he passed. "Please God, don't let him get us!" Jon and I thought. Of course, Ray could smell our fear and sometimes he got me, and sometimes he got Jon.

When I was the chosen victim he picked me up by my scrawny neck, held me at head level, and yelled into my face, "Arrrgggghhh, I'm Darth Vader!" Then he shook me like a wet noodle and let me fall to the floor in a dazzled heap. He performed this little ritual as a tribute to "Star Wars" when Darth Vader picked up one of his men by the neck and killed him. Having my neck stretched wasn't so bad and I was always glad to get away relatively unscathed. Jon was never as fortunate.

When Jon was little, Steve and Ray nicknamed him Knobs because his ears were so big. Unfortunately, Jon's knobby appendages seemed to beckon to Ray who became obsessed with them. When Ray attacked Jon, he actually lifted him off the ground by his ears! I would not have though it possible had I not witnessed the foul deed more than once. On one occasion I remember thinking to myself, "How fascinating. Jon can be lifted by his ears and they don't even rip off his head! Absolutely amazing."

Worse than being picked up by the neck, or even by the ears, was when Ray made a fist (with his middle knuckle protruding above the others) and rapped us soundly on the top of our skulls. We first heard a sharp crack and then felt a piercing pain. This tradition of Ray's was very painful and extremely annoying. We even preferred when Ray threw us into the lake or chucked us into the snowbanks. Anything was better than the knuckle treatment.

To demonstrate how evil Ray was, he even thumped Jon and me on Christmas Eve. After sleeping for several hours, we both woke around midnight due to the holiday excitement. Jon whispered to me in a quiet voice, "Let's see if Santa Claus left any presents yet." His suggestion sounded like a good idea so we prepared to creep out of bed clad only in our jockey shorts.

As Jon and I rustled out of our covers, we heard Ray roll over. However, we both decided that because Ray was on the top bunk and so far from us, he was harmless (Jon was in the middle bunk, and I was in the trundle bed; a giant drawer-like bed that slid underneath Jon's bunk). We slithered out of our beds with confidence.

We "snuck" through the back bedroom and made it to Mom and Dad's room when all of a sudden we heard Ray shout, "Get back to bed right now!" Before we knew what happened, we heard something whirring through the air. An instant later, Jon was hit in the back with a combat boot and dropped like a dead parakeet. I stood motionless and stunned at my comrade's fate. Another whir sounded and I skillfully ducked the spinning boot. After the second near miss we both sobered up and made a mad dash for our bunk beds. We did not move from them until morning and any visions of sugar plums dancing in our heads were quickly replaced by black dancing combat boots.

Getting clobbered on Christmas Eve was not an isolated incident. One Christmas my godfather gave me a pistol that shot plastic disks the size of pennies. For some reason I called it an "Ogioge" gun (pronounced Oh-Gee-Oge with hard g's) and called the disks Ogioges. Back in those days they knew how to build quality toys because when I shot Jon and Karl, the disks left really big welts. Yup, those truly were the good old days when toys could cause bodily damage and really put an eye out.

Needless to say, by the end of Christmas day Ray claimed the Ogioge gun for himself. Worse yet, toward the end of the week, Mom and Dad went shopping in Glennallen and left Ray to watch us. Bad idea.

Not ten minutes after Mom and Dad left, Ray lined Karl, Jon, and me up against the closets in the back bedroom. Then he growled, "Just like the Germans used to do to the Jews [we had no idea who or what Jews were]. Close your eyes!" The three of us didn't utter a word and closed our eyes. Long agonizing moments passed before we heard the sharp clicks of the pistol and felt the plastic disks slice into our skin. We howled and tried to flee, but he blocked the back bedroom doorway and said, "It'll be worse if you try to escape." We didn't doubt him for an instant so we lined up again and repeated the ritual until *he* was tired.

I could say that Ray wasn't as bad as my stories portray him, but I would be lying. The truth is, he was a bad, bad apple rotten to the core. But, now that he is older, he is very pleasant and often smiles. His attitude is very cheerful and relaxed, and he is always ready to have fun.

I've often wondered why Ray's attitude did a 180-degree turn. And although I cannot say for sure, I think that the change has something to do with him not having to deal with three younger brothers who acted more like magpies than humans.

Mr. Plaque

Living far away from Glennallen had its advantages and disadvantages. The numerous advantages, including isolation, freedom, silence, and peace, greatly outweighed the three largest disadvantages: no police protection, no fire department, and no communications to contact anyone else for help.

Our family remedied the first problem by owning a lot of guns and being highly proficient with them. In our area, and throughout most of rural Alaska (the bush), there are no police. What I mean is that although most areas technically have a police force consisting of one or two officers, they are required to patrol literally hundreds of square miles (as was the case in Glennallen) and are therefore overextended.

If any sort of emergency occurs, the one or two officers cannot be counted on to be in their headquarters and might be as far away as 150 miles from the incident. Hence, our police force (and many others like it across Alaska) is rendered nearly useless and the law falls into each individual's hands. Self-defense and extreme independence are the keys to survival in Alaska.

Though the problem of police protection was easily overcome, the threat of a fire was never banished. If a fire started in or near our home (within a fifty-mile radius), there was absolutely no means by which to report or stop it. True, Glennallen boasted a volunteer fire department, but they were inadequate at best (which they proved to the community time and time again) and could only be reached by phone.

In the event that the team was contacted, they would roll out of their cozy beds (like molasses in January trying to turn a corner) and arrive at the burning house a few hours later or when they felt like it. Once there, they would tangle hoses, trip over one another, and attempt to put out the fire with a few gallons of frozen water. Perhaps I am exaggerating their incompetence, but after talking to our friend Dusty (whose house burned down near Glennallen) and several others, this was the consensus.

Nevertheless, without a phone we could not even attempt to rouse the Glennallen amateur fire department, and even if we could have we might have regretted it. In addition, insurance companies refused to insure our home and property against fire damage because we didn't have a real fire department. So, if a fire started anywhere remotely near our home, our family was screwed and we knew it.

In an effort to remedy this haunting problem, Dad repeatedly told us kids, "Don't play with fire." We knew the consequences were serious if we did, and we knew what would happen to the forest, the animals and our house as well. Although we were armed with this knowledge, we still took each and every possible opportunity to play with fire.

I guess we were intrigued by fire because we often saw Dad burning trash in the trash barrel. In addition, we occasionally had cookouts in the fireplace and enjoyed making a big bonfire in order to incinerate our hamburgers and hot dogs ("caveman style," as Dad used to say). The hamburgers would be charred black and have long, hard stalactites attached to their bottoms. Similarly, the hot dogs were encased in a black coating of carbon while still perfectly frozen inside. But I digress, and need only point out that burning the trash and having campfires often excited the firebug in each of us boys.

We were all very interested in flames and because Dad said not to play with fire, we played with it. Steve and Ray once started a fire by the north end of the lake and were the large-scale pyromaniacs. Karl burned models, plastic GI's and dolls and thus was the perverted pyromaniac. Jon and I were small-time criminals and simply enjoyed striking matches and watching them burn. Each one of the brothers had his specialty and took great pride in it.

On many occasions, Jon and I went into the garage and stole little boxes of "Strike Anywhere Matches." Afterwards, we walked up to the drainage ditch of our lake and struck a single match. Next, we threw the lit match on the ground and shouted, "Look! A fire! Smoky Bear doesn't like fires!" Finally, we ran over to the burning match and stomped it out.

Sometimes Jon and I just watched matches burn themselves out on the ground (to see if dropping a lit match in the moss really would start a fire like Dad said). Still other times we struck matches underneath the hobby shop where it was dark and private. This was a prime spot because no one would ever think to look for two kids starting fires while wedged underneath a shed (the crawl space was only about a foot and a half high).

The only beings who witnessed our questionable deeds under the shed were the copious numbers of spiders and the all-encompassing and sagacious Draggy (the family's small black Labrador dog who stayed cool under the hobby shop). He would gaze steadily at Jon and me with his glowing orange orbs, then dig a circular nest in the soft dirt and settle in to continue watching us with critical eyes. Although Jon and I never thought about what would happen if we actually started a fire under the shed (we would have been doomed), I believe Draggy did think of this potential disaster and that is why he watched over us so intently. Needless to say, Jon and I were morons and Draggy was the wise one in this situation (and many more over the years).

One day, after Jon and I grew bored with striking matches in the forest, under the sheds, and even under Dad's scrap metal pile, we thought of a new place to go. Without pausing to consider the safety of our idea, we headed for the trees. No, not into the forest again, but instead we headed for a tree fort situated high in the limbs of three large poplar trees. Steve and Ray had built this tree fort on Barney's property about ten years prior to our brainstorm and at this point it was quite rotten. "This is the perfect place to start fires!" I crowed as we settled into the well-rotted, high tree fort.

"Yeah, it'll be a real challenge getting them going way up here," Jon added.

Thus, one summer day Jon and I found ourselves in Steve and Ray's old tree fort with a few boxes of Strike Anywhere Matches. At first, we just lit them and watched them burn. After a bit, I grew bored of this activity and decided to stack the matches on the tree fort's floor and create little fires about three inches high. This task being successfully mastered, I took small twigs and stacked them in order to create larger blazes about a foot high.

Starting these little fires was fun, but certainly not as much fun as doing "the dragon." The dragon (not to be confused with a hot cocoa incident outlined in another chapter) was created by opening a whole box of matches about a quarter of an inch and placing it on the floor. Then, one lit match was inserted into this opening and allowed to instantly catch all the other matches on fire. The matches blazed and fire erupted from the narrow slit in the box, and Jon and I were entranced by the dragonesque nature of the phenomenon.

Although pleasurable, doing the dragon quickly diminished our supply of matches so I went back to starting little campfires on the tree fort floor.

"Jon, you should start one of these fires," I said.

"No, I'll just strike matches," he answered as he continued striking them halfheartedly. Poor Jon, he was afraid of getting his fingertips burned and held the match at the farthest point possible from the head. As a result, he found it difficult to actually ignite a match and often broke them in two (due to the leverage exerted on the end of the match). When it was finally lit, Jon watched a match burn for only the briefest period of time before vigorously waving and extinguishing it in the air.

In one of these spasmodic fits of fear, Jon shook the match too close to my head and caught a portion of my hair on fire. I felt a miniature heat wave roll across my forehead, smelled burning flesh and reached up to touch my cranium. Yellow particles of burned hair cascaded through the air and my worst fears were confirmed. Jon just pointed at me and laughed.

I was both angry and annoyed with Jon, so I decided to keep him from striking matches and lighting my hair on fire. I told him, "Build a small fire like me."

"No way."

Then I used my acute mental skills and quickly thought up a lie. "Jon, if you don't start a fire, Mr. Plaque will get you," I threatened.

Mr. Plaque was the evil cartoon character that the tooth lady (Mrs. Burgey) at school showed us in order to encourage us to brush our teeth. It never did scare the Chmielowski boys enough to make us brush, but it did scare Jon into starting a small bonfire. I'm not sure if he really believed my lie, but the desired results were produced nonetheless.

Jon and I both had small fires brewing in the tree fort and were really enjoying ourselves for a time. It was sunny out, the wind was blowing nicely, and in general it was a perfect summer day to start fires in high, rotten tree forts.

All of a sudden Jon exclaimed, "There's Ray!"

I looked in vain and asked, "Are you sure?"

"Ya, I saw him on the road, but then he disappeared," he said gravely.

We both became worried and put out our fires. After stamping out the last of our embers and noting the nice black holes in the floor, we heard Mom yelling at the top of her lungs. "Jon and Joe, come home! Jooonnnnn, Jooooeeeee, come home NOW!" We quickly shimmied down the tree trunks and sprinted home.

Mom met us outside the porch and demanded, "Where have you boys been?"

"Oh, just around the yard," I lied.

"You were playing with fire weren't you?"

70

"No," we lied in unison.

"Don't lie to me. Joe, your hair is singed. How come?"

"Oh, I burned it on the trash barrel," I casually lied again.

"No you didn't. The trash barrel isn't burning,"

"Dang she's crafty," I thought before countering, "Oh, I burned it a *while* ago on the trash barrel."

"No one has burned the trash today!" she rebutted in victory.

"Dang, I'm dealing with a crafty old mom and there's no way of winning," I thought silently. Jon and I then pleaded guilty to the charges of "playing with fire" and accepted our fate. We knew what was coming and thus we awaited Dad's return from work with jangled nerves and puckered butt holes.

Dad came home at supper and said, "OK boys. Your Mom told me you were bad. Now bend over the couch." We put our hands on the couch and then he took the big wooden spoon and gave me a beatin' first.

"F!" he yelled as he gave me a whack. "I!" whack. "R!" whack. "E!" whack. "FIRE, FIRE, FIRE!" whack, whack, whack. My backside stung like fire and so did my hands as I tried to cover my butt with them.

I ran in a few small circles and screamed, "Oooooowwwwwooooo!"

"Cry nicely," Dad said, as usual (whatever that meant).

"Oooooowwwwwooooo!" I continued to cry as I streamed out of the house. Once outside I jumped up and down and yelled and screamed and cried some more. I then waited to hear Jon's cries and yells and when I did I felt much better. Jon soon came running out of the house and we spent the whole evening crying, moping, and making plans to run away. We even cut down a few trees at the north end of the lake and started to lay the foundation of our secret cabin. By the time night came we were worn out and went home. "We'll finish it another day," we agreed.

It wasn't until some time later that Jon and I had the nerve to ask Mom how she'd known that we were playing with fire.

"Ray told me."

"How?" we pressed.

"That afternoon, Ray was on his way to the gravel pit and heard your voices. He then saw you two playing with fire and he ran home," Mom explained.

"That traitor told Mom in order to get us in trouble and watch us get our butts beat," I said to Jon.

"Yeah, I hate him."

Mom looked both of us in the eyes and said, "Perhaps Ray hates his little brothers and wants them to get their butts whipped, or perhaps maybe he cares about them and doesn't want to see them hurt. Go outside and think about it."

We went into the yard and thought about what Mom said, and after a couple of minutes of contemplating her wisdom we decided that Ray was the meanest brother in the whole world for getting our butts whipped and for deceiving Mom into thinking that he actually cared about us. "What a jerk," Jon and I repeated to ourselves as we headed to the garage in search of some matches.

Boss Hogg

Boss Hogg was Karl's nickname, and our family derived it from the old TV series "The Dukes of Hazard." Boss Hogg, one of the main characters in this weekly program, was extremely fat, lazy, and a conniving politician. Hence, Karl was gifted with this nickname that fit him like a snug pair of jockey shorts.

Karl was the third of five brothers, in the middle of the birth order. As a result, Mom referred to him as her "cream in the Oreo cookie." She also made this cookie analogy to somehow indicate that Karl was a sweet child. I was never fooled though, and I firmly believed that Karl's loads of white fat rolls resembled the cream in an Oreo cookie more than his demeanor did.

Karl was obese at a young age, but weight problems were certainly

Boss Hogg (aka Karl) took great pains to make every single day of my life a living hell.

the least of his worries. In order to hide his fat rolls, he wore a loose T-shirt that inevitably untucked itself from his waist. His free-flowing, wrinkled T-shirt made him look like a huge, slovenly ghost and Karl would have been much better off wearing a normal-sized shirt. In addition, when his T-shirt came untucked, his baggy boxer shorts pulled out too. Thus, Karl strutted around our house and Gakona Elementary School with more underwear exposed than concealed.

Worse even than his clothing problem was the fact that Mom shaved Karl's head (like the rest of us poor sods). However, instead of looking clean-cut or military-like, Karl resembled a monstrous tic. His small cranium coupled with his disproportionately large, bloated body made him nearly identical in appearance to that insect which attaches itself to a helpless victim (usually a brother) and receives free transportation and blood at its host's expense.

Furthermore, Karl sported the most hideous glasses imaginable. The lenses were about half an inch thick and made his eyes look buggish, while the frames were composed of some kind of super-industrial, black plastic material—which made him look like a cross between a physics professor and an enlisted soldier from the 1950s. Worse yet, Karl somehow managed to break these optical devices right down the middle above the nosepiece. Hence, he either had chewing gum, scotch tape, or black electrical tape (when Dad went high-tech) adorning the middle of his glasses.

As if being cursed by his physical appearance was not enough, Karl was doubly cursed by his personality and demeanor. He turned the air blue with cuss words (and farts too, I might add), swindled others, complained incessantly and wailed like a siren. In fact, he yelled, cried, and complained so much that Dad gifted him with the title "Voice of the Copper River Basin." Originally, our local radio station (KCAM) invented and used this title, but it fit Karl much better and our family swore that he could be heard on the other side of the valley.

Due to Karl's immense bulk, he was obsessed with comfort. For example, the first year we received the Alaska Permanent Fund dividend check, Mom made us buy futons because Karl, Jon, and I had been sleeping on the floor. When they arrived Karl and Jon slept on them the first night, and I burrowed underneath mine (so as to remain on the floor that I loved). The next morning, Karl woke up, went to the garage and returned with a big sheet of yellow foam. He then unzipped his futon and stuffed it with this extra foam. His futon, which had been a mere eight inches thick, was now well over a foot thick and resembled a kielbasa (stuffed Polish sausage) more than any type of sleeping mat.

In a related incident, Karl, Jon, and I bought brand-new, top-of-the-line, BMX bicycles. About thirty minutes after receiving them,

Karl went to the garage and returned with some foam and proceeded to stuff his bicycle seat.

On another day in a different year, the three of us built tundra forts at the north end of our lake. I stole old sandbags from the garage and packed them with grass to create a makeshift mattress. Jon imitated my idea, but Karl did not. Instead he swindled the old "Daddy Umpa" pillow from Mom and Dad and carried it to his fort. This pillow was a huge, orange, corduroy pillow (1970s style) complete with arm-rests, and was at least two feet thick. He also obtained some sofa pillows, from God knows where. That luxurious ratfink always managed to be comfortable, even in the worst conditions. Jon and I despised him for that.

One time I stayed the night at David Dawson's (my best friend's) house and he showed me how to build a crow's nest. A crow's nest, according to David, was simply a modified tree fort that was very small and built high in the trees. Thus, the tree fort resembled a crow's nest on an old sailing ship. I took David's design home with me and I built a crow's nest by our lake. It was about ten feet up in the spruce trees, had a triangular platform and was just big enough to stand on. Karl saw my work and liked the idea.

Needless to say, he wanted one too, but because he wasn't agile enough to climb the trees, he forced me to climb them for him. I shimmied up them very high and then constructed the foundation of his fort and helped him complete the rest. When it was finished, it stood about twenty-five feet off the ground and had a spiked ladder up the side of one tree. Additionally, the fort had a panoramic view of our lake, a view of the Wrangell Mountains (from the second floor, which he never used because his weight was too grand), and most importantly, it was large enough to accommodate a lawn chair. Yes, he actually installed a lawn chair in his "crow's nest" so that he could rest his bulk and enjoy the labors of his skinny little brother.

Karl's exploitation of his younger brothers was not an uncommon or isolated incident. Once, he cooked up this really good story about building a big tree fort along the south side of the lake. Like idiots Jon and I readily agreed. Karl gave us the big wooden ladder, the nails, and the boards and we set off through the forest and swamp.

Karl, who was not only the oldest but was also the biggest person on this expedition, had his hands full. He carried the hammer. When I questioned him, he said, "I'm only carrying the hammer, because I'm the one with the good idea and I'll be doing mental labor equivalent to the physical exertion that you guys are experiencing."

When we arrived at our destination and set the first board into place, we heard Mom yell, "Boys come home!" Her voice carried on the wind across the lake like a dreaded siren. As a result, our tree fort expedition came to an abrupt halt.

Without really thinking, Jon and I foolishly imagined that Karl would help us carry the now useless burden home. Instead, he simply smiled and said, "Nope, you guys brought that stuff out here, not me. You carry it home!" Then he trudged off towards the house with his hammer and left Jon and me with all of the other building materials to carry back.

After this incident and many others like it, it was my opinion that Karl was not only lazy, but that his ultimate goal was to gain complete domination over Jon and me. He reminded me of a king in an old 1950s, black-and-white movie—stereotypically obese, evil, and in general a royal pain in the butt—and it seemed that Karl always wanted his little brothers to do his work so that he could lounge around and collect more lipids. He was very successful in his endeavor until the day I rebelled.

After being bossed around for years, at the ripe age of nine I decided that I had had enough. When Karl wanted me to do something and I said no, he countered with the argument, "You wanna be a GI don't you? Well, a GI would do this chore." Like any young boy, I dreamed of joining the army, and thus I did whatever he commanded.

One day while Karl and I were playing at the drainage ditch, His Largeness became parched and he decided that he would like some water.

"Joe, run back to the house and get me some water," Karl demanded.

"No," I replied nonchalantly.

"You wanna be a GI? Huh?"

I thought for a couple of seconds and then yelled, "No, goddang it! I don't wanna be a GI anymore!" I left Karl standing there looking stupid—phase one of the rebellion was complete.

Jon sparked phase two a couple of weeks later when Karl was shooting his BB gun into the lake. Jon and I spotted him, and we wanted to shoot it too. We asked Karl if we could and he smiled that big politician smile and said, "Sure you can, but you have to let me shoot you in the butt first!" Well, that didn't sound too good to us, but we really wanted to shoot his BB gun. We both turned around and bent over.

Karl shot Jon first and he sprung into the air like a jackrabbit. His breathing rate increased tenfold and he danced around the yard in a spectacular fashion. Then I got nailed. It took the wind right out of my lungs. My cheeks stung for a good ten minutes, but I thought, "The reward will be worth it."

Jon got to fire the BB gun first and he hit a lily pad. I fired next and my BB landed in open water. The subtle splash caused by the BB did not seem worth the excruciating pain I had just gone through, but I really enjoyed shooting Karl's rifle.

"Wanna shoot it again guys?" Karl asked.

"Yeah!" we both answered in unison and reached for the gun.

"No way! You have to bend over again. I have to shoot you in the butt each time you want to shoot my gun."

"Dang," I thought as I grabbed my ankles.

Jon and I each got peppered in the backside again and I was allowed to fire my one pathetic shot into the water. At this point, Jon reached his critical-anger threshold and was sick of Karl's tyranny. He took the gun and pretended that he was going to shoot into the lake. Then, at the last second, Jon turned around and shot Karl right in the buttocks. "All right!" I thought excitedly as I began running from the scene of the crime.

Jon did what I had always wanted to do. The chains of tyranny had been broken and the slaves were free. "Oh, happy day!" I thought to myself as I continued running. But maybe I should have thought "Oh, happy moment," because Karl *did* own the BB gun, and it was only a matter of time before he regained his senses and hunted us down.

Revenge Is Sweet

Growing up, Karl and I rarely got along. I'm not sure why, but our personalities just seemed to clash. He was a lazy dictator and I was an annoying little brat who could provoke a sloth into a dead run. Needless to say, there were many confrontations, but I will only detail three incidents that particularly stand out in my mind.

The first took place on a sunny or rainy afternoon, I don't remember which, but that is unimportant. Karl, Jon, and I were playing behind our two sandboxes in a fenced area where all our Tonka toys (trucks, graters, cats, cars etc.) were kept. After some time, Karl yelled, "I found a huge rock over here, guys!" Jon and I approached him and looked at where he pointed and sure enough, there was a big rock just sitting on the ground.

We spent the next few minutes circled around the rock in a ring formation just staring at it. It was peculiar because in our area of the Copper River Basin, there are literally no rocks in the soil. We have hills and flats composed of glacial silt hundreds of feet thick, but absolutely no interesting rocks such as the one Karl had just found.

While we were staring at the rock dumbfounded, for some odd reason, Karl picked it up and in one fluid motion hurled it into the air. It was a big rock, about the size of a bowling ball, and it was white with black specks on it (granite most likely). I didn't see it fly into the air, but I did hear a sickening and dull crack echo through the yard. In addition, I felt an intense pain explode through the top of my skull and travel down through my spine to the very core of my being.

I crumpled under the blow (I was only eight years old and weighed 50 pounds), and wobbled on unsteady legs. I then howled in pain, confusion, and rage.

"Why'd you throw that dang rock!" I wailed.

"Shhhh. Don't worry. You're all right. It doesn't hurt. Don't go in the house, Joe. Don't tell Mom," Karl whispered in soothing tones.

I didn't tell Mom on Karl, not because he said so, but because it would have done no good. In this case, Mom could not right the heinous wrong that had been done to me. In addition, she probably would have gotten pissed at me for getting hit on the head by a large boulder and I would have gotten in trouble. Thus, I waited until the pain subsided, collected what wits I had left, and formed a strategy in my rattled brain.

I decided to pretend like I harbored no ill feelings toward Karl and I wandered away to the front of the house. I then secretly hid behind the brown propane tank beneath our kitchen window and waited for my enemy. I waited for hours for him to pass, but eventually he did and I capitalized on the opportunity.

I sprang from my hiding place with a fist-size, gray rock in my hand (Dad imported some shot-rock from Hogan's Hill and laid it along the house to keep squirrels, rabbits, weasels and other critters from making homes under it) and started running at Karl full speed. I cussed at him, muttered and readied my arm to launch the rock. Karl took one look at me and ran the opposite way into the woods.

I saw him disappear into some vegetation at the end of the pissing path and heard him stop. I took aim, calculated his whereabouts, and let the missile fly. It soared through the air, into the leaves and found its mark, which was indicated by a dull thud.

"Yes! I got him!" I thought with jubilation as I began to scramble toward the house.

Karl howled and came tearing out of the bushes after me like a wild boar. So began a day-long battle which consisted of chasing one another, throwing rocks and sticks at each other, and cussing incessantly all the while.

The second major event took place one day when I was outside the house and heard Karl and Jon on top of the kitchen roof. I was curious to see what they were doing and decided to scale the kitchen walls instead of using the ladder leaning up against the back of the house. True, I was skinny, but I was also tough and scaling this wall posed no problems for me.

I approached the wall confidently, hopped up on the big spool table where we put our dishes out to be cleaned by the birds and squirrels, crawled on to the window box where we planted beans in the summer, and proceeded to jump repeatedly until the tips of my fingers found a hold on the roof. Finally, I wiggled my hands onto the green tar-papered roof and did a chin-up.

Looking over the roof I saw Karl and Jon talking and laughing, and

I decided that I wanted to join them. I just began to pull myself up when Karl reached into his pocket and pulled out a match (he always carried a big wad of matches in his pocket so that he could set fire to anything he desired). He struck the match and threw it toward me. It bounced twice on the roof and on the third bounce landed directly on the back of my hand.

As I stared at the flame burning my hand I decided that I'd better do something quickly. "I can pull myself up, but that will take too long and I will get burned. If I let go, I will fall and get hurt," I reasoned. But in the next instant, reasoning went out the window and my instinct took over. I let go of the roof while simultaneously shaking the lit match from my hand.

Though I plummeted only six feet to the ground, when I hit I

While hanging from the roof, Karl threw a burning match on my hand and forced me to plummet to my doom. Shortly after the incident, Karl and Jon proudly survey their handiwork.

landed wrong and pain shot through my ankles and legs. Furthermore, I noticed that the back of my hand was badly burned and it was red where the match had been. I looked up expecting to hear apologies and remorse, but instead saw Karl and Jon laughing like hyenas. I was physically hurt, slightly burned and utterly humiliated. At this point, I vowed to myself that this sick and perverted injustice could not be left unpunished. I had to do something.

I planned my assault carefully. I went into the house and selected the largest bottle rocket from our huge fireworks supply. The head of the missile was composed of thick plastic, had a sharp point at the end and was about six inches long and twice as big around as a man's thumb. I hid it in my shirt, went to the hobby shop and selected the best toy rifle we had (an old one with a wood stock and hollow metal barrel). Later on in the day I spied Karl around the corner of the house and lit my rocket's fuse.

I then confronted him about the roof incident and let the great messenger of justice fly. It screamed shrilly and sped at him quickly with a shower of sparks. I had originally aimed at his head, but the missile took a disappointing dive and careened into his upper thigh. As it drilled slowly into Karl's leg, he danced like a little ballerina until it exploded with a resounding *Pow!*

"I'm going to kill you!" he howled in pain.

What sweet music to my ears. Additionally, my eyes feasted on the pain, surprise, and fear etched on his face (which must have closely resembled my face when I fell from the roof). Better yet, my spirits were further bolstered when he pulled down his pants to inspect the damage and found a silver-dollar-size bruise on his leg. I was proud of myself for not only getting even with my older brother, but for also leaving a semi-permanent mark.

The last notable confrontation took place indoors. I may or may not have done something to provoke Karl, but one evening I found myself sweating profusely while hiding in Mom's "hanging clothes closet." I heard Karl looking for me, and as his footsteps neared, I began to fear for my life.

I heard Karl hesitate, turn, and stop. I could picture him peering into the corners of the room. After a long stretch of silence, I thought the coast was clear and relaxed. Just then, he yanked open the door hard and peered directly at me. "Oh crap!" I thought. But before he could see me hiding behind Mom's blouses, my animal instincts took over (my desire to live and see another day was ingrained deep into my psyche) and I balled my fingers into a tight fist. I lunged out of the closet and hit Karl directly in the nose.

His nerdlike, taped wire-frame glasses with tinted lenses shot from his face like a rocket. I zipped by him like a weasel and bolted into the living room. Karl was blind without his glasses and had to look for them before he could locate and properly beat the crap out of me.

This was just the chance I needed, and it gave me enough time to tell Mom and Dad. Unsurprisingly, my pleas fell on deaf ears and with no other choice I slipped behind our tall winter curtains that hung in the living room. "I'm so skinny, and the drapes are so long, he'll never find me here," I thought to myself confidently. But those were my last thoughts as I heard his labored breathing and felt his pudgy but strong hands around my scrawny neck.

Chuck-Chuck Cars

When I was very young, before Karl and I developed a dislike for one another, we occasionally played together. One of our favorite activities was making things out of Lincoln Logs such as trappers' cabins or cars. We especially liked building cars and ramming them, but they easily came apart and never rolled very well. With a little thought we successfully overcame these problems by using a toy that fit our needs exactly: Legos.

Once we hit upon the idea to use Legos instead of Lincoln Logs, we had no trouble designing sturdy cars that we called "chuck-chuck cars." We called them chuck-chuck cars because we vigorously rammed them (by rolling or "chucking") against one another as hard and fast as possible. Often the cars missed each other and hit our knees and as a result we kneeled on pillows as a safeguard. When the cars did collide, they came together with a resounding *Crack!* and were then either unaffected, loosened, or reduced to rubble. If neither car was incapacitated, we would chuck them towards one another again and again until someone's car exploded. Whichever opponent's car exploded was deemed the loser.

Our initial design was based on the standard rectangular Lego which is four prongs long and two prongs wide. With this basic building block (the most common block in old Lego sets) we designed a smooth rectangular box with no moving parts or useless pleasantries. Granted, our "cars" had wheels, but they in no other way resembled a real car. In short, they were very simple, extremely durable rectangular boxes on wheels. They didn't look like much, but they were lethal.

Despite our cars' excellent design, we noticed that after several ramming sessions they still disintegrated (it was against the rules to tighten the blocks between heats), and so we built new ones. This time we duplicated our design but compressed the blocks with all our hand and arm strength. This proved a little better, but was still not good enough for our high standards, and we began standing on them. Of course, Karl weighed a solid two hundred pounds (versus my forty-five) and therefore he could compress his car far tighter than I could. I lost every competition. As if he wasn't already defeating me time and time again, he further improved his design by putting a spare wheel on the front and back of his car. Additionally, he took off the rubber tire, but left the red, four-pronged rim (in essence, a battering ram) on the front. This gave his car a big, dull spike for extra smashing power. It also hurt extra bad when it hit my kneecaps (which made him laugh).

On one occasion, for some reason or another, Ray happened to watch us duel. I am not sure why he took the time out of his busy schedule to watch his little brothers play, but maybe he really loved us. More than likely, he was amused at watching us smash something, or perhaps the sight of a chuck-chuck car slamming into our knees pleased him. Then again, it's certainly possible that he was waiting for the rare instance when a chuck-chuck car left the floor and sailed into an opponent's arm, chest or head. Nevertheless, I can't say for sure why Ray was there, but it just so happened that one day he watched us duel.

After our heated duel Ray pulled me aside. I think that what followed may be the only kind, selfless, sincere deed that Ray ever did while living at home. He showed me how to improve the design of my chuck-chuck car, so that I could defeat my archenemy!

Ray's idea was very simple and herein lay his genius. He searched through the big Lego jar when Karl wasn't looking and pulled out all the flat sheets (a sheet is four prongs wide, eight prongs long and half as thick as a standard block). He then compressed two flat sheets, put two sets of wheel blocks on top of them and filled in between the wheel blocks with standard blocks (making a rock-solid base). Ray compressed five more sheets and put them on top of the base that contained the wheels. Finally, he put battering rams on both sides of the car, and voilà! The ultimate and unbeatable chuck-chuck car was born.

The strength of the new car was due to its simplicity and seven-ply sheet design. By virtue of the sheet's nature, they adhered to one another with a tremendous suction, and formed a more solid car with fewer stress points and cracks. In addition, the small cracks that did exist were all horizontal and therefore parallel to the force of impact. Hence, the only possible way my car could come apart is if the sheets were somehow peeled apart like an onion (a vertical force was needed). The odds of that happening were about one in a million.

Karl and I dueled later on that day, and I proudly kicked his butt. Time after time I destroyed his car with my secret weapon. He later improved his car, and much to my amazement it was very difficult to defeat. I carefully scrutinized the design and found that he had painted it. He did not paint it for aesthetics, but instead for the glue-like qualities that characterize model paint. In effect, the outside of his car was glued together. I even noticed that he had taken model glue and cemented the Legos themselves! No matter, I still beat him and that pissed him off to no end.

"You better tell me your secret," he threatened that afternoon, "cause if you don't, I'm gonna beat you up at five o'clock tonight!" His threat fell on deaf ears and I refused to answer him. I never did figure out why Karl didn't look at my car and see the sheeted Legos, but then again, at this age he was famous for his mouth, not for his intelligence. As the day wore on, I became frightened and as suppertime approached I gave in to the tubby tyrant. As soon as I explained the secret sheet design to Karl, he built one himself (with utter disregard to copyright laws). We were now back on equal terms (not quite, because when he stood and jumped on his car, it was not coming apart) and the wars began with fresh hatred and enthusiasm.

The days and weeks passed and we began to tire of smashing chuck-chuck cars and incurring brutal injuries. But one day, much to our pleasure, Karl's best friend, Danny Lausen visited. We threw ourselves into our work with newfound vigor and told him that we were building chuck-chuck cars. Of course, he didn't know what a chuck-chuck car was, but like any self-respecting boy he said he'd like to play. After more than an hour Danny had built an elaborate Winnebago camper that was entirely hollow and contained all the interior furniture and appliances. Needless to say, this delicate and vulnerable piece of crap had Karl and me wrestling to see who would challenge him and destroy his hard work. After much bullying, His Hugeness got the best of me and Karl dueled Danny.

Poor Danny, he never knew what was coming. Karl's glued and sheeted chuck-chuck car tore through the beautiful Winnebago camper and reduced it to smithereens. Seeing an hour's worth of work destroyed in one second took its toll on Danny. He looked stupidly at the smashed creation while I rammed what was left of its lifeless form. I never asked Danny permission to do this dastardly deed but I didn't care. Nope, I never even hesitated in repeatedly smashing his unmoving wreck with my car. What blood lust and passion I felt as Karl watched me approvingly and Danny looked on with eyes of sorrow.

After the Winnebago incident, Danny never played Legos with us again. Furthermore, Karl and I retired our sheeted cars because there was no greater achievement we could hope to accomplish with them. After all, humiliating our unsuspecting friend was far more gratifying than any duel we could have had with our chuck-chuck cars.

M&M

When I was young, my family had a lot of nicknames for me including: Skin and bones, Jockey, Jock-Strap, Miler, Joey, and Choco. They called me Choco because I was a confirmed chocoholic and not afraid to admit it. My weakest desire for chocolate easily superseded an average chocoholic's strongest desires. In fact, my disease may have been the worst case ever documented in Alaska's history.

I ate chocolate at every single opportunity. Starting in kindergarten I ate Cocoa Puffs cereal every morning until my first day of college at West Point (for some unknown reason the U.S. Army does not like to distribute Cocoa Puffs to its troops). When available during the holiday season, I ate vast quantities of chocolate chip cookies, fudge, brownies, chocolate pie, chocolate-covered pretzels and chocolate-covered cherries. Over Easter break I ate my chocolate rabbits and chocolate eggs so quickly that I was like a tornado tearing through a trailer park. When possible, I saved my meager earnings and purchased chocolate candy bars from Sourdough and Gakona Lodge.

If the latter evidence is not convincing enough to support my premise that I was a severe chocoholic, I will further illustrate my passion for chocolate by relating an odd but very convincing tale.

I loved chocolate, but I often went without it because our family was poor. Thus, on one occasion, I was so desperate for chocolate that I actually believed Steve and Ray when they told me there was an M&M lodged in the spark plug cap of our snowmachine. I put my finger in the cap and they turned over the engine. Instantly a spark zapped my finger and I howled in pain. Not only was I humiliated and angry, but what was even worse was that I failed to procure the desired M&M.

My older brothers said convincingly, "No, really Joe! It's up there. You can't see it, but it really is. Here, try again!" I was only four years old so I readily believed my trustworthy brothers. I confidently wedged my little finger as far inside the spark plug cap as possible in search of the elusive M&M. Once again they cranked the engine. *Zap!* Those ratfinks knew that I was a chocoholic and

Karl (left), Steve (rear), and Ray (right) are huddled around Dad's Arctic Cat snowmachine which has its hood opened. "Hey Joe! There's an M&M in the spark plug cap. Put your finger in there and get it out."

they capitalized on my disease in order to generate a few cheap laughs. The shock wouldn't have been so bad had I actually retrieved the missing M&M, but as it was, I walked away empty-handed and in considerable pain.

A short time later I was innocently sauntering on the path from the porch to the outhouse (see property map, Appendix B) when Karl intercepted me and asked, "Hey Joe, I got an M&M. Wannit?"

I failed to notice Karl's big politician smile and I never questioned the fact that he had only a single M&M. More importantly, I neglected to think about why he was giving me his one and only M&M. All that mattered was that Karl had a real M&M plainly displayed in the palm of his hand and he was going to give it to *me*.

I was so ecstatic that I instantly snatched the M&M out of his hand and popped it into my mouth. I chewed the delectable tidbit so quickly that I nearly swallowed it before realizing that it tasted awful. The chocolate flavor I anticipated was replaced by a very acidic grass-like taste.

"Aaahhhhh!" I moaned helplessly as I spit out the tainted M&M. Karl stood directly in front of me laughing as he pointed at my twisted and contorted face.

"Ha, ha, ha! You idiot! You just ate a rabbit turd!" he announced triumphantly.

"No way," I mumbled. Outwardly, I could deny his accusation all I wanted, but deep down inside (especially deep inside my mouth) I knew that he was right. He had tricked me fair and square. There wasn't a dang thing I could do but accept defeat and inquire as to how he pulled off such a devious and clever shenanigan.

Karl proudly explained that earlier in the day he had found a fresh and still glossy rabbit turd behind our house. Then, using a fine brush and white model paint, he carefully painted a small white "m" on the turd. Knowing my uncontrollable desire for chocolate, he offered me the treat and as he anticipated, I indulged without hesitation. Karl had done many cruel things to me over his long and very fruitful career as an evil tyrant, but capitalizing on my choco-disease was by far his crowning achievement.

The Dance Macabre

Hey guys, let's do something cool!" Karl said.
"Uh-oh," I thought, "this sounds bad."
"C'mon guys, we have to do something!" he whined again. Jon and I looked at one another and decided that we were bored enough to hear him out.

Karl and I inspect our twelve-inch GI Joe dolls. "Hey Karl are you sure we should burn these things? They might be collectors' items some day!" "Yeah, you're right. Let's burn my Planet of the Apes dolls instead."

"What should we do?" Jon asked.
"Just listen, I've got a really neat idea ..."

Karl went into our hobby shop and emerged with a Planet of the Apes doll and some string. The doll was about one foot tall, had cotton clothing and movable arms and legs. It was definitely a collector's item, but we didn't give it any thought. Karl then smiled slyly and whispered, "C'mon guys, let's go back to Barney's!" Jon and I obediently complied and followed him on the narrow trail through the woods to Barney's (we often went to Barney's to perform things in secret because Mom and Dad never looked for us there).

After a minute's walk through the woods we arrived at the abandoned single-wide trailer and Karl led us to the back of it. "Something really good must be planned," I thought. I truly believed that Jon and I were in for something spectacular because we rarely ventured behind Barney's trailer (due to the nasty swamp and thousands of mosquitoes). Despite the harsh conditions, we pressed on eagerly to see just what sort of surprise Karl had painstakingly planned.

Once safely behind the trailer and away from the prying eyes of older brothers and parents, Karl began working quickly and vigorously. First, he scrounged around the ground and the trunks of the sickly black spruce trees until he found two sticks, each about two inches around. One stick was a bit longer than the other and he laid the two on top of one another to form a crude cross. Then he used the white string to tightly tie the sticks together. Afterwards he scrounged on the ground for dried grass. He ripped up clump after clump of straw and put it in a little pile on the ground. Finally, he took the Planet of the Apes doll and lashed it to the makeshift cross. What followed next would have made Edgar Allen Poe very proud.

Karl took the cross, stabbed it into the ground (with the crucified doll attached) and laid out all the dried grass and twigs beneath it. Then he pulled out a little container of diesel (from God knows where) and doused the doll, cross and grass. He pulled out a match from his everfull pockets and struck it. He tossed the match casually onto the grass and flames erupted quickly. After the initial shock of a large-scale diesel fire wore off, Jon and I watched with interest as the scene unfolded before us.

The original blaze died down quickly as the fuel oil was consumed, but soon the grass and twigs caught fire. After a couple more minutes, a small but truly splendid blaze burned smartly. Karl watched the fire like a madman. He looked at the crackling flames and grinned at us with a feral smile. He watched as the doll's clothes caught on fire and the cross itself began to burn.

Apparently this delighted him because he began screaming, "Aaaahhhhh! Aaaaahhhhh! Hhhhhelp!"

At first I wondered, "What in the hell is he screaming about?" Then I caught on. He was pretending that the doll was being burned alive (like during the European witch trials) and Karl was ad-libbing the screams.

"Aaaaahhhhh! Hhhhhelp!" he screamed again. Then as the blaze grew, he clenched his balls in his right hand (Karl had a habit of grabbing his nards when he was either excited or angry) and began jumping up and down.

"Aaaaahhhhh!" Karl screamed in a very high-pitched tone. "Hhhhhelp!"

Had a child psychologist been present, he or she would have been bewildered by observing a 200-pound, bald, twelve-year-old boy with big black nerd glasses clenching his balls and dancing around a burning crucified doll, while his two younger brothers stood in rapture. It was quite a sight, I assure you.

As the blaze grew and then began to dwindle, Karl's cries and excitement dwindled too. The dying flames did not inhibit Jon and me, but instead inspired us. Before the fun was entirely over, we decided to join Karl and started screaming, "Aaaaahhhhh! I'mmm dying ..."

It was actually quite fun. However, I must hastily add that we did *not* clench our balls; we left that ritual solely to Karl. We all screamed in unison until the blaze was entirely burned out and the only thing that remained was a charred cross and a melted corpse. We extinguished the fire properly (mustn't play with fire around here) and insured that all the evidence was safely buried. Finally, we straightened our clothes, took a deep breath and headed home through the woods. No person ever discovered our evil deeds or witnessed our highly secretive dance macabre.

Eggs

When Dad was away working as a laborer in the summer, we were forced to cook for ourselves (Mom's culinary skills were somewhat limited). Of course, we made only simple dishes such as grilled cheese, Top Ramen, Campbell's soup, peanut butter and jelly, mayonnaise-and-bread sandwiches, and the infamous fried-egg sandwich. Karl and I especially loved to eat fried-egg sandwiches because they were quick and easy to make, and in our opinion, were a gourmet treat.

One morning, Karl and I woke up and decided to have fried-egg sandwiches for breakfast. We poured vegetable oil in an antique, black, cast-iron pan and turned the propane stove on high. Our eggs were soon saturated with grease and ready to eat in no time. We each put a generous amount of mayonnaise on two pieces of bread and slapped the dripping, crispy eggs between the limp slices. Once the sandwiches were complete, we thoroughly enjoyed them.

Lunchtime approached and we found ourselves disenchanted with the thought of Top Ramen or grilled cheese. We had had those dishes all too often and could not think of eating them again. After much thought and even more debate, we decided to go with fried-egg sandwiches. They tasted excellent for breakfast and no doubt would be as delectable for lunch. With these thoughts in mind, Karl and I once again prepared the marvelous greasy egg sandwiches and indulged our cravings.

The afternoon wore on and dinner approached. Since the official cook (Dad) was absent, we were forced to prepare our own dinner. Karl and I were very hungry and needed something quick (we could not cook complex dishes). Once again, the thought of Top Ramen noodles for dinner seemed monotonous, and nothing else piqued our taste buds. We decided that if the fried-egg sandwiches tasted so good for breakfast and lunch, they could only be better for dinner. In the past we had eaten a good deal of fried-egg sandwiches for dinner, lunch, and breakfast, but never for all three meals in a row. We broke a Chmielowski household record that day.

Karl and I were proud of our heroic feat and enjoyed a quiet evening of play. Later that night we went to bed and slept soundly with our stomachs full of eggs. In the morning when we woke, Mom said, "Holy cow, boys, the room smelled like eggs when I passed through this morning."

Jon added, "I thought you were cooking eggs, Mom."

Mom shook her head no, and looked at Karl and me. We both smiled. Then Karl lifted his leg and let a thick, sulfurous fart dribble out, as we went to the kitchen to make breakfast.

"What should we have, Karl?" I asked.

"Brrrrrpppppp," he farted. "Hmmmmm, eggs sound good …"

I voiced my agreement with a fart, "Brrrrrrppppp," and poured the oil in the pan.

Lonesome Polecat

All members of my family were eccentric in their own way, but Jon easily outdid us all. Whereas Steve was Mr. Sensitive, Ray was perpetually pissed, and Karl was a hedonist dictator, Jon was a loner (even by Chmielowski standards). Granted, I did spend some time playing with him, but usually Jon preferred to be alone. "He's a lonesome polecat," Mom and Dad used to say.

Due to his self-imposed isolation—as if living in the middle of nowhere wasn't enough—he had quite an active imagination. At the tender age of four he would put the inside of his elbow on the tip of his nose and let the remainder of his arm hang limply. Then he would stomp around the house making elephant sounds.

Soon after mastering the elephant impersonation, Jon decided that he liked dinosaurs (fifteen years before *Jurassic Park*). He would arch his thumb like a raptor and twist his index and middle fingers into claws. Then he would growl like a Tyrannosaurus Rex and stomp around the house in this fashion for some time. No one in the family bothered Jon when he behaved in this manner because he was entertaining himself and that was great. Truthfully, though, who in their right mind would have attempted to get in the way of an overweight, bald-headed six-year-old who was howling and gnashing his teeth, and slashing at the walls with his talons? It just wasn't prudent.

On several occasions I remember Jon and me pretending that we were dinosaurs and spending hours on all fours in the yard. We grazed, growled, and ate grass as well as leaves (we even tried other hors d'oeuvres, but personally, I do not recommend either spruce tree sap or willow bark for any young dinosaurs).

Later in Jon's impersonation career, he put his arms at his sides and kept them very stiff. Then he bent his wrists upward and pointed his fingers out and pretended that he was a snowmachine (or as the

93

folks in the Lower 48 say, snowmobile). The idea was that his arms and hands were skis. Jon tore through the house making engine noises, "Brrrrrmmmm, brrrrrmmmm!"

Next, he suddenly stopped, and taking his right hand he curled all his digits inward except his index finger. Then, as he made revving noises he rotated his extended index finger in a clockwise fashion in imitation of a snowmachine's speedometer. Sometimes Jon would rev up his engine and watch his finger/speedometer for as long as twenty minutes or more.

Jon also impersonated helicopters. He used the same arm and hand ski mechanism as he did for the snowmachine, but for a helicopter he would bend at the waist and put the skis under his body (just like a real helicopter). In addition, his sound effects were different and he would chant in a diminishing tone, "Pooka, pooka, pooka, dooka, darn, darn ..." as if the chopper were receding into the distance.

1977: Jon at age five riding his Kitty-Kat snow-machine on our lake.

The craziest thing Jon tried to imperson-ate was the ptarmigan bird. For this special task, he had no weird arm movements or crazy sound effects, just a couple of authentic bird wings safety-pinned to the shoulders of his winter coat. Mom gave him the wings from one of Dad's hunting kills and Jon wore them with pride. As a matter of fact, he spent nearly a week jumping off our spool table, picnic table, and truck's tailgate trying to fly. Though he had no success at flying or even gliding, he did have infinite success at skinning his knees.

My family must have considered Jon crazy, but I must admit that I did not think that he was insane (especially because his wings were real) and I was convinced that if he'd just tried to jump off the garage roof, he could have flown.

"The extra air will help you," I stated persuasively, but to my great disappointment Jon never leaped.

Jon was also good at crying, wailing, and using body language to communicate how pathetic he felt when the mood—or Dad—struck him. In cases like this, he could outperform some of Hollywood's best actors. He was so good that he even taught me all his tricks and as a team we could minimize our physical or emotional pain while simultaneously maximizing our self-pity.

For instance, after receiving a good spankin'—usually for playing with fire or throwing snowballs—Jon and I would mope around together for hours. We cried, wailed, whimpered and made pathetic animal noises hours after the pain had subsided. We made

Jump off the garage, Jon! Your wings will work ....

noises like, "Mmmmm, Owwwwwooooo, mmmmmmm, hiccup, bbbbbbmmmmmm ..." and so on and so forth. When one of us stopped and seemed to be coming out of the delirium, the other guy gave a short "mmmmmmm ..." and the whole process would start again for hours.

Our whimpering and whining sessions often carried on a whole afternoon. Just the two of us, moping around the yard and house, feeling sorry for ourselves and as if the end of the world was near. It was times like these that we said, "Yeah, if we were dead or gone, Mom and Dad would be sorry. Let's run away."

Jon and I would wander to the north end of the lake and attempt to build some sort of pathetic tundra teepees to live in until we were old and dead. Inevitably, we tired quickly and returned home at suppertime. Although we were never successful at running away, moping around with Jon was quite a bonding experience and he was very good at teaching me how to feel lonely and unloved—just like a lonesome polecat.

High-Speed Cook

Jon loved food as much as Dad, but unlike my father, whose patience knew no bounds (especially when he was preparing a delectable meal), Jon's eagerness and primitive cravings for food compelled him to act rashly. Jon just could not wait for a pot to boil or a meal to cook. He had to have his hunger satisfied now. Because of his compulsive-obsessive behavior, Jon often found himself in interesting situations.

In our front yard we had a permanent fire pit surrounded by cinder blocks and large rocks from Hogan's Hill (the only source for rock within ten miles), all cemented together with gray glacier mud from the lake. About once a month, the family gathered at the campfire pit and had a spectacular cookout. The fire blazed, camp robbers robbed our food, and the dogs lounged nearby waiting for treats.

1980: The High-Speed Cook (aka) Jon with a bad hair day.

The family's favorite cookout food was hot dogs and Dad, Mom, Steve, Ray, Karl, and I would roast them patiently until they were golden brown. Not Jon, though. He took a frozen hot dog from the pack, forced it onto a long thick wire, and thrust it wholly into the flames and glowing red coals. After searing his hot dog for thirty seconds, he removed its charred, black, ash-encrusted form from the fires of hell and commenced eating it right off the wire!

More amazingly, the inside of the hot dog was frozen like a rock, while the outside sizzled like hot bacon. Without paying heed to frostbite or burns, Jon consumed the thing quickly and efficiently and speared another in order to subject it to the same thirty-second ordeal. It was by this method that Jon earned our respect in the food consumption area and none dared slow him down or cross his path.

To prove that the hot dog ritual was not an isolated case, a close look at his grilled-cheese preparations will suffice. As usual, one day Jon's hunger could not wait and he threw a large pad of butter (close to a quarter stick) into a small pan (the same size as his sandwich) and turned the propane stove on high. The pan was so small that the blue flames from the stove wrapped around it wholly, and Jon was satisfied that he could prepare this meal quickly.

In anticipation of his soon-to-be-done sandwich, he ran to the back bedroom for some potato chips. When he returned, yellow flames a foot high were consuming his grilled cheese while smoke billowed up to the kitchen ceiling. Jon reacted quickly and put out his sandwich, flipped it over, finished burning it, and without hesitating consumed it with pleasure. Granted, it was a little more charred than usual, but "At least the cheese had time to melt," I thought wryly. Owing to this incident, Jon earned the nickname "High-Speed Cook" and he took great pride in it.

Though Jon often found himself in odd predicaments similar to the grilled-cheese fire, the family never judged him and he pursued his eccentric ways in peace. Jon's naïvete, good heart, and gentle nature only made us smile and shake our heads in mild disbelief. However, his knack for disaster and his desire to be the best high-speed cook he could be; truly amazed us, and left Mom and me aghast at what Jon did one day.

Aunt Kathleen, who lived with my Uncle Ray in Anchorage and occasionally visited us in the countryside, was seated at the table playing cards with Mom. I was sitting in the "Queen's Chair," and Jon was in the kitchen hastily assembling a fried-egg sandwich (high-speed style, I might add). While his eggs burned nicely in the cast-iron pan, he frantically scraped the inside of the mayonnaise jar to extract his usual quantity of white stuff for the bread (a full one quarter inch thick on each slice). While thus engaged, he tried hard to scrape under the lip of the jar and as a result the metal knife built up a lot of tension in the blade and handle. What happened next the gods could not have foreseen.

I heard a metallic twang, and witnessed a glob of greasy mayonnaise hurtling through the air. The glob sailed through the small window that connected the kitchen with the living room (see house map, Appendix A), ducked below the ceiling, and landed right on the back of Aunt Kathleen's head. I looked to my left and saw Jon's eyes bulging and his hand covering his mouth. I looked to my right and saw Aunt Kathleen scratch her head as if a mosquito had alighted there. "What in the world?" she questioned as her fingers came in contact with the slimy substance. Mom stood up and investigated, only to report that the mysterious goo was mayo. Both of them looked at Jon who just smiled and shrugged his shoulders.

Jon's successful assault on Aunt Kathleen was the talk of the family for some time, similar to the talk of a small town when one of its inhabitants wins a lottery. The story was told and retold with awe, amazement, and respect for Jon. It was stretched and exaggerated until everyone commented on the odds of such a great feat.

Everyone was forgetting, though, that we were dealing with Jon, a unique human by most people's standards, and by his family's. Hence, a good, or not so good, mathematician could tell you that the odds were phenomenally high that he would successfully flick mayo across a room into his aunt's hair. Any betting man, or even a fool, if he had known Jon personally would have gambled his mother's life on such odds. This is why I wasn't surprised when one day Aunt Josie came to visit and a similar calamity befell her.

Aunt Josie was playing cards with Mom, sitting in Aunt Kathleen's favorite chair (mistake no. 1), with her back to the kitchen (mistake no. 2), and was wholeheartedly absorbed in the game (three strikes and you're out). I was in the Queen's Chair and Jon was in the kitchen, hastily (always hastily, mind you) building a grilled-cheese sandwich. With one swift stroke of his mighty butter knife he lopped off a quarter stick of butter and somehow, I'll never know quite how, managed to catapult his load from the knife.

"Déjà vu," I thought to myself.

The hunk o' butter sailed through the air according to the now established flight path, and pounced deliberately on the back of Aunt Josie's skull. Like Aunt Kathleen, Josie reached up and was both mystified and horrified to find a wad of grease in her hair. As I said, she was both mystified and horrified, but not at all shocked or surprised to look up and find Jon smiling sheepishly and shrugging his shoulders apologetically. After all, Jon was Jon, and the family knew that odd events often and coincidentally transpired around the High-Speed Cook.

Attempted Murder

In the Chmielowski household, when one of the boys lost a tooth, the genie came. No, not the tooth fairy, the genie. Not automatically though. Nope, as anyone knows, the genie had to be summoned. That's what Mom said. In order to insure that the genie came (and with him some money or prizes), the boy who lost his tooth would take a special lamp and rub it.

The lamp was an old brass piece, probably purchased in a junk catalog, and sat on our windowsill. The lucky boy took this lamp and rubbed it while crouched in a secret location. The lamp could not be rubbed while anyone else was around, and you had to say secret words such as, "Genie, genie, come tonight. Bring me something very nice." This chant was usually repeated three times as one concentrated intently on the desired prize. In addition to these words, some really magical incantations could be uttered such as, "Please bring me a really good prize, *please!*"

This task was accomplished during any portion of the day, morning or evening, and the only thing left to do was wait until the next morning. Upon waking, the lucky boy looked under his pillow and discovered the genie's hidden treasure. Sometimes the genie would leave a pile of change, a small prize, or nothing. Yes, sometimes the genie left nothing. That dang genie either ran out of prizes or just plum forgot about the tooth so recently lost. I don't think he really ran out of prizes; after all, he was a genie. So that meant the tooth thing slipped his mind, and perhaps he did not concern himself with the misery and agony associated with losing teeth. The heartless weasel. Well, the only course of action was to ask Mom what happened.

"Oh, I don't know. Maybe you didn't look hard enough," she said.

Then Mom would go into the bedroom and look through the covers and under the bed and miraculously produce the sought-after treasure. "Here it is!" she exclaimed, and everything was all right. The genie was forgiven and life went on.

The boys always wanted an extra prize and the genie was one potential gift giver. All you had to do was lose a tooth! So naturally any one of the boys was always wiggling, pulling, and making every effort to lose a tooth on any given day of any given month. The boy who got lucky (or was overly ambitious, as the case may be) and was able to remove a tooth, held his grinder up like an idol. "Ha! The genie will come to me tonight and I will get a prize!" Having said this the fortunate boy grabbed the lamp and retired to a secret place to perform the ceremony.

I remember one of these situations when Jon happened to be the lucky boy and Karl and I stood gaping at his good fortune (and toothless smile), while he gloated over his future wealth. Karl and I were so jealous that we could not stand the injustice done this day.

We entered the house, grabbed the lamp, and commenced working on a hasty plan right away. Karl grabbed some toothpicks and chewing gum, and I collected a glass of water. We opened the main compartment of the lamp and wedged several toothpicks into the wick-hole that penetrated into a smaller compartment. Next, we filled the small compartment with water and let the fluid seep into the wick-hole. Finally, we plugged up the wick-hole on the small compartment's side with toothpicks and sealed both sides of the hole with chewing gum. There, it was done. The deed was done, and although Karl and I were nervous, we felt good about our accomplishment.

Jon found the lamp and took no time in bawling when he saw the wicked act that Karl and I had just completed. He could not comprehend the desecration that had taken place. Worse than that, he could not comprehend the fact that he would not be getting any prizes. You see, the wick-hole in the lamp was the only logical place where the genie could live (because we could not see inside of it), and hence, Karl and I had potentially drowned the genie. If not, without a doubt we had sealed him within his dwelling so that Jon could not receive any prizes! Jon was horrified and now it was our turn to gloat.

Karl and I made a good effort at killing the genie, but it did not work. Furthermore, Jon was able to unplug the wick-hole and perform the ceremony in secret. That night the genie came and Jon found a prize in his bed the next morning. Karl and I were both very disappointed but we learned an important lesson. You can't kill a genie.

Skin and Bones

When I was young, my family said that I was nothing but a sack of skin and bones. In fact, I was so skinny that the first year I wrestled (kindergarten), I was 35 inches tall and weighed 35 pounds. That year, when I went to the doctor for my sports physical he told Mom that I was "a pound an inch." The doctor's observation only confirmed what my parents and brothers always feared. I was bony, skinny, anorexic, starving, and it was just a matter of time before I died or the wind blew me away.

Like any good parents, Mom and Dad tried to encourage me to eat. They employed many tactics such as coaxing, rewarding, threatening, punishing, pleading, laying guilt trips, cussing, etcetera. They tried their hardest, but I still would not eat. In fact, I was so unlike my father and brothers that the family (and Mom too) claimed I was the mailman's son, and hell, we never even had a mailman.

Perhaps some of my eating problem was psychological, but most of it was physical. I could not eat certain types of foods without my body revolting and on the rare occasions that I tried, the effort always ended in failure. Inevitably, the bile in my stomach rose up into my mouth and I would either gag openly or swallow my puke silently.

I explained this odd phenomenon to Mom and Dad, but it never sunk into their brains and they continued their efforts in vain. On one occasion, Mom didn't let me leave the table because I would not eat her lasagna. I sat at our table from supper (five o'clock sharp every day without fail) to ten o'clock and adamantly refused to consume the vile stuff. Actually, my body refused to allow the cheesy substance down my throat and when I finally did try to swallow, my stomach had a mind of its own.

First, it contracted, and then it sent bitter bile up to intercept the intruder from above. The piece of lasagna was met somewhere in the midthroat region, was stopped successfully, and was then escorted back up to the friendly territory of the mouth. The taste of regurgitated lasagna and acidic bile mixed together caused me to retch and I never attempted to eat lasagna again.

In addition to loathing lasagna, I hated the following foods and then some: green beans, spinach, peas, all cooked vegetables (except corn), beans, chili, steak, cheeseburgers, nuts, all breads (except store-bought white bread), jelly, all condiments (except mayonnaise), tacos, burritos, moose, caribou, roast, ribs, fish, ham, anything barbecued, all soups (except Dad's beef soup), stew, casseroles, macaroni, seafood, and anything I considered to be weird or unidentifiable. The only food that I really enjoyed, and that sat well in my stomach, was certain types of junk food.

I could eat enormous quantities of chocolates (without nuts or anything weird on or in them), chocolate cake, and chocolate pies. All other nonchocolate candies and sweets I considered to be as evil as liver and onions and I would not touch them on pain of death.

Thus, I survived on a steady diet of chocolate when the opportunity presented itself, but mostly I went hungry because Mom wouldn't let me indulge in junk food if I didn't eat her "real meals." During hard times like these, I sneaked into the meat shed and stole a couple of slices of frozen Wonder bread from the freezer. I hid under the platform by our lake and consumed them greedily. I sustained myself in this manner for quite some time and even managed to keep my secret by cautiously extracting no more than three slices of bread from each loaf.

Eating slices of plain white bread and the occasional candy bar did not help me grow or gain weight and I quickly became the runt of the litter. My parents, brothers, and all the kids at school remarked on my diminutive nature every day of my childhood. As if that wasn't bad enough, my head was shaved like a cue-ball and I had a huge gap between my front teeth a full quarter of an inch wide (Karl called me Skip Stevenson in reference to the old TV show "*That's Incredible*" because of my gap or skip). Furthermore, my lack of experience with nonfamily humans left me especially vulnerable to the kids at school.

Though the cards were stacked against me, I balanced the deck somewhat with my natural abilities. At a very early age I could outrun both Karl and Jon, I could climb any tree (skinny, fat, short, or tall), scale any building without a ladder, and hide in places that would elude the best Labrador dog (no real Alaskan has a hound dog). In addition, I had a quick wit and I used it.

When I was four years old I was jealous of my brothers because they got to go to school. I would mope around the house with nothing to do and I had to stay at home all day with Mom. But, that same September, Mom scrounged up some school supplies (from the Glennallen correspondence department), and even excavated an ancient wooden desk from the attic of the high school wood shop. She then presented these two gifts to me for my birthday and I thought they were the best birthday presents I ever received.

The old green desk opened at the top and had a swivel chair. The supplies contained reams of lined papers, arithmetic problems, and a red magnifying glass in the shape of an elephant. I was happy to have all of the "school stuff," but I really fell in love with the magnifying glass. I stared at it constantly (though not necessarily through it), and played with it like a toy animal.

As soon as Steve, Ray, Karl, and Jon got on the school bus at 7:10 a.m., I thought they were instantly at school and I started my studies diligently. I worked through the day, took a lunch, and then worked until they arrived home on the bus around 4:20 p.m. Mom tried to explain to me that my brothers went to school only from 8:30 a.m. to 3:00 p.m., but I did not understand her and kept my schedule throughout the year. I wanted to be just like my brothers, and even more important, I wanted to be good at something that didn't depend on my size.

That year, Mom taught me simple mathematics (counting, writing numbers, addition, and subtraction) and many other skills. However, she refused to teach me how to read on purpose because she figured that if I began to read at four years, I would get bored in school and there would be trouble. So I spent my entire pre-kindergarten year at home with Mom studying math and logic games five days a week. During that year of home schooling, I honed my wits until they were razor sharp and I felt confident in myself.

When I attended kindergarten, Mom was right and I was bored. I despised the childish arithmetic Mom assigned (Mom was the kindergarten teacher this year and had to follow the school district's work and schedule policies), and I hated the mandatory nap time even more. I told Mom that I hated kindergarten and she attempted to help me the only way she knew how.

Mom tried to enroll me in first grade with Jon, but the child psychologist said I had too short of an attention span and that I couldn't do the work. She based her opinion on a test she administered and I failed.

"Which one of these items is unsafe?" she asked me. "The ladder, the toy, or the cup?"

"None of them," I answered (how was I supposed to know that a ladder was considered "unsafe" when I climbed them all the time and Dad told us to use them to shovel snow off the roofs?).

"Which one of these items is unsafe? The kite, the hammer, or the pocket knife?" she asked next and pointed to a series of three pictures.

As I sat silently I pondered her question thoughtfully. I knew it wasn't the pocketknife because I had one in my pocket that Dad gave me. Furthermore, I knew it wasn't the hammer because I saw my Dad build things with hammers and I myself even helped my brothers build tree forts with hammers. Perhaps it was that dang kite thing that I had never seen. It looked like it could strangle the hapless kid in the picture or even suck him into the sky by that rope tied to his arm.

"The kite, definitely," I responded with confidence.

"What is missing in this picture?" she asked finally and pointed to a telephone.

I looked at it for some time and then answered, "I don't know."

She smiled at me and said, "Obviously, the receiver cord is missing."

That one flew over my head because we didn't have a telephone, I never talked on one before, and I had no idea what a receiver cord was. I failed the test miserably.

After failing the first grade entrance exam, my only other option was the "Jon option." That is, the first day Jon attended kindergarten he did not like it and said, "I don't want to go again."

"Well, you don't have to," answered Mom and so she let Jon stay home.

The next year he went to first grade and said, "I don't like it, I'm going to stay home this year too." But poor Jon could not, and so he embarked on a tremendously nerve-racking and mind-boggling school career. Unlike Jon, though, I looked forward to first grade (what I considered real school), and decided to stay in kindergarten in order to be near Mom and as close to my brothers as possible.

When I finally did go to first grade, I was not disappointed. My teacher, Mrs. Browder, taught us to read, write, and do even more math (multiplication tables and simple division). True, I was bored at times, but because there were only three first-graders (David Dawson, Liana Charley, and I), we received special attention, a tailored curriculum, and help from the upper-graders (second- and third-graders who were in the same room). I learned a great deal that year and became best friends with David Dawson.

Throughout first grade and the rest of my elementary years, I took academics and wrestling (people my size and weight) very seriously. My love for both of these activities deepened and became my entire life in junior high, high school, and even college.

My body and mind became stronger and though I was a bit lanky, I was neither weak nor weak-willed. Being a sack of skin and bones as a child shaped the person I am today and gave me inner strength beyond any physical attributes.

1982: Three Natives and a Polak earn gold and silver medals at the state wrestling championships in Anchorage. Left to right: Darin Gene, Skin and Bones, Robert Craig, and Harvey Jackson.

Miler

Miler. That was what they called me. They being my brothers, of course. Actually, they being only my brother Karl. But regardless, I had earned my nickname and I was proud of it.

Growing up without running water naturally meant that we had no plumbing and therefore had an outhouse. However, our outhouse

I (aka Joe) was a sack of skin and bones with a shaved head and no front teeth. So what? I could piss a mile and that __had__ to be worth something ...

became quite unpleasant smelling in the summer, not to mention the pesky flies that incessantly buzzed us. In addition, during the winter months when all of the brown material was frozen and did not smell, we encountered a different problem. The fudge tended to form a stalagmite sort of formation that would rise up from the hole in the ground by as much as four feet. Sometimes it got so tall as to make us nervous when we sat on the seat and we prayed that our butts would not scrape the mysterious formation. But enough about outhouses; suffice it to say that we used it only when we needed to pitch a load.

As a result, from my earliest childhood days I would leak outside. I would leak on trees, plants, shrubs, rocks, ants, snowbanks, paths, or wherever was convenient or pleasant. Eventually, I found out at about the age of four that I had a certain gift. I was able to urinate incredible distances and hit small targets at the same time. At first only I knew about my super powers. I would stand and whiz like a madman, four, five, six feet distant. Soon I honed my skills so that I was whizzing in excess of twelve feet. I would angle my golden stream at forty-five degrees and let her go. What fun I had as a child. Sometimes I would spy a target, perhaps a wood chip, a branch or a large black carpenter ant, and space myself deliberately ten feet away. Then I would do my duty and improve not only my long-distance abilities but also my precision. In time I found stationary objects boring and the ants could not move quickly enough to avoid my yellow death. I had to find something new and challenging.

Outdoor buildings provided the answer to my dilemma. I would stand next to a building, maybe the generator or screen shed, and whiz in a parallel line with a wall. The goal was to see if I could make the top arc of my stream bisect the invisible plane formed by the roof of the building. In a relatively short period, I could accomplish this task with little effort. Sometimes, just to prove that my abilities were no hoax, I would actually whiz onto the roof of a building and reaffirm my supernatural powers.

It was during one of these power trips that my brother Karl discovered my unusual urinating abilities. I can't remember when or where it occurred, but I do know that I was whizzing madly when Karl came up and said "Goddang! You can piss a mile! Man, we should call you Miler!" And so he did. That was my nickname and I was downright proud of it.

As I grew older, I found that my skills and potential knew no bounds and I became bored with life and whizzing. I had to do something. I couldn't let all my talent go to waste. There had to be some crowning achievement, some climactic ending to the years of rigorous training I had put myself through. I was ready for retirement, but I could not justify quitting without a grand finale. In this quest I was not disappointed when one day the opportunity presented itself.

I must have been nine years old when on a sunny day I decided to climb Dad's big, uncut-wood pile (see property map, Appendix B). I was standing on top of the pile and felt the urge to whiz. "This will be nice. I should be able to get four extra feet of horizontal distance due to my increased altitude," I thought. I knew that the horizontal gain was about four feet because I was just as much of a veteran at pissing off roofs as I was at pissing onto them. In addition, pissing off a roof is almost the same as pissing off a woodpile, so I knew my calculations were accurate.

While I was mathematically engaged, the most magnificent thing happened. Jon was walking below the pile, minding his own business, and did not see me. "What luck. He may be out of range, but I'll give it a whirl," I thought to myself with delight.

I whizzed like I never whizzed before, and that afternoon I truly lived up to my nickname, the Miler. My golden stream shot out into the sunshine, cut a beautiful arc across the blue sky and fell right on my intended target. I still remember the question mark etched on Jon's face as he brushed his hair and looked for the rain cloud. Poor Jon, he probably would have never known his ill luck had I not started ranting hysterically like a little monkey.

"Ha, ha, ha," I laughed at my big brother, "I pissed on your head!"

Even though Jon was twice my size, I felt undaunted because I was on top of the woodpile and could easily outrun him. I don't remember if he ever beat me up, but I do remember that I retired after the woodpile incident and I do remember that Jon was quite pissed.

Draggy

All true Alaskans have dogs (usually large ones) and our family was no exception. From the early years when my father homesteaded our land, to the later years when I graduated from high school, our family always kept one or two dogs. Their job was primarily to offer companionship, but they also helped with hunting and trapping, and they kept watch over our house and family.

Our dogs were treated as members of the family, save when they were being worshipped like gods by us younger boys. The first few dogs (Trouble, Sorrow, Pokey, and Bruiser) I do not remember because they passed away years before I was born. However, our last three dogs (Boy, Fang, and Brutus) I remember very well.

Mom and Dad bought Boy from a GI in Anchorage in March of 1971, and he was the only dog they ever paid money for. Boy was a small black lab with very short and shiny fur. I am not sure why my parents named him Boy, but we had scores of nicknames for him including our two favorites, Draggy and Father Rawhide.

Jon and I used to worship Draggy and would spend hours following him, petting and combing him, and even sleeping on him (we used his back hind leg as a pillow). We nicknamed over eighty body parts on him including: cow ears, salt and peppers (area dotted with holes where his whiskers emerged on his lips), bores (nostrils), humdigger (fur under his chin), mountain point (knob on the back of his cranium), possessors (muscles on the sides of his head), pad-pads (feet or paws), rape-rapes (soft, muscular area of the back leg), Coleman lantern (his penis, which would occasionally glow red and alert us to run for our lives), and on and on. I mention this extensive list of nicknamed body parts simply to demonstrate how many hours and days we doted on our favorite dog.

Boy, like most labs, was very intelligent. Also, like most labs, he enjoyed lounging by a warm stove and would only occasionally go outside to relieve himself or take a short walk with Dad. In addition, Boy (like all our previous and future dogs) was never chained up, never wore a collar, and was never forced to stay at or near home. He had free rein of our property and literally hundreds of square miles of Alaskan wilderness. Needless to say, he would disappear into the forest a full half mile when going to the bathroom, and sometimes many miles when searching for porcupines or squirrels. Like all our other dogs, Boy had a life to be envied for its freedom and wildness.

As good as Boy had it, though, and as much as we loved him, we were still cruel to him in a childish and naïve way. I remember Karl, Jon, and I once locked him in our big hobby shop and slid some lit fireworks under the door. They whistled, fizzed, and zipped about with vigor and when Boy finally emerged his eyes were like saucers and he moved quicker than the rockets we launched at him. Hence, we dubbed him with yet another nickname, "Rocket."

Inspired by Boy's theatrical abilities, on another occasion we locked him in Barney's abandoned trailer and repeated the barrage of fireworks. We opened the door afterwards but this time he didn't emerge. We went inside the smoky building and found him huddled underneath an old bed. We spent several minutes coaxing him out and when he did emerge, he low-crawled on his belly all the while eyeing us suspiciously. This sight weighed so heavily upon our hearts that we never scared him with fireworks again.

Sometimes when we went for walks on the highway, Boy tried to follow. "Go home!" we yelled at him, but because he was so loving and obedient he wouldn't listen. In a case like this, we picked up handfuls of dirt and rocks and threw "buck shot" at him. After being stung by the rocks he would turn and go home. We didn't want Boy to be hit by a car or a truck, so sending him home with a peppered butt was for his own good.

At times we were overzealous throwing rocks and we often took pleasure at trying to hit Boy when he was marking a tree, or wading in a deep swamp (which we nick-named "Brontosaurusing"). I even went so far as to throw a big rock (about two to three inches long) at him once for not going home. I didn't think I would actually hit him, but the rock flew true and hit him squarely in the ribs. He looked at me, turned his head away and walked slowly home. I never forgot the way he looked at me with those wise, golden eyes. He seemed to be utterly disappointed in me, as if he really was my father. I think the rock hurt Boy's feelings more than his body, and it hurt me even worse than it hurt him.

I threw that rock when I was very young, and after the incident I truly understood "Father Rawhide" and treated him with all the respect he deserved. Karl and I would take him to Sourdough Creek with us and he crawled in our forts (which were simply excavated beaver holes in the banks). He nestled in the rear of the caves and when we lit candles his eyes glowed in the dark. We also took him fishing and swimming at Gulkana River, and raspberry picking on Hogan's Hill. He enjoyed these little trips immensely except for the mosquitoes and horseflies that buzzed him. He expertly snapped them out of the air and ate their bodies with great relish.

Draggy lived a long and fruitful life. Excepting the fireworks and rock incidents, he was well treated and loved by the whole family. In addition, he aged like fine wine and by his fifteenth year was still quite healthy, albeit a bit gray around the muzzle. His golden eyes still sparkled with wisdom and his connection with the family had grown inconceivably strong. I thought he would live forever, and I really expected him to be around when I was gray.

In October of 1985, Steve and Ray came up from Anchorage and decided to drink some beer. Karl and Jon joined in, but I didn't since I was only twelve years old. They all had a good time and drank until very late. Then, in an effort to sober up, they took a walk on the highway about one o'clock in the morning. In their drunken state they didn't notice the ever watchful and obedient Father Rawhide slip out the door and follow them.

I am not sure what happened, but I was awakened at about three in the morning to the sound of Jon puking and howling. Apparently, Jon's first experience with alcohol did not treat him so well (he was thirteen years old), and I was definitely glad I did not take part in the celebration. Something else was wrong though, and Karl and Ray were babbling about Boy.

"Boy got hit by a truck," They moaned in a drunken stupor.

The words hit me in the gut and left me with an empty feeling. I double-checked the back bedroom and sure enough, he wasn't there. I cried to myself in bed, trying to figure out how I would go on without him. He watched over me as a baby and as a boy, and was my best friend as a young man.

"Why the hell did my brothers have to get drunk? It's their fault!" I thought again and again.

The next day was sunny and cold, a typical Alaskan autumn day. The sky was crystal clear and the light hurt my eyes. Karl and I took the blue truck up to Rose Bud Hill and parked it by the black carcass that was once Boy. He wasn't mangled or visibly violated; only his empty stare and the telltale trickle of blood from his lips gave a clue to his state.

I saw the black tire marks where the semitruck had put on its brakes and a spot of brown where Draggy's life had ended.

"C'mon, let's take him home," Karl said. Karl grabbed his front legs and I grabbed his back legs and we lifted his stiff body into the back of the truck. "God, he was a light little bastard, huh?" Karl remarked.

"Yeah," I answered and watched as my breath turned white and floated away. I stared after it for some time in a daze and then studied the asphalt and the highway's berm where Draggy had lain. I reached down and picked up two gray pebbles with brown stains on them and also a lock of black fur. I put these items in my pocket and hopped in the cab of the truck.

We hauled Draggy's dead body behind the outhouse to a big hole. The hole was about four feet in diameter, five feet deep and had filled with water that was now frozen on top. Steve and Ray dug it years ago as a reserve outhouse hole, but it would now serve just as well as a grave. I don't know where all my other brothers were, or where Mom and Dad had gone, but none of that mattered.

I reached down and petted Draggy as he lay on his side near the watery grave. Where once his body had been soft and warm, it was now hard and cold.

"I love you, Draggy," I thought to myself. "I'll never forget you. I love you," was all that I could think again and again. I then knelt beside him and kissed his salt and peppers and his possessors one last time.

"C'mon, Joe, let's put 'em in."

I stood up and we shoved his body into the hole. His carcass easily broke the thin veneer of ice and floated in the gray water. The sight sickened me.

"Let's get some rocks," Karl suggested. We went along the house and found several large rocks and carried them back to the hole. We dropped them on his body. Each of the rocks landed with a dull thud as they hit his ribs and forced him to sink. After four rocks we could no longer see Father Rawhide's body, and he left my life forever.

"Hey, maybe we can get the skull in a few years," Karl joked halfheartedly.

"Yeah," was all I could say as I stared into the gray murkiness. As I turned my back on the hole I reached into my pocket and rubbed my bloody pebbles.

I kept those two pebbles and the lock of fur in a little box and have them to this day. For years I blamed my brothers for Boy's death, but maybe I should have thanked Draggy for my brother's lives. Who knows, if the truck hadn't hit Boy and slowed down, it could have just as easily hit a few drunken kids on a lonely highway. Even in death, Father Rawhide demonstrated wisdom, obedience, and love.

The Outhouse

I disliked the outhouse and took great pains to minimize my time within or near it. Nevertheless, after years of repeated use I was intimately familiar with its details and quirks. It was 4 by 4 by 8 feet in dimensions and constructed out of very stout one-by-fours, one-by-twos, and two-by-fours. Unlike our other outbuildings, the outhouse wasn't Dad's work (thus its solid construction) but instead he retrieved it from the Paxon campground in 1964. Afterward, he blasted a hole behind our house with a few sticks of dynamite, set the outhouse over the hole, stained it red and called it good.

The walls inside the outhouse were painted white, but exhibited a greenish hue because the roof/ceiling was simply a piece of green corrugated Plexiglas. This roof/ceiling was one of the state's nifty ideas and was of the same material used to fabricate the walls of a modern greenhouse. Thus, not only were the white walls of the outhouse bathed in puke-green light, during the summer the energy from the sun penetrated the roof/ceiling and cooked the contents of the outhouse quite efficiently.

To keep the outhouse user's attention off the overwhelming smell, Mom and Dad hung a pleasant nature painting on the wall right above the throne. It depicted a crystal-clear brook flowing through luscious green trees and was so serene that it often made me indignant because its beautiful appearance was always eclipsed by the noxious outhouse odors.

The source of these unpleasant aromas was the throne. The throne was a green plywood box that served as the official toilet. It had a wooden lid on hinges that covered a roughly elliptical hole (the hole's shape was similar to that of a genuine store-bought ceramic toilet). Within the hole itself lurked some of the most ghastly sights imaginable.

In the summertime, the hole was not only well respected, but most normal individuals feared it. This fear was spawned by several factors. First, high temperatures and long days worked on the outhouse's contents and produced a fierce methane smell that could kill a small bird. Second, from far and wide this horrible smell lured flies in search of room and board. These pesky insects would burrow in the turds and breed until they practically owned the outhouse. Great care had to be exercised not to rile them up while going to the bathroom (otherwise some of the larger ones would repeatedly buzz and bump your butt in their zest to escape). Of course, when the actual bomb hit the pile down below (made a splat sound if landing on its comrades or a splash if landing in water), the whole colony mobilized. A wise person would either wipe very quickly or lean to one side to allow them an egress. Third, the mosquitoes in the summer would follow everyone into the outhouse and tank up on the helpless victim straining with concentration.

It is true that our outhouse was to be feared in the summer, but it is also true that it was to be just as much feared in the winter. Granted, there were no mosquitoes, flies, or simmering turds in the winter, but there were three major problems that were just as bad or worse. First, due to the cold we almost always wore warm clothes to the outhouse. This was a big inconvenience getting dressed and an even bigger one unbundling and unhooking in the outhouse. Second, the cold itself was enough to make your butt pucker up and keep any turds from sallying forth. Shivering uncontrollably in the dark at fifty below tends to break a person's concentration. Finally, the biggest problem was the "stick-a-log."

The stick-a-log (named by Karl) was a stalagmite-type mass of frozen feces that rose from the hole's depths eight feet down. At its base it was as round as the hole (two-foot radius) but it narrowed to a dull point like a giant chocolate pudding pop. The stick-a-log was so tall that it often came within mere inches of the throne's hole and the butt of any person sitting down. It was Dad's duty to break the magnificent natural structure in order to protect his family and friends. Still, even with Dad's aid, the stick-a-log never stopped growing in the winter and it was a constant threat to all the brothers' physical and psychological well-being.

Although it was not technically designed for stick-a-log protection, I would place a white Styrofoam seat (one of Dad's awesome inventions) on top of the throne to create an additional two-inch buffer between my butt and the turd-cicle. In actuality, Dad intended that the Styrofoam seat be used for warmth. From some source or other (the pipeline, campground, or side of the road), Dad procured a hunk of fine-grained Styrofoam and cut an elliptical hole in it. He then sanded and smoothed it so that it fit on top of the wooden outhouse bench perfectly. Thus, our butts never had to touch the permanent wooden bench.

We didn't use the white seat for sanitary reasons, but instead to keep our butts from freezing during the winter. As most Alaskans know, and especially those who have outhouses, when the temperatures drop to forty and fifty below, the cold sting of a wooden outhouse seat can be rather unpleasant. Good old Dad remedied this problem with the Styrofoam seat and as a result our butts were always warm (most visitors didn't know this trick and they literally froze their butts off in the outhouse while pondering stupidly over the odd Styrofoam contrivance at their side).

Other than the sickly green walls, an annoyingly peaceful picture, and an odd Styrofoam seat, there were only a few other items within our spartan outhouse. There was a kerosene lamp hanging on the front wall to the right of the door (which was never lit at night because no one would take the time to light it in the cold or stench or both), a roll of toilet paper (hung from a wooden roller which was attached to the right wall), a can of Raid on the bench to the left (to eliminate any pesky flies or dangerous stinging insects), and a small, white, knitted Irish hat (with a green plastic clover leaf) that hung on the left front wall opposite the throne. Mom and Dad kept an emergency roll of toilet paper under this little hat and to my knowledge it was never moved or used. In addition, there was a speckled blue-brown indoor/outdoor carpet on the floor as well as a plethora of living things.

Yes, living things. More specifically, there was an entire ecosystem within the outhouse itself. There were the flies that nested and reveled in the basement; there were the mosquitoes that enjoyed the blood of the human victims; and of course there were the large spiders that could not pass up the opportunity of hunting insects in such a highly populated area. Furthermore, other random insects such as bees, wasps, yellow jackets, and flying beetles would often become entrapped in the outhouse. Hence, as a general rule (except in winter), while I strained at the stool (teeth clenched and lungs on fire), I had to constantly shoo away large flies, hungry mosquitoes, dangerous wasps, and rappelling spiders. Of course, I had to minimize these extraneous movements because they taxed my muscles enormously and forced me to use precious oxygen that I didn't have and could not replace until I gained my freedom.

The outhouse is something that I will not ever forget. Everyone I have run into during my extensive travels thinks that they are terrible, but these people have not been required to use them in extreme weather conditions for eighteen years as I have. I would agree that they are somewhat inconvenient, but they are not altogether unpleasant or unusable. Granted, I would prefer using a flush toilet over an outhouse any day, but if I had been born to that luxury, I would not be a true Alaskan.

The Elf in our Attic

Owing to our almost complete isolation from civilization, Mom and Dad had free reign over our thoughts and could even control what information was fed to us. Mom and Dad were all we knew and they were gods. They were all-encompassing, all-knowing, omnipotent and—little did we know—very mischievous and highly prone to using their twisted imaginations (usually at our expense).

To prove my point, Mom and Dad convinced Ray and Steve that Santa Claus was real until they were eleven and twelve years old, respectively. As if that was not enough, they replaced the traditional tooth fairy with the genie in the lamp. Furthermore, on more than one Easter holiday, Dad rolled the old iron wheelbarrow all over the snowy yard to simulate the Easter Bunny's cart tracks. These cart prints combined with the wild rabbit tracks that we often found near the house, were very convincing evidence that the Easter Bunny was real.

On one occasion, Dad accidentally dropped some Easter candy while bringing it from the garage to the house (in preparation to filling our baskets).

When Karl spotted the candy on his way to the pissing path, he returned and asked suspiciously, "Dad, why is there candy on the ground?"

To this question Dad quite cleverly answered, "Oh, a fox was probably chasing the Easter rabbit and he spilled some candy trying to get away." This short, logical answer once again confirmed our belief in everything that Mom and Dad had told us.

The Easter Bunny games and other shenanigans played by my parents were small-time when compared with the Patrick incident. Once, when Mom and Dad were bored and most likely afflicted with cabin fever, they came up with the granddaddy of all pranks. First, Dad retrieved a little green elf doll about one foot high from the garage. Then he collected some thin monofilament fishing line, and a small fishing hook (a treble hook without the lure). Finally, he tied the line from the top of the window to the doll and somehow rigged the whole apparatus so that it looked like the little elf was climbing a rope with a grappling hook. Dad ran the fishing line from the window, around the house, in through the front door and into his hand. Thus, with a flick of his wrist, the small fairy would dance and appear to climb the rope.

Jon was three years old when he walked into the living room and noticed the small man (but not Dad's hand, nor the fishing line). He stood in awe and his excitement could not be contained. Jon called Karl and he too saw the miracle of all miracles. They had both heard the tales from Mom, Dad, Steve, and Ray but still they couldn't believe what they were seeing.

"I wanna get him, Dad!" Karl yelled.

"No! Don't move or you'll scare him away," Dad replied. They took Dad's warning to heart and watched in silence until the little man departed. Quickly thereafter, Dad conveniently went to the outhouse and when he returned all evidence of the mysterious elf was gone.

Karl and Jon were convinced the little man was real and that it was none other than Patrick Begorra whom Mom and Dad had taught Steve and Ray about. Of course, it was Mom and Dad's intent for my brothers to think this, and they encouraged them accordingly. The story of Patrick was fabricated by mixing a character from a Walt Disney book *The Borrowers*, a plot from another book called *The Gnome from Nome*, and typical Chmielowski imagination and logic.

They told Karl and Jon (as they had told Steve and Ray years earlier) that the elf's name was Patrick Begorra and that he came from Nome. On his travels, a big snowstorm hit and he was forced to seek shelter in our attic. He was shy but liked our family very much and in particular he loved kids. To show his appreciation and love for us, he would sometimes leave a small present (or a prize as we used to say) when a certain candle was lit.

What luck! We had a homeless elf from Nome freeloading in our attic without invitation, and he gave out prizes for no reason at all! Life couldn't be better for the boys, and it did not take much effort on Karl's part to convince me of the sighting as I grew up. After all, when there are gifts involved all children are eager to believe any tall tale and we certainly were no exception. We fell hook, line, and sinker for Patrick.

To receive a prize, a selected boy (whoever asked Mom for permission first) would light "Patrick's" candle before bedtime. Patrick's candle was blue, and it was set in an ornate, blue, glass bowl. Upon lighting the candle, we would go to bed while it burned and this was a signal to Patrick that one of us wanted a gift. When we woke in the morning, whoever lit the candle the night before would find a small present in his bed. Sometimes we would find a plastic toy, some candy, money, or nothing. As with the genie of the lamp, sometimes Patrick's Alzheimer's would kick in and he would forget our prize. Upon further investigation though, Mom always ferreted out the "missing" prize from some mysterious portion of our bed, and she would save the day.

We all believed in Patrick for some time primarily due to Karl's and Jon's eyewitness account. In addition, the footprints we would sometimes find inside the house (compliments of Dad) were also convincing evidence that Patrick was real. Furthermore, at any point if there was ever a doubt about Patrick's validity, Mom erased it at once with her twisted, psychotic propaganda (which, incidentally, would have made Hitler green with envy).

"Boys, you can't tell other kids about Patrick because he is shy and will leave if you do. He is our family secret and cannot be revealed to anyone. Also, if you ever stop believing in Patrick he will leave our home and take up residence in another. Then you will never receive any more prizes from him!" The idea that our prize factory would move to another kid's house made us determined not to betray Patrick.

As the years rolled by and we began to question our beliefs, Patrick was Mom and Dad's ace in the hole.

"How does Santa fit down our six-inch stove pipe?" I once asked.

"He doesn't. Patrick lets him in through the door," Mom replied matter of factly.

"Well, how does he unload all the presents so quickly and without us hearing?" I countered.

"Patrick helps him."

"So I guess he helps the Easter Bunny too!"

"Yup."

"Dang! Patrick sure gets around!" I finished, exasperated.

"Mm-hmm ..." Mom mumbled without looking up from her book. Thus, in the face of such unshakable logic we were fully convinced that all Mom's and Dad's magical characters were real.

Eventually, all good things come to an end and we stopped believing in Santa Claus because he had too many holes in his story. Although, I must admit, being close to North Pole (a town in Alaska just south of Fairbanks) and finding reindeer (caribou) tracks in the snow did prolong our beliefs longer than those of the most gullible city kid. The Easter Bunny's story was very strong due to hard physical evidence such as cart tracks, rabbit tracks, and rabbit turds in the snow. But the bunny was canned because his story was too similar to the already false Santa. The genie went down rather easily when he didn't die during "the great drowning" and his story did not hold water. Of course, if there was no Santa or Easter Bunny to let into the house and help, the helper must not exist either.

Based on our own strict line of unshakable logic, we chose to stop believing in Patrick (although his story was the most believable of them all). As our belief faded, so did Patrick Begorra and he packed his little bags and left our home.

Not to worry though, because my brother Jon recently told me that Patrick got caught in a snowstorm a few years back and he is now living in the crawl space of his Anchorage home. Rumor has it that his son and daughter are favored by Patrick, and when they light a special candle, they too receive little prizes.

The Veteran

Even though the flush toilet had been invented nearly a century ago, a man had been put on the moon, supercomputers had been invented, and the twenty-first century loomed just over the horizon, our family still used an outhouse. We were not proud of the fact that we used one every day of our lives from 1960 to 1997, but we endured the inconvenience and embarrassment. For me, personally, the outhouse was not so bad because over the course of my childhood I took the time to develop a series of clever tricks that minimized my suffering and allowed me to perform my necessary bodily functions in relative comfort.

The outhouse was always eager to take advantage of any hapless cheechako or overconfident sourdough that passed through its door.

In order to access the outhouse from home, I had to get dressed appropriately (depending on the weather), go outside, and run down the "outhouse path" more than a hundred feet south of our front porch. Once there, the little red-stained building instilled fear in my heart and I often thought twice about entering. If the circumstances were urgent enough (i.e.,

I had to take a dump and was nearly exploding), I gritted my teeth and prepared myself to do battle with the outhouse.

First, I performed some preparatory but very necessary precautions before even getting within five feet of the outhouse (which was perpetually encompassed by a horrible methane odor, and which, I deemed the death zone). These precautions included unbuttoning my brown corduroys, unzipping them and stretching their elastic waistband. Then I inhaled and exhaled five times very rapidly to oxygenate my blood (like the ancient sponge divers). While I was still dizzy and somewhat high from this ceremony, I took one huge final breath of pristine Alaskan air and followed it up with as many extra gulps of air I could force down my already bursting lungs. Finally, I prepared myself mentally and opened the red door very quickly (to create a vacuum and suck out any unsuspecting hovering insects).

Inside the outhouse, time was of the utmost essence (hence the reason why I unbuttoned and unzipped my pants ahead of time) and every move was calculated perfectly and executed with lightning-fast precision. One mistake could be fatal in such a harsh environment and I would carry out my duties in the most expedient manner possible. Although flirting with death every time I needed to defecate, I was always calm about my situation because I considered myself well trained after years of experience. I was a veteran, and as such, I could pitch a load and leave without ever having to inhale the toxic air within or remotely near the outhouse (let me point out that friends, visitors, and cheechakos are *not* veterans and therefore they are subject to all of the intrinsic perils of the outhouse).

As a seasoned veteran, in one fluid motion I quickly jerked the door open, grabbed the white Styrofoam seat, slapped it on the throne, and sat down. Then, while I was holding my breath and still very dizzy, I closed my eyes, clenched my teeth, flexed my stomach muscles and used the large volume of air in my lungs to push my diaphragm downward and force out a turd (forcing a turd never took me long, because I always waited until the last possible second to use the outhouse). As soon as I felt that a log was approaching fast, I reached to my right and unrolled about three feet of toilet paper, ripped it off, and placed it in my lap. Then I continued straining so hard that sometimes I launched my turds like little missiles.

Well before the turd could even fall eight feet and splat amongst its comrades, I quickly and efficiently wiped my butt (no-wipers were always considered good, whereas greasers could mean trouble) and discarded the utilized toilet paper down the hole. At this point my breath would be running out and I began letting out air in short bursts to keep my lungs from hurting. While thus engaged, I was very careful only to let air out, and never once did I inhale the outhouse fumes.

While emitting air like a pressure cooker I stood up, quickly dropped the white seat on the floor to the left, slammed down the wooden lid (in order to keep any large flies safely in the basement while simultaneously stirring them up for my brothers), threw open the outhouse door and burst forth from my small prison. I slammed the main door shut (to keep the smell and insects inside) and ran like a madman from a burning building until I was outside the death zone. Finally, I inhaled fresh air, pulled my underwear and pants up (there wasn't time in the outhouse to mess with trivial things like clothing), buttoned and zipped my trousers and straightened my shirt.

This everyday experience seemed to last for hours, but in truth, if all things went well I could perform the entire ritual in one lungful of air (less than one and a half minutes). Sometimes, however, in dire circumstances (right after someone used the outhouse or summer temperatures had recently soared into the 80s or 90s and the turds were cooking) I resorted to the shameful but very safe two-stage tactic.

In the first stage, I took a big breath, entered the outhouse, and lifted up the throne's wooden lid. Then I set up the Styrofoam seat, stretched out the toilet paper to a length of three feet (and left it hanging freely from the roll), exited the outhouse and moved to the safe zone. Finally, I unbuttoned and unzipped my pants and relaxed. In the second stage, I performed the ancient sponge diver's trick to oxygenate my blood and induce dizziness. I entered the outhouse, performed my duties, used the pre-unrolled toilet paper, and exited (with pants down). Although not as prestigious or elegant as using the one-stage veteran's method, the two-stage method was advantageous because it almost always guaranteed that I would not have to draw a horrible second breath within the outhouse.

In some rare instances I ran out of air. This occurred if I did not properly oxygenate myself, insects bothered or stung me (*Gasp!*), the toilet paper repeatedly ripped on the roller (during the one-stage method only), or Karl threw rocks or snowballs at the outhouse (ruined my concentration and he knew it). In rare and desperate times like these, I resorted to my bank robber trick. This clever tactic consisted of pulling my coat or shirt over my mouth and then exhaling all my carbon dioxide into the sealed coat. Afterwards, I inhaled my old air through my mouth and thus never had to breathe any of the outhouse's noxious vapors. The second breath of carbon dioxide only lasted me an additional thirty seconds, but it was just what I needed to escape and survive.

Suffice it to say, I was not only provisioned with clever precautions such as the sponge diver's technique, the one-stage strategy, the two-stage tactic, and the bank robber's trick, but I was also armed with the confidence that my outhouse survival skills were perfect and that it could never defeat me. However, just when I considered myself an invincible veteran, the outhouse surprised me.

Late one winter's night I had to use the outhouse so I put on Dad's slippers, grabbed a flashlight and ran outside in the stinging cold.

"I have no need for clothes 'cause I'm so fast!" I thought as I sprinted under the starlit sky. Upon reaching the border of the death zone I quickly performed a shortened sponge diver's trick, entered the outhouse and did my duties. Halfway through completing my job a loud blast ripped through the air and snow exploded through the screen window (there were two windows in the outhouse, both of which were covered with only a fine metal screen).

"Dang him!" I muttered under my breath as I heard Karl's muffled laugh and quick retreat. *Smack*! Another snowball impacted the screen window and cold powder covered my naked body. I went into a frenzied rush because not only was I freezing, but I did not have a shirt on to perform the bank robber's trick.

"Holy crap! I have to get out of here," I thought to myself. Without considering the flashlight that I had wedged between my thighs (it kept the inside of the outhouse nicely illuminated while allowing my free hands to dispense toilet paper), I jumped up to exit.

As I extended my body I realized my mistake. It was too late, however, and all I could do was watch helplessly as the flashlight slipped between my legs and fell into the great black abyss. The horror and dread that I felt in that short moment could never be put into words. Worse yet, when I looked down the hole, the flashlight was still shining somewhere far below and its light cast an eerie glow on the monstrous stick-a-log. With a cold body and heavy heart I dragged myself to the house and made the announcement that I lost the flashlight down the hole.

Everyone in my family laughed with delight (especially Karl) and teased me as I donned warm clothes and gathered the necessary equipment for a flashlight rescue mission. They laughed because they knew exactly what I knew. None of the fancy techniques or tricks I had hitherto contrived would save me now. The outhouse had bested me; the veteran was doomed.

TV Sucks

Our home was so small and so short on storage space that Mom and Dad were forced to economize space any way possible. One way they accomplished this incredible feat was to spread our enormously extensive food and grocery supply throughout our house. We stored food not only in the kitchen, but also on our front porch (in an old icebox), in the freezer shed (in a large freezer), in the living room (in tall cabinets) and in the back bedroom (also in cabinets). Our food supply had to be large enough to feed a family of seven and furthermore we had to stockpile it because we rarely went to Anchorage to shop (we also rarely shopped in Glennallen because the prices were between double and quadruple those of Anchorage).

In Mom and Dad's bedroom they kept dried goods such as crackers and Milkman in the tall grocery cabinet and all the canned goods in the TV cabinet (see Appendix A). The TV cabinet was about four feet high, two feet deep and made out of wood. Perched atop this cabinet was an ancient black-and-white television from the early sixties. Mom and Dad had had the thing since before I was born, and I am not really sure why they kept it. It was big, ugly, nearly unusable (no constant electricity and only one snowy station available), and it constituted a health hazard.

Yes, it was a real health hazard. I do not mean that it had a frayed cord or shoddy wiring, what I mean is that its incredible bulk could be dangerous to an unsuspecting victim such as myself. Recall that when I was five years old, I weighed only 35 pounds and was 35 inches tall. One afternoon Mom sent me into the back bedroom to retrieve a can of corn and I obediently followed her order. I ran into the back room, kneeled on all fours, opened the TV cabinet and *Bam*! My backbone nearly snapped in two! It seems that in my haste

124

to carry out Mom's order, I neglected to notice that the television's cord was hanging directly in front of the cabinet door. Thus, when I opened the door, the cord got caught in the spaces between the boards (Dad's homemade furniture always had gaps between the boards) and the snagged television was pulled forward. It plummeted four feet and landed squarely in the middle of my back.

Keep in mind that this was an ancient TV and undoubtedly weighed more than fifty pounds. When it landed on all thirty-five pounds of me, my vertebrae seared with pain and I was nearly crushed. Despite my incredible suffering, I did not dare yell or cry, because I thought Mom would give me a sound whoopin' for making the television fall. I bore all my agony in silence. Much worse than the pain was the touchy predicament I now found myself in. The TV was perfectly balanced on my back (as I was still on all fours) and the weight of the beast was quickly sapping my strength. I could not call out for help, lest my shameful deed be discovered, yet I could not stand the suffering much longer. Something had to be done. Someone or something had to give.

While maintaining the television's balance, I slowly lowered myself onto my elbows and then extended myself into a facedown prone position. Then, holding my breath I quickly slithered out from beneath the evil thing and steadied it.

"Thank God! I'm alive and Mom doesn't even know that the TV fell," I complimented myself. "But wait. Uh-oh. I still have to get the dang thing back on the cabinet!" With a heavy heart, a heavier television and Mom's desk chair, I went to work.

Thanks to my superhuman strength (due to the adrenaline rush), after a few minutes of hard labor I managed to wrestle the behemoth back into its accustomed place. At this point, my back was bruised, cut, and now very sore from lifting such a great weight. Disregarding my war wounds, I quickly grabbed a can of corn (insuring that the cord did not get caught this time), put a smile on my face, and sprinted back into the living room. This incident lasted for hours in my mind (pain tends to extend time), but in reality, it probably took only about two minutes and Mom never questioned my suspicious absence.

Ever since that traumatic day when our television set nearly took my life I have detested TV. Perhaps I would have gotten over the incident if further run-ins with television had been positive, but as it turns out they were always negative. For instance, when Dad cranked up the old Lister generator and we actually had an opportunity for viewing, we received only one station. Furthermore, because we lived in the middle of nowhere, that one station always came in very snowy. Finally, because the reception was so bad, our family had to assemble a three- to six-man team in order to receive and maintain a halfway decent picture.

The team was composed of a minimum of three men and was a huge project. The first person's job (usually Dad), entailed cranking up the generator by hand and waiting for it to halfheartedly come to life. He would then flick a switch that turned on the electricity to the house. Once the electricity was on, the other members of the team sprang into action.

The eldest brother present (or the one with the best TV eye) stationed himself in front of the television as "the looker." His job was to turn on the TV, assess the picture, and monitor the reception. Ninety-nine point nine percent of the time the picture was so snowy that not a single thing could be discerned. Thus, the looker summoned a younger brother and posted him at the bathroom window (the only window in our house that actually opened). The person stationed in the bathroom was known as "the yeller" and it was his duty to relay any commands from the looker to "the antenna man." The antenna man (usually Steve) climbed a ladder onto our roof and posted himself in front of the antenna. His job was to adjust and rotate the antenna according to the yeller's commands. What came next would have made the three stooges look like geniuses.

The looker or lookers (usually about three brothers and one Dad) scrutinized the television's reception with care. Then, with great sagacity they concluded that the picture was indeed bad and something had to be done.

In an even tone Dad yelled, "Bad!" and the brother stationed at the bathroom window yelled at the top of his lungs, "Bad!" Finally, the brother on top of the roof rotated the antenna left or right a few degrees and waited for a verdict.

"Still bad!" the lookers intoned in unison.

"Bad!" the yeller relayed, and the antenna man rotated again.

"Worse!" the lookers exclaimed.

"Worse!" the yeller repeated, and the antenna man rotated once more.

"Terrible! Go back the other way!" the lookers screamed.

"Go back!" the yeller hollered, and thus, the unfortunate person on the roof rotated the antenna back to the starting position and the entire process repeated itself.

"Bad!"

"Better."

"Back!"

"OK."

"Other way!"

"Worse."

"Better!"

"More!"

"Good enough."

"Come down!"

After five minutes or thirty minutes (depending on the weather), the reception was deemed OK and the team could disperse and commence watching the one snowy channel. Most likely a really bad show like *"The Cliff Hangers"* or *"The Mummy"* was on, but that was all there was so we watched it with keen interest. After half an hour of watching nebulous forms dancing on a snowy background, Dad would inevitably turn off the generator in order to conserve fuel and preserve our sanity.

Throughout my childhood I believed that all families had to tune their televisions with an experienced TV team and I could not understand why anyone would work so hard for such a little reward. Furthermore, I could not understand why any sane person would actually want to keep such a large, heavy, potentially lethal piece of equipment in their home. To me, the concept of television seemed ridiculous and at a very early age I firmly decided that TV sucked.

The Pissing Path

The outhouse was feared by all and used only in dire circumstances (i.e., we needed to pinch a loaf *bad*). As a result, when one of us had to take a piss, we never went to the outhouse. I repeat, we did not go to the outhouse for a trivial task such as taking a leak. Instead, we went somewhere convenient, private, and open. We went to "the pissing path."

The pissing path was a windy and narrow path that branched off our driveway near the garage (see property map, Appendix B). It was about one and a half feet wide and was bounded on either side by dense willows and black spruce trees. In the summer, the leafy foliage provided cover from prying eyes, and in the winter the snowbanks sheltered the whizzer from public view (the rest of the Clan or an occasional visitor). Dad gave the pissing path its illustrious name and he used it religiously. On the other hand, us boys used it only when it suited our fancy. We usually whizzed behind the log pile, in the yard, or wherever was most convenient depending on the time and situation.

In order to take a leak during the day, we took no unusual precautions or special measures. We simply found a spot on the pissing path or in the trees and relieved ourselves. Problems arose every winter, when yellow spots began dotting the landscape. Dad periodically remedied the situation by reminding us to use one area at the very end of the pissing path. Granted, this particular area was tinted a deep golden hue, but it was easy to cover with fresh white snow and was preferential to random yellow spots scattered throughout the yard.

When we needed to take a leak at night, this was a different story and required fantastic measures. Let me relate a typical, but true whizzing incident. Keep in mind that the incredible events outlined in this story (including Karl's ruthless shenanigans) were not isolated incidents but occurred regularly every night or every other night. This tale details a ritual rather than an anomalous incident.

On a cold and dark winter's night, the whole family was gathered peacefully inside our home. Mom and Dad were quietly reading and all five of us boys were playing diligently. It was late, about 10 p.m., and pitch-black outside. I was playing with my Lone Ranger doll by myself when Karl abruptly asked, "Hey Joe! Wanna take a piss?"

"Naw, that's OK," I replied and continued to play.

"C'mon Joe! Are you sure?"

"Ya. I don't have to piss!"

"Ya you do. C'mon, let's go!" Karl persisted.

"No."

"You'll have to go when everyone's asleep and then you'll have no one to go with. Let's go!" I saw his logic and reluctantly put away my toys and prepared for the ordeal.

Our first step was locating a good flashlight. Although Mom and Dad had just given each of us five boys a personal flashlight for Christmas, we somehow misplaced all of them. Karl and I made a halfhearted effort to find one of the missing lights, but after thirty seconds of fruitless searching we ran into the back bedroom and grabbed Dad's big flashlight. Dad's flashlight was the largest, brightest, handiest, and readiest flashlight at any given time. It was always in the same place, was never missing, and could be counted on in emergencies such as this.

Once we procured Dad's flashlight, our second step was to find a good pair of shoes quickly (the pressure was building in Karl's delicate bladder). We searched for a couple of minutes for our moon boots and shoepacks, but they were wet and the inserts were missing. But Dad's white bunny boots were handy, and so too were his slippers. Typically I went for the slippers because they fit more snuggly than the bunny boots, but the slippers were still six sizes too large.

On this particular night Karl managed to snag the slippers first and I was stuck with the white army boots. For those readers not familiar with bunny boots—these are Arctic army boots made of white rubber and are supposedly warm to sixty below zero. They weigh about ten pounds each, have a nozzle to air them up, and are about a foot and a half high. At the time of this particular excursion, I was eight years old and weighed fifty pounds. Needless to say, these boots easily constituted one fifth of my total body mass, and were a tad bit large for me.

Walking with bunny boots took a good deal of concentration and effort. When I lifted my right foot, the momentum of the huge boot sucked me forward abruptly. When my foot reached the ground, it anchored itself instantly and I had to force my left foot forward (only to be jerked forward even further by that boot's momentum). In this manner I attempted to walk/run/hobble out of the house.

Imagine if you will, an anorexic eight-year-old with pipe cleaner legs, standing in his baggy jockey shorts and huge bunny boots. Except for the well-worn jockeys, he is entirely naked (because it is too inconvenient to find clothes and he thinks he will be outside for only a second), armed with a little flashlight (because Karl got the good one), and already shivering even though he is not yet outside. Also, picture if you will, a larger, obese pre-teenager who is smiling a wicked smile. He is clad in large tentlike boxers, sports many fat rolls, and is wearing black nerdlike glasses. He has on Dad's sleek brown slippers and is carrying a huge halogen flashlight. This is how the stage was set on this particular night, just as it had been on countless others.

"Boys, don't leak down my shoes," Dad said nonchalantly.

"Don't worry, we won't," Karl whined.

"Where are your flashlights?"

"Oh, I don't know … somewhere," Karl mumbled as we approached the door. We got to the big door and no sooner had we grabbed the cold iron latch than Dad said, "Don't let the Higee get you! Ha, ha, ha!"

"Oh, Dad. We don't believe in him any more," Karl said furtively.

"Well then, don't let Danny and Regis get you!"

Dang. Dad always had to bring out the big guns didn't he? To make things clear, the Higee (pronounced with a soft "g") was a fictitious monster (or was it?). It had big teeth, a lot of hair, and resembled a mysterious animal head that hung in Gakona Lodge. Jon was the one who coined the word Higee and it was he who was the most obsessed with the monster. Although Karl said we didn't believe in the Higee, the truth is, we did. Maybe we didn't believe that it looked exactly like the stuffed head in Gakona Lodge, but we couldn't deny the fact that a monster lurked somewhere in the cold black night.

Worse than any Higee were Danny and Regis. Once their names were mentioned, no pretense of courage was garnered and we fell silent and lingered at the door for a while.

I had been to church only once in my life as a child. That one time was to see the two Sipary boys buried (while driving their fixed-up Firebird they were involved in a head-on accident near Glennallen Lodge). Not only had Karl, Jon, and I never been to a church, but we had never been to a funeral or seen a dead person. The images of our childhood friends, Danny and Regis, could never be torn from our minds and we dwelled upon their fate often. Dad said that they were always outside somewhere waiting for us …

130

At this point, Karl and I hesitated, but after a minute His Tubbiness needed to relieve the pressure on his king-sized bladder. So, Karl opened the latch and pulled the door inward. Instantly, a huge cloud of white smoke billowed inside the house. This was our cue to exit quickly. The extreme cold that night (thirty, forty, or fifty below), caused such smoke and condensation that it was not possible to see outside when the door was opened. Regardless of what monsters waited unseen outside, it was ungodly cold out there and Mom was nice and warm inside. We decided that monsters were preferable company to a cold and angry Mom. We hustled outside into the frigid blackness.

Once outside, the cold was so extreme that it stung and bit into our flesh. We were not worried—this was just standard operating procedure for going to the "bathroom." Karl and I wasted no time pondering over the cold and we ran into the silent night. The whole way down the pissing path we shivered and flashed our lights left, right, up, down, sideways, forwards, backwards, diagonally, into the trees and into the driveway. We resembled an energetic pair of air traffic controllers.

We performed our dazzling light show in order to keep the monsters, axe murderers, and Danny and Regis at bay. The night was so impenetrable that nothing could be discerned unless it was in the direct beam of Karl's big flashlight (mine was pathetic and useless). The weak glow from the kerosene lights inside the house threw off our concentration, as did the occasional flickering shadows.

Karl and I took our positions and whipped 'em out. We kept flashing randomly and quickly, all the while trying to make pleasant conversation. "Ya Joe, I don't believe in that crap anymore," Karl said.

"Me either," I replied smugly. We watched our yellow arcs cut through the night air, and marveled at the immense amounts of steam they emitted. It's a wonder that instead of yellow spots around the house there weren't yellow ice arches! After a bit, we were not only finished doing our duties—we were nearly frozen.

I was going into convulsions shivering while Karl stood unfazed and protected by his numerous layers of lipids. Just when our confidence had peaked and our fear subsided, we heard the door open and Dad's deep, monotone voice, "Dannnnny and Regisssss are commmmmminnnnnng! Oooooo! Ha, ha, ha!"

My heart fell inside my jockey shorts and rattled around a good bit. We looked at each other, frozen with fear and anchored to our doom. Our blood stopped and horror welled up from our stomachs into our throats. We couldn't make a sound or scream.

"Oh, God. I hope they don't get me! I hope they don't get me! I hope they don't get me!" I thought again and again. Dreamlike, I attempted to move, but was unable.

At length, Karl somehow managed to set his bulk into motion. In a phantasmagoric scene I watched Karl pull up his sagging underwear, turn toward the house, let out a loud scream, "Bbbbbmmmmmmmm!" and quickly unfurl his arm toward me. No, he wasn't trying to rescue me—he was trying to knock me down. He deliberately tried to push me into the snowbank (where we had just squeezed out a few drops), so that all the waiting monsters could have me as a snack. Karl figured that a small child squirming in a yellow snowbank would be an easy kill. He figured that the monsters would eat me first and leave him to escape. That ratfink!

I tried to avoid his ill-timed and devious attack, but I couldn't sidestep his pudgy hand. As a result, he sent me reeling into the yellow snowbank. I never really had a chance to avoid falling because I couldn't move my huge white boots. Those dang boots were like cement shoes and I toppled like a rotten tree. Furthermore, even if I had managed to slip my feet out of the concrete-like shoes, I would have stepped into the cold snow with bare feet. Perhaps not a bad idea, but then I'd have to take all that precious time to put the bunny boots back on, and in that short period the ghouls and monsters would be on top of me for sure. Thus, I fell into the cold golden snow, rolled to my stomach, pushed myself to a standing position and let out a feeble scream. With the aid of two quarts of adrenaline, I managed to get my huge boots moving. Once in motion, I was an unstoppable juggernaut and covered ground quickly.

Yup, once I got those bunny boots going, they were self-propelled due to their immense mass and fantastic momentum. While running at maximum velocity, I was able to cover ground in leaps and bounds (literally, due to the boots).

"Surely, at speeds such as these, the monsters can't catch me!" I thought to myself. "Ya! I must be cruising! I can even feel the air rushing on top of my head I'm going so fast!" It never really dawned on me that because I was nearly bald (my hair was less than one sixteenth of an inch long) I could always feel the wind on my head whether standing, walking, or running. It was only when I was running that I tended to notice the air on my head and that observation made me run even faster.

"Fifty feet, forty feet, thirty feet, I'm almost there!" I thought. "I'm going to live! I'm going to ..."

"Ah, crap!" I screamed. Somehow a bunny boot (owing to its momentum and free will) shot off my small foot like a rocket. The fact that my legs were pipe cleaners and my feet were six sizes too small for the boots certainly didn't help matters.

132

"Oh, no. Oh, no. Oh, no ..." I whimpered as I scrambled to collect my missing bunny boot.

"Now I'm doomed for sure," I thought darkly. I could hear them coming. I could hear the Higee and the axe murderer. I could hear Danny and Regis stepping softly over the snowbanks, coming to get me. There was no doubt in my mind that I was going to perish.

With my life at stake, I looked for the missing shoe. "Maybe if I don't turn around they won't get me," I hoped. It's common knowledge that if you ignore monsters they often delay their murderous actions and give their victims hope of escape. They do this for sport, I think. Anyhow, I eventually retrieved the missing shoe from a soft snowbank and never even considered putting it back on my foot. Instead, I ran across the yard with one boot on and the other cradled in my arms. A not-so-careful observer would have noticed that in addition to my naked body being wet and covered in snow, I had prominent yellow stains on the front of my jockey shorts. There was absolutely no chance I would have ever noticed these trivial inconveniences as I ripped open the screen door and slammed into the big wooden door.

"What the ... is the handle frozen?!" I thought wildly. Nope. I wasn't nearly so lucky. Realization hit me in the bony ribs and I knew that Karl was inside the house holding down the dang latch.

"Ha, ha, ha ..." I heard him cackling. "Danny and Regis are gonna get you! Ha, ha, ha..."

"Karl, open the dang door!" I squealed as the skin on my hands stuck to the cold dry steel.

"Ha, ha, ha ... the Higee!" Karl yelled through the thick door.

"Kar-rl!" I shrieked. Then a calm voice intervened.

"Karl, let him in. He's freezing out there," Mom said calmly.

"Do I have to?"

"Yup."

"OK. Danny and Regis ..." he said again and then paused a full ten seconds for dramatic effect. I heard a faint click as he released the latch. I jerked open the big door, ran inside and slammed it shut so quickly that not a single ounce of smoke entered the house.

Once inside I was nearly frozen (covered in snow from Karl pushing me and from searching for the lost shoe), pale white with fear, and in shock from entering a well-lit and overly warm house. My heart pounded visibly in my skeletal chest, my knees shook uncontrollably and my body was racked with fits of shivering.

"Ha, ha, ha!" Karl laughed again. "You idiot! I beat you back! You were so scared!" he yelled in my face.

"No I wasn't," I replied calmly as I gulped down my adrenaline and pulled the lone bunny boot off my foot.

"Ha, ha, ha," Dad chuckled, "You were both scared witless. Now put the light and my shoes away." While Karl and I followed his orders I vowed to myself that I would never take a piss with my evil brother again.

"That's it. He pushes me every single time we take a piss and he always leaves me for the monsters," I thought. "No more. Tonight is absolutely it. Never again!"

These thoughts and thoughts similar to them burned in my mind after our nightly pissing ritual. They remained with me until the next night when Karl soothed them away by sincerely asking, "Hey Joe. Wanna take a piss? C'mon. If you come with me, you won't be alone and the monsters won't get you. I won't leave you *this* time. Really, I won't ..."

Karl is pictured here masterminding one of his countless evil plots. Why on God's green earth did I ever trust that big politician smile?

134

Fang

Fang was crazy, there was no doubt about it. Since the day a friend of the family gave him to us as a puppy, Fang never operated with a full deck of cards. Granted, he got along well with our older dog, Boy, but Fang's eccentric behavior taxed the family's patience to the limit and exasperated us to no end.

What was so peculiar about Fang's character was his obsession with engines. For example, if he was sleeping in the back bedroom of the house and Dad started a motorized machine in the front yard, Fang went nuts. He immediately awakened, barked like a rabid dog (in a very high pitch and shrill tone) and then bolted outside. Once outside, he kept barking while simultaneously seeking out the devilish noise. After detecting the source, he quickly moved in for the kill. He would get as close to the machine/engine as possible and attempt to bite it. Needless to say, employing the seek-and-destroy tactic with a chainsaw was somewhat hazardous to his health.

Fang was a crazy old dog who would chase our snowmachines, bite at Dad's running chainsaw, and pick fights with big Brutus. Hence, we kept him locked in the back bedroom for his own protection.

If Fang had gone crazy only around chainsaws, we would have

considered ourselves fortunate. Instead, he completely lost his mind when any motorized tool or vehicle was activated, and as a result, he barked at and bit the following: the blue truck, the Ford Maverick, Ray's motorcycle, Karl's motorcycle, the trail blazer (a huge motor-cycle-type thing surveyors use to drive through rough terrain), any snowmachine, the ice-auger (a device used for drilling holes in ice), the lawn mower, the generator, the snowthrower, Jon's remote-control airplanes, and so on. Poor Fang—had he lived in a normal household, where noisy engines are a rare occurrence, he probably would have been sane. Alas, the Chmielowski compound was anything but normal and because one engine or another was always running, Fang's mind and muzzle were also running.

Fang often chased Karl and Ray on their motorcycles and would try to bite the wheels. On more than one occasion he approached the machines too closely and was accidentally run over. After each such incident we thought he was gravely injured but he never was. Fang would just spring up, shake it off, and continue his assault on the engines o' death.

Fang was also run over by snowmachines time and time again. As we raced across our frozen lake, he ran alongside us and barked at and bit the snowmachine's skis. He was highly skilled at attacking the skis and could do so even when we drove into the forest. He bit and barked at the skis while successfully dodging spruce trees and beaver stumps (pointed tree stumps carved by beavers). His lips and tongue often froze to the cold steel, and sometimes his neck got caught under a ski or the wood sled (a sled towed behind a snowmachine that is used to haul firewood). Needless to say, these and all other physical injuries either bounced off Fang or did not register in his delirious mind.

Fang was run over by the trailbreaker, his lips got caught on the rotating blade of the ice-auger, and trees fell on him when he was too close to the chainsaw. Fang was even shot once! The incident oc-curred one afternoon when I was walking down the highway shooting soda cans with my .22 rifle. Without warning, Fang sprang out of the bushes and right into my line of fire. My bullet bounced off the road and ricocheted into his stomach. He yelped, hid in the trees, and then emerged a couple minutes later seemingly unaffected.

After many accidents over many years, we discovered that Fang was nearly indestructible and he earned countless nicknames such as: Crazy Old Man, Bicycle Seat Head (his head was long and narrow and re-sembled a ten-speed bicycle seat), and Dilapidated Old Crock. In truth, the family did not consider Crazy Fang to be as respectable as the exalted and wise Father Rawhide (our older dog Boy/Draggy). Hence,

Fang never received quite as much attention as Draggy and therefore, with good reason, was often a very jealous dog.

After Draggy died in 1986, Fang ruled supreme and did not have to share his kingdom with anyone. He was happy being the only dog in the house and would have enjoyed this ideal situation if it hadn't been for Brutus. Brutus was a 120-pound, jet-black, shorthaired New Foundland "puppy" we adopted a year after Draggy's death. Although Brutus was much larger than Fang (a seventy-pound, wiry lab mix), he was constantly bullied by our fearless older dog. This situation didn't last too long and after less than a year Brutus realized that he was both bigger and stronger than Fang. Once again, Fang was low dog on the totem pole.

At first, full-scale fights were rare and when they did erupt we simply pried Fang and Brutus apart and kept them separated. In time though, fights became so commonplace and fierce that we often put Fang in the back bedroom for his own protection. We kept him in the room by placing a homemade baby gate in the doorway. Fang felt confident in his chamber and whiled away most of his days sleeping on a thick rug, moaning about his aching bones, barking at engines outside, and eyeing Brutus enviously. He sometimes put his narrow, gray muzzle between the bars and watched the household with his one good eye. He closely resembled an ancient, grizzled jailbird and soon took on yet another nickname, the Jailbird.

For the most part, we let the jailbird out of the back room only to relieve himself, eat, and take walks. On such occasions we always provided him with a personal escort in order to discourage fights. But try as we might, the body guard tactic never worked because Fang felt so at ease with his protection that he would actually taunt Brutus. Inevitably, they would battle and Fang would get the worst of it.

Brutus beat Fang in every fight, but the stubborn old fool would never back down or quit. More than once, Brutus had Fang pinned on the ground (by the throat) while Fang gasped his last dying breaths. Somehow, we managed to peel Brutus's jaws off Fang's throat before death actually occurred. But after each such rescue, Fang's eyes flew open, he sprang to his feet and he began attacking Brutus with fresh vigor.

Fang never learned his lesson and one time Brutus even hauled him off into the woods for a sure kill. Fang hung from Brutus's powerful jaws like a dead rabbit and Brutus gave him a good shaking in order to do him in. As Fang was kicking his life's last kicks, Dad miraculously separated him from Brutus's maw. Upon separation, no one was surprised when Fang attempted to restart the duel of death.

Owing to such bloody battles, Dad purchased a self-defense flashlight that also squirted mace. The company advertised that it would stun, disable, and knock down an attacker. Dad figured that it would do the same or possibly worse to a dog (a nose that can detect three-month-old urine must be pretty dang sensitive). After receiving the device in the mail, we eagerly waited to test it out on the next fight. Our desires were soon rewarded when a particularly good rumble broke out the very next day. During the heat of the battle we sprayed each dog's nose, mouth, eyes and face at point-blank range.

We fully anticipated them yelping and slinking off into the bushes but nothing of the sort happened. Instead, neither combatant was slowed at all and if anything, seemed to fight harder, each convinced that his opponent was unleashing some secret weapon. Even household ammonia failed to separate them and we had one heck of a time stopping the fight.

On this very occasion, while we were prying the dogs apart, Fang bit my right hand in order to stay engaged with Brutus. I drew back quickly and found two clean holes punched in me. One was at the base of my thumb and the other in the back of my hand. Disregarding pain, I eventually succeeded in nullifying the fight but I was not too pleased with Fang.

Because of the perpetual fighting and no sure way to stop the violence, our family permanently relegated Fang to the jail in the back bedroom. He spent his golden years there, and despite being isolated, he was comfortable, well fed and near the family. Even so, I often felt sorry for the old jailbird and in order to cheer him up I sometimes played with him.

On one occasion, I let Fang out of his penitentiary so that we could play outside. Once outdoors, I procured a stick and proceeded to get him so riled up that he was near to bursting. He was overflowing with energy, entirely mad, and raring for a good chase. Having anticipated his condition, I had formulated a plan earlier. I would run as fast as possible about one hundred feet, jump on our swinging trapeze bar (at our house we had a tire swing *and* a trapeze bar), and easily kick my legs up and over it. I would be like an Olympic gymnast and support myself with my arms as the bar rested easily against my stomach.

"I've already accomplished this trick a million times from a standstill; a running start won't be much different," I confidently thought to myself. I pondered a bit more and thought, "And after I successfully accomplish my escape, the demon dog will get his excitement and exercise for the year, while I get an adrenaline rush and tons of glory. I will be just like a courageous bullfighter."

Everything did not go as planned and thank the gods I wasn't wearing tights and Fang wasn't a bull. Although I had a brilliant plan in my head, what actually happened was quite dismal. The events unfolded in slow motion and this is what I remember. First, I got Fang really riled up and pissed off. Then I ran one hundred feet with him close on my heels and I jumped for and grabbed the freely swinging trapeze bar. Finally, I attempted to kick my legs over the metal bar but failed miserably.

At this point, my plan went out the window and the situation became grim. I had performed the gymnastic maneuver of mounting the bar a million times, but I had always done it from a standstill. I did not take into account my forward momentum when I ran, and because of this, I could not force my legs over the bar regardless of my agility or strength. The freely hanging bar caused me to swing forward a good ways, and then back just as far. While swinging back, my only thought was "Uh-oh!" and indeed, it was well founded.

As I swung backwards, Fang leaped into the air, and at the apex of his jump he bit me. I felt his long, yellow fang pierce my lower back and I fell to the ground in a heap. Fang stood over me triumphant, barking, and giving me little fleabites here and there. Seeing my predicament, Jon and Karl laughed at me as I screamed for help. In good time, they pulled Fang off my back and revived me. After a quick inspection I found that I had received a well-placed, well-deserved, fang-hole in my back fat roll (although I was extremely skinny, Fang had just found my only patch of fat). Owing to the trapeze incident, I found new respect for Fang regardless of his age or physical condition.

Fang lived for several years after the trapeze catastrophe. During this time he moaned and groaned as if he was going to die but he never did. In short, he was like the Energizer bunny and kept going, and going, and going.

Longevity can last only so long and one day Fang escaped his jail cell and ventured up to Uncle Joe's cabin. To his delight, he found that Uncle Joe was revving up his truck and backing out of the driveway. Fang was in heaven and without hesitating he began barking wildly and biting at the tires.

Unfortunately for Fang, the bliss was short lived. Due to his one blind eye he did not see the truck tire before it ran over his back. He squealed, sprang to his feet and hid in the bushes. Sure enough, after a few minutes he came out alive but he was badly wounded. We took care of him for several months afterwards, but in the end, Uncle Joe's green truck won the battle.

It is true that Fang is no longer with the family, but it is also true that I will never forget him. How could I? He left me with long-lasting memories and three very prominent fang scars.

Tarzan

I have no idea where we got the thing. I never saw one anywhere else in my life. Only the Chmielowski Clan would own such an odd contraption and only the Chmielowski Clan would have the audacity to use it.

What I am alluding to is our infamous Tarzan swing. The Tarzan swing consisted of an inverted T-shaped handle attached to two wheels. These wheels were about four inches in diameter and were bound on either side by metal plates. This pulley device was threaded onto a cable (hung between two trees) and could roll freely over the cable. In essence, our Tarzan swing was similar to a gravity-driven tram. However, unlike the trams used at ski resorts and mines, our device was built for only one person (hanging by his fingers) and had no brakes.

The cable was strung from a large spruce tree (more than fifteen inches in diameter) to a medium spruce tree (seven or eight inches in diameter) and spanned the entire length of our lawn (a stumpy/swampy strip of ground that just happened to have a few blades of grass on it). The cable itself was steel and about as big around as a grown man's pinkie. It was attached to the big tree some twenty-five feet off the ground, and it was attached to the smaller tree about four feet off the ground. Thus, over the length of our stumpy yard (about seventy-five feet), the cable had quite a steep slope. Using algebra, slope can be calculated from the following mathematical formula: $m=(Y_1-Y_2)/(X_1-X_2)$. Substituting the above values into the slope equation shows that $m=(25-4)/(75-0)=(21)/(75)=$pretty dang steep.

A telescopic aluminum ladder was placed in front of the large tree to allow access to the top of the cable, and a thin mattress was affixed to the smaller tree in order to cushion the inevitable impact. A slender nylon rope hung from the pulley device so that after the ride we could grab the rope and guide the pulley all the way to the large tree. Then, while holding the rope and keeping the pulley device stationary, we would climb the ladder, grab the T-bar, and jump.

What happened after jumping always happened very quickly. One moment we would be suspended motionless twenty-five feet above the ground, and the next, we would be ripping (I don't use this term lightly) across the yard at a high velocity. Before we could successfully count five heartbeats we would run out of cable and be forced to react quickly. A visitor unfamiliar with the Chmielowski Tarzan swing, would mentally bounce back and forth between two possibilities: 1) Should I stay on the swing and risk the thin mattress that seems to be much thinner than I anticipated? 2) Should I release my death grip from this hell-spawned pulley device and take my chances plummeting to certain doom?

More often than not, the unfortunate cheechako (inexperienced fool) would foredoom him- or herself by using the following logic: The mattress at the end of the swing must be there to stop me; otherwise, why would the Chmielowskis put it there? Only idiots would strap a mattress to a tree if it was not really going to cushion the impact. Thus, I'll stay on the ever-accelerating Tarzan swing and bounce harmlessly off the mattress!

That exact line of reasoning was responsible for a serious injury. One summer, when Mom and Dad had a cookout, a female pipeline worker went down the Tarzan swing. She tried to stop herself by using the thin mattress and *Wham!* She broke her leg. Of course, what she never knew, all of the boys (true veterans) knew very well. Staying on the Tarzan swing was certain death. The only real means of survival was to let go and endure the sharp stumps, mud, and relatively low drop height.

The fall was not really that bad once you knew exactly when and where to jump, what stumps to avoid, and how to roll when you hit. It was common sense as far as we were concerned, and if some imbecile wanted to ride the swing, let him or her feel the full effect! The beauty of the Tarzan swing (and Dad's raw genius) was that it combined height, astronomical velocities, adrenaline rushes, drops, rolls, timing, and much more. The Tarzan swing packed the punch of a theme park ride, was entirely free and could be ridden as often as desired.

Like the rest of my brothers, I loved the challenge of the Tarzan swing and eventually I mastered it. By age eight I could easily outdo my brothers (mere amateurs) and I often put my feet behind my head while I raced down the cable. More specifically, immediately after jumping off the ladder, I elevated my legs horizontally until they were perpendicular to my chest. Then I brought them up higher until my feet were on either side of the whizzing cable. Next, I tucked my feet between my hands (that were gripping the inverted T-bar), until they touched my ears. Finally, for the grand finale, I extended my feet beyond my ears an additional two feet. Hence, I would fly down the cable, turned nearly inside out, smiling and knowing that danger awaited me (the tree with the flimsy mattress stuck to it).

I was definitely not a fool. Nope, not me. I was smarter than a weasel and quicker than a cat. Whizzing at nearly twenty miles per hour and with only ten feet of cable left, I let go of the bar and rotated in midair. My feet came down quickly and *Bam*! I hit the ground, rolled, got pierced by a stump or stick, and jumped to my feet triumphantly! All these complex maneuvers were performed in one fluid movement. I was an expert, the best of the best, and I am being modest.

On one occasion, I climbed the ladder in front of the big tree and decided to show Jon my latest gymnastics trick. As I stood on top of the aluminum ladder I drew myself up to my full height (about three and a half feet), took a deep breath and leapt into the air. I instantly began ripping (again, I don't toss around this term lightly, especially in a serious and life-threatening situation such as this) down the cable. The air rushed by my face, the pulley wheels hummed, the cable blurred and … *Kachunk*! The goddang Tarzan swing jumped its track. The pulley wheels somehow managed to come off the cable, and the cable was wedged between the wheels and the thin plate of metal holding them together.

As I hung freely over twenty feet of nothingness I instinctively tried to bicycle my legs and wiggle the wheels free. No luck. I shook my body. The stubborn Tarzan swing refused to budge. I gyrated, writhed, shook, rotated, screamed, yelled, bounced, and cursed. Nothing. Jon just stood on the ground looking up at me and laughed. I hung there for a minute or more doing rotations and what not, and then I decided to try and grab the cable in order to shimmy down the length of it. I let go of the pulley with one hand and grabbed the cable.

"Owwwww!" I screamed in pain, "The cable's too thin! Help, Jon!" The cable was way too narrow to grip and it contained so many fine metal strands that shimmying down it was definitely out of the question. I had no choice but to maintain my waning grip on the Tarzan swing.

I pleaded again with Jon for help and then I cursed and moaned. At length he deemed it was an urgent situation and Dad's help was enlisted. Jon found Dad napping on the sofa, and pulled him out of the house grumbling.

After clearing his eyes and getting his bearings, Dad stood under me and simply said, "Let go."

"No," I replied.

"Let go and I'll catch you."

"No," I said again. I would have hung there all day, but the muscles in my hands and forearms burned so badly that I had to let go. I closed my eyes, released my grip and put fate into Dad's hands. As always, Dad was true to his word and he easily caught me. I survived the heart-pounding incident unscathed and unbruised (except for my ego).

I do not remember exactly what became of the Tarzan swing. I believe that as we grew older it became less and less spectacular and eventually it fell into disuse. I do recall, however, seeing it mixed in with the Tonka trucks in the fenced yard behind the fuel drums. It simply rusted there for a number of years before eventually disappearing. Perhaps it was overgrown by moss, or perhaps a jealous friend stole the thing and set it up at his house. If the latter case was the fate of the Tarzan swing, the thief sure got a lot more than he bargained for.

Rock and Roll

David Dawson was my best friend for as long as I can remember. We met each other our first day in kindergarten (a one-room trailer adjacent to the Gakona Elementary School) and from that day forward we were inseparable. It is incredible that out of a class of only three students (Russel Longfellow, David Dawson, and I) David would be the greatest kid in the whole world. Had I gone to a kindergarten with one thousand kids, none of them would have compared to David. I was very fortunate to have such a good friend in an otherwise lonely and isolated world.

David and I spent as much time together as possible. While in school we always sat by each other and at recess we always played together. After school we shared the same seat on the bus even though his was the first stop and mine was the last (his ride lasted two minutes and mine lasted an hour). Occasionally we spent the night at one another's house because this was the only possible way we could share time together (living twenty-six miles apart with no telephone communication tends to put a damper on budding friendships).

Once, while staying at David's house in the summer, we decided to climb Gakona Hill. This hill is very steep, dangerously eroded, and the highway is carved right into its near-vertical face. Furthermore, because Gakona hill is composed of gray glacial silt and because it is constantly baked in the hot summer sun, it is very crumbly—an accident aching to happen. Needless to say, the hill beckoned to David and me, and in no time we had climbed more than one hundred feet up its face.

Once we neared the top of the bluff, we became bored and began milling around in the "Dawson heat" (a term coined by Karl and me to indicate an intense dry heat that only encompassed the Dawson's house and surrounding Gakona area). While we were precariously balanced on the face of the crumbling cliff, we began rolling rocks down the hill just to see how far and how fast they would go. Most of them were small and jagged so they did not roll very well and were quite a disappointment. They would slowly bounce down the hill and then get caught in a five-foot ditch separating the bluff from the road.

The engineers who designed the Tok cutoff (the official name of the road that we were bombarding) had probably foreseen the fact that rocks would work loose during rainstorms and roll onto the highway. Therefore, they had dug a ditch paralleling the road that easily remedied nature's little accidents. What they hadn't foreseen was two mischievous kids purposely rolling rocks down the hill. Furthermore, they hadn't anticipated what I saw with my own eyes: the granddaddy of all rocks.

The rock that I beheld so reverently was the size of a basketball, speckled with white and black dots, and rounded like a sphere. It was protruding from the face of the hill in such a manner that I swear it called to me: "Joe, roll me down! I belong in the Copper River with my brothers. Rooooolllll mmmeeeee!" And so, with little thought and less effort I gave the magnificent thing a hearty downward shove.

The second after I pulled it free, I thought to myself, "This one ought to roll nicely." Indeed, my intuitions were correct and I was ecstatic as I saw the speckled juggernaut speed downhill. What was not intuitive to me at the time was a fundamental law of physics which states: p=mv. In other words, momentum equals mass times velocity. In the rolling rock's case, the mass was certainly large and its velocity was undeniably very high. Hence, by multiplying the large mass by the high velocity, the momentum of the small boulder was incredible as it went sailing towards the highway. "This one may make the road!" I thought as I witnessed the rock leap vigorously over a wide horizontal protrusion.

The thought barely crossed my mind when I heard David yell, "Joe! There's a car coming!" I looked to where my friend pointed, but could see nothing. After waiting for just one heartbeat I could make out a car rounding the corner near the Gakona River Bridge and close to Dwayne Shelton's house.

"Too far away," I said with a professional air. "Besides," I added to myself, "the rock won't make the highway. None of the others did." Other than estimating and reassuring ourselves, there was nothing either of us could do so we just watched the events unfold in slow motion.

As the car approached the straight stretch, the rock barreled downhill. Eventually, the car crossed the rock's path, and with perfect timing the granite boulder bounced out of the ditch and smashed right into the car's rear wheel. David and I distinctly heard a loud crash, a pop, and a screech. The car came to a grinding halt, and dead silence followed.

"I guess I figured that all wrong," I muttered.

"Crap, man! We're gonna go to McLaughlin," David moaned. Of course, he was referring to the juvenile correction facility in Anchorage, and the mere thought of it drove daggers of terror into our hearts. I stared stupidly at him for what seemed like an eternity, and the only thing that registered in my mind was his bugged-out eyes and wide-open mouth. Somewhere in the back of my foggy brain I realized that we were both paralyzed and it wasn't until hearing some movement from the car below that our senses took over and we leapt into action.

We ran wildly along a narrow ridge until David found a small vertical crevasse in the face of the bluff. We stopped immediately and wedged ourselves tightly into it. David crouched directly in front of me in such a manner that the only thing I could see was the back of his shaved blonde head. I literally could not see around his head because it was so enormous that it blocked my entire field of view (David's head was of such legendary proportions that his mother must have been a goddess to pass him through her birth canal).

"Dang it. I can't see around your bowling-ball head!" I whispered urgently. David didn't reply so I attempted to use my keen sense of hearing to determine the car's fate.

Once again, I had no luck in this endeavor because all I could hear was David laboriously breathing like a cigarette smoker running a marathon. It sounded as if he was drawing his last breath and would start hacking and dying at any moment. "Blaaa, blaaa, blaaa," he wheezed. As if his breathing wasn't enough to drown out any noise (save that of a helicopter), between gasps he would whine something about jail or McLaughlin or our parents. All the anticipation and not being able to see or hear what was going on caused blood to beat in my temples furiously and my heart to sink deep into my jockey shorts.

After nearly a minute of intense anxiety, David whispered that an old man and two old ladies had just extracted themselves from a large, four-door vehicle. I shifted my position and managed to glimpse around David's head just in time to see them looking around in circles. They seemed infinitely perplexed and peered at the sky as if a meteor had struck their car. After assuring each other that there were no more meteors, the old man surveyed his damaged vehicle and began walking along the side of the road. As he progressed closer to our hiding place he peered up at the bluff mystified.

He spotted us cringing in the tiny crevasse and yelled up at us, "You guys ought to be shot for this!" A little extreme perhaps, but at

146

this point David and I felt so guilty that we would have agreed with him. In fact, we felt so terrible about my wicked deed that we stood up and made a hasty descent down the hill. We ran to the car, apologized, and eagerly helped them change tires.

It turns out that the old folks had driven up from the Lower 48 (Michigan to be exact) and that day was their first day touring Alaska.

David Dawson and I pose in our Gakona Elementary wrestling uniforms. How could two innocent looking boys do such dastardly deeds?

"Welcome to the wild state of Alaska," I thought as the old man asked where he could get his wheel fixed. "Ummm, up the road there's a lodge and you can get your flat fixed there."

"No!" he replied hotly, "Where can I get the wheel fixed?" It took me a second to grasp what he was getting at, but when he pointed at his crooked rim understanding hit me like a big rock.

"Oh. I'm not sure about that," I replied meekly and David shrugged to indicate that he was as clueless as I was. I looked into David's eyes and could sense that he was thinking the same thing as I, "Let's get the hell out of here!" At an opportune moment when the three "old crocks" were deciding what to do, we bid them a hasty farewell and good luck on their vacation. We both secretly hoped that they were all right but did not want to stick around long enough to get into more trouble.

When we got home we never mentioned the incident to David's parents or mine. We just kept our mouths shut and prayed that we weren't reported to McLaughlin or the Glennallen State Troopers. It turns out that we were never turned in or punished for committing the heinous crime of rolling rocks down Gakona Hill. Instead, we escaped justice and were free to roam the countryside committing even more dastardly deeds and forming a stronger friendship, which would never die.

Camping is Hell

As Jon and I grew older, we grew closer. We were always on the bus together, in the same school and we often took classes together too. That's why, when we finally reached puberty and the urge to go camping swelled in our veins, we went into the great unknown together.

We went camping only once in our life, but it was a memorable experience. I remember Jon and I making up our minds to go and thinking that we were "going to go where no man had ever been and where no signs of man could be found." In addition, because our home life was akin to camping, we had to improvise in order to really rough it. We shunned all camping equipment (mostly because our family didn't own a scrap of camping gear) and we avoided taking any of the amenities from home out of fear that our father and brothers would label us suburbanites or Lower 48ers.

After packing our meager belongings at night, Dad suggested going to Secret Lake, behind the pipeline pad. We agreed it was a good place to go, because, after all, what boy would turn down camping at a lake that was secret? We prepared ourselves for a long and arduous trek and slept fitfully due to our excitement.

Dad said to leave at 6 a.m. because it was a long walk. The next day, we followed his instructions and left at six but were at Secret Lake by nine.

"Dad must have walked here in his old age and really took his time," I remarked to Jon.

"Yeah, we're here early."

At any rate, we were at Secret Lake and decided to set up our camp in order to kill time. After all, I reasoned, "We are camping, so we should actively make camp."

First, we set up our sheet of plastic as a shelter. We strung a line between two trees and draped a blue plastic tarp over it (the blue tarp is a very precious commodity and is almost as indispensable to Alaskans as duct tape). This blue tarp was our shelter and we never even considered using a tent because we were convinced that only city people used tents.

Next, we dug a small hole in the ground and started a campfire. By this time it was almost noon and we were starving, so we went to the lake to go grayling fishing. Dad said there would be a mess of fish in the lake this time of the year. After fishing for some time and only pulling in weeds and sticks we decided that Dad didn't know what he was talking about—regardless of the fact that he had fished, trapped, and hunted on this lake for three decades. We decided that we would retire to our camp and eat some of the emergency food we'd brought with us.

Jon and I cooked a couple of hot dogs and ate them plain (we had no bread or condiments, because only suburbanites use these luxury items). I pulled out an ancient can of sardines Dad had given us (probably from the gold rush) and we ate them too. Between eating dry hot dogs and mummified sardines, and continually breathing the sickening smell of burning peat moss, Jon and I became ill and nearly hurled. At this point, it was only one o'clock in the afternoon, but we thought it would be best if we rested and relaxed.

As we lay in our plastic prison, a wicked wind sprang up and was funneled right into our shelter. Naturally, the ends of our makeshift "tent" were open and acted like a perfect wind tunnel. As we tried to rest, the walls of our blue tarp would expand to their maximum capacity and then snap back and contract to such an extent that we almost suffocated when the wind changed directions. This pulsating shelter was certainly less than pleasant and so we went to work on constructing a windbreak.

First we climbed a tall spruce tree and cut off many limbs with a hand axe. This occupied our time for about an hour until Jon cut his hand and we had to return to camp. Then, with some old logs and tundra, we constructed a wind block for the entrance of our shelter and were very proud of our accomplishment. We crawled into the revamped blue tarp shelter and were confident that we could finally get some rest.

As I began to doze off in the afternoon sun, (it was like a sauna in there), I could not rid the smell of burning peat moss from my nostrils. It was then that I realized that the campfire was smoldering underground and the smoke was being funneled right into our plastic contraption. I got up and after some effort I put the remainder of the fire out.

Once again I lay down exasperated. I was hot, exhausted, sick to my stomach, and ready to sleep. Jon was in the same condition and said so several times. Despite a large root under the small of my back, I finally managed to get to sleep, but not for long.

Soon I awoke to a loud, repetitive thumping noise. It was Jon. His bottom half was in his sleeping bag while his bare top half was propped by his elbows on the ground. He was pounding the ground furiously with his right fist.

"What are you doing?" I asked.

"I'm smashing ants," he responded. We had camped directly on an anthill with a tent that had no floor.

I tried to tell Jon not to worry about it, and after nearly an hour of pounding he heeded my advice. It was now suppertime, but we were too sick to eat dinner. We had nothing better to do, so we stayed in our shelter the remainder of the day. Around 11 p.m. when the sun was just starting to go down, I actually fell soundly asleep. But my luck didn't hold and at one in the morning I was rudely awakened by Jon packing his backpack.

"What on God's green earth are you doing?" I asked.

"I'm going home."

"No way. Let's go to sleep and go home in the morning."

"Nope, I'm going home now," he repeated. We packed up our entire camp and trudged home through the dense forest and mosquito-infested swamps in the wee hours of the morning.

Jon's huge pack and suburbanite fishing rod caught on every branch that night. He was frustrated the whole way home, and to make matters worse, Brutus (our lovely camping dog whom I neglected to mention earlier due to his persistent absence) was some miles off barking like crazy.

"I think I heard something," Jon said. I ignored him and we moved on.

I'm not sure at exactly what hour we got home, but Karl was standing outside the house and said, "Did you guys see the bear?"

"Nope," we answered thankfully and pushed our way past him to get inside our warm and cozy home. We were so glad to be home that we just stripped off our clothes, burrowed in our blankets and fell asleep.

An hour later Dad woke us up because Brutus had come home looking like a walrus. He had found a porcupine earlier and now had hundreds of quills protruding from his face. They were stuck in his muzzle, lips, nose, nostrils, tongue, mouth and gums. It was currently six in the morning and we had to pull every quill out of him, one by one.

"Camping sucks. I don't know why people like it. I'm never doing it again. This is my first and last camping trip," Jon stated as he plucked a quill out of Brutus's slobbery lip. Thus, Jon and I ended our perfect adventure, and our perfect hell.

Purple People Eater

When Karl was young, Mr. and Mrs. Browder (our elementary school teachers) gave him a parakeet named Clipper. The bird was green with a yellow head, and had a very pleasant demeanor. A few months later, Clipper was walking on the floor eating little pieces of dirt when he unexpectedly darted under Karl's foot and ceased to exist. I saw his green body stained by a trickle of red blood issuing from his head. Karl was traumatized and heartbroken, but mom saved the day. She comforted him and said that she would buy a replacement bird. A few weeks later, she drove to Anchorage and kept her promise.

When Mom returned from the big city, she gave Karl a brand-new purple parakeet. She said that this particular parakeet was the pick of the crop because she had rigorously screened all of the candidates herself. "How did you pick 'em Mom?" Karl asked excitedly.

Mom answered, "Well, when I went to the pet store and asked the owner to retrieve one of the parakeets, they were all scared and flew to the far side of the cage. Except this one. This purple bird stood his ground and bit the store owner ferociously!" My brothers and I looked at the purple parakeet and then at one another. We knew that he was the perfect bird for us.

Officially, Karl named the new parakeet Grover, but that name never stuck. Instead, we called him the Purple People Eater, Caddy Shack, Crevasse, or Cad. Although Cad was naturally rebellious and short tempered, my brothers and I tormented him so much that he soon became a wicked little bird. We did not intend that he become malicious, but in our innocent efforts to express love, we accidentally created a monster.

The first and least of Cad's worries was what we termed "smuggling." Smuggling entailed reaching into the birdcage while he was sleeping or minding his own business, gently grabbing his body (so that his feet perched on our thumb), and extracting him from his peaceful dwelling. Cad was then at the mercy of the smuggler, and he could do nothing but squirm and chirp.

Sometimes smuggling Cad was not so easy and when we put our hand in the cage, he would ruthlessly bite our fingers. If biting failed to repel the smuggler, he would resort to hopping and fluttering around the cage in an effort to elude his potential captor. Eventually, if all else failed, he would chirp in a low melancholy tone, "Beeep, beeep, beeep, beeep, bwuub, bwuub, bwuub." Cad's last-ditch effort was not only directed at the smuggler's conscience, but at Mom and Dad who always told us to put him back in the cage.

When we did successfully smuggle Cad, we had a lot fun with him (usually at his expense). First and foremost, we would gently touch and kiss him. We would kiss his delicate head, tiny tomato seed eyes, warm and cardboard-like back, and stomach (or "stomata" as Karl used to say). Sometimes, Karl would place Cad's back in his mouth and suck like a vacuum cleaner so that the bird helplessly adhered to his lips. Cad's miniature chicken legs would peddle furiously while the human predator growled like a Tyrannosaurus Rex. After Cad's nerve-racking experience, Karl would allow the petrified bird to perch on his index finger.

Seemingly finished, Karl was just beginning. Next, he would put the bird's head and upper torso into his mouth and pretend that he was going to eat the poor little morsel. Cad could not fly away, because Karl blocked his retreat with his hand. When Cad had been held in this position for about thirty seconds, the cornered bird would become possessed (his eyes turned white and his pupils dilated). Once fully possessed, he would chirp softly and carefully pick small things off the smuggler's teeth. He would use his beak and tongue to gently massage Karl's molars, lips and gums. When Karl was lulled into a false sense of complacency, Cad would inevitably "get grip" (Chmielowski slang which meant to bite down hard) on a soft piece of skin.

When Karl opened his mouth to yell, "Owwww!" Cad gained his freedom and flew to his perch. Cad got grip more times than I can remember and it is truly amazing that Karl never learned his lesson. Humans often claim to be more intelligent than animals, but in my life's experiences, the opposite has been proven time and time again.

On one specific occasion, Cad got particularly good grip on Karl's tongue and made a daring escape. My brother's face was bright red with pain and embarrassment while the bird's countenance reflected mirth mixed with satisfaction. Karl, Jon, and I could not overlook Cad's hideous crime so we took great pains to catch him. We stationed one brother in each of the house's three main rooms and chased him relentlessly. We tried to exhaust him but he never seemed to tire and eventually he found a high perch out of our reach. When the situation looked good for Cad and bleak for us, Karl found a squirt gun and drenched the purple parakeet. Cad became so waterlogged that he could no longer fly and Karl smuggled him with relish.

Once Karl got his hands on the belligerent culprit, he thought of a proper punishment. One of Karl's favorite tortures in situations such as this (i.e., if Cad bit Karl, defecated on Karl, or fled from Karl) was "dunking." He got the idea of dunking from reading about the New England witchcraft trials in the late 1600s. In Karl's case, he did not want to drown Cad, but instead, thoroughly humiliate him.

So Karl opened the copper boiler on top of the wood stove and checked to make sure the water was room temperature. Satisfied that the water was indeed lukewarm, he quickly and completely dunked Cad in the boiler. Even after the hideous torture, the bird still seemed to be laughing. Karl gave him another dunking.

If Cad's crimes were truly unforgivable (a shit-and-run for instance), we would torture him in more creative ways. Sometimes we would put him in a cage so tiny that he could barely turn around. We would hang the cage from the ceiling and glare at him in his small prison. If the claustrophobic conditions did not seem to frighten the parakeet, we would push his cage so that it swung like a pendulum. If he still did not crack, we would twist up the cage's string and set the whole thing spinning wildly. Finally, if all previous efforts failed, we would invoke a special combination torture: the spinning-pendulum.

Eventually, after many such torture sessions, Cad gnawed through the cage's delicate wooden bars and we were forced to think of a new torture. At length, Karl and I decided that the bingo cage was perfect. Our bingo cage was originally designed to mix the balls from our home bingo game, but we thought that it would be better used as a torture device. The cage was spherical (six inches in diameter) with metal bars (no possible way to chew through them) and it had a crank (to spin the whole cage). Cad fit like a charm in the bingo cage and his tiny feet grabbed onto the wire mesh when we spun the apparatus. The centripetal force glued him to the walls and round and round he went. When we released him he exited on wobbly legs and flew into the walls and windows.

When Cad was good, which in our opinions was rare, we would play with him. We would smuggle him and put him under our shirts because he tickled our stomach and chest when he walked. He would also chirp softly, "root around" (scratch with his claws) and occasionally get grip on a patch of skin. Of course, if he bit us, playtime was over and we tortured him appropriately.

154

We often thought that Cad was bored sitting in his cage all day so we constructed a maze for him out of Legos. The passages were three inches wide, and the maze itself was approximately four feet by four feet. We laid a sheet of clear Plexiglas over the entire thing so that we could monitor his progress as he searched for the exit. Additionally, once we placed him in the front entrance, we blocked his retreat with a portable Lego wall.

Cad crawled through some of the passages, but mostly he just stood still and picked on the corners of the Lego blocks. Occasionally, he saw the futility of his situation and he tried to dig through the plastic floor by vigorously rooting. When Cad stalled too long in a given area, we would shake the whole structure in order to encourage him towards freedom. After nearly an hour, he continued to exasperate us and he made no attempt whatsoever to sincerely solve the puzzle. So, we gave him a dunking.

Cad's unceasing trials and tribulations made a tough bird even tougher. He would swoop into the turtle's bowl just to bathe in the foul brown water. Worse than that, he *enjoyed* drinking the murky stuff more than the clean water that we provided for him in the cage. Also, Cad would eat anything and he made no qualms about landing on our dinner plates and snatching food from us. He would consume bread, cereal, cookies, steak, vegetables, and even his larger cousins such as the chicken or turkey.

On one occasion, Cad was so eager to eat Karl's cereal that he leaned over the edge of the bowl too far and fell into the milk. With only his head above the floating Corn Flakes, he waded all the way across the bowl and hopped onto the opposite edge. He shook the milk off his wings, turned around and continued to eat. On a different occasion, Cad scalded the bottoms of his feet when he attempted to land on a pot of boiling soup. Dad hit the nail on the head when he observed, "He's a tough little bird and getting worse every day."

Cad was not only tough, but he was also very homely. Due to some sort of French molt disease (which parakeets are particularly prone to getting), he lost all the feathers on his stomach. Our bird books said that his feathers would eventually grow back, but they never did. Poor Cad, he had a bald belly and we were completely powerless to help him.

As if Cad's featherless belly was not bad enough, he lost even more feathers. This time the cause was not a European virus, but our newly adopted Newfoundland dog, Brutus. Two weeks after we brought Brutus home, Cad was walking on the floor picking at wood chips and noticed the 130-pound black dog sleeping nearby. Without hesitating, he boldly hopped over to Brutus and bit him on the end of his nose. Prior to the biting incident, Brutus had regarded Cad as a harmless curiosity. After the incident, it was all-out war.

A day later, I witnessed firsthand one of the most spectacular events in Chmielowski history. While I was warming myself in front of the stove, Cad was on the floor eating pebbles and Brutus was asleep in a corner. Quicker than a heartbeat, Brutus's eyes popped open and he leaped more than six feet towards the parakeet. He pounced right on top of Cad with his front paws and I heard a loud squawk as feathers flew everywhere.

When the feathers settled and all was quiet, I gingerly approached Brutus and saw a pink parakeet leg protruding from under a massive black paw. At that moment, I lost all hope for Cad and Brutus lifted his paw to gloat over the dead bird. But as he shifted his weight, an amazing thing happened; an alien creature had replaced Cad!

This new creature emerged from the chaos on wobbly legs and slowly took off into the air. It was small and purple, had two wings, and just like Cad, it had a bald belly. But unlike Cad, this odd creature had no tail feathers whatsoever and strongly resembled a purple egg.

The purple egg hovered for three seconds above a stunned Brutus, did a 360-degree turn, and rose vertically six feet. Then, it flew forward at an incredible speed and attempted to land near the kitchen. The poor creature had no tail feathers to slow its momentum and it could not land. As a result, the egg continued flying in broad circles (the thing couldn't turn tightly because it had no rudder) until it crash-landed on the living room windowsill. Brutus looked both delighted and disappointed.

Eventually, over the next six months, the odd creature grew tail feathers and mysteriously metamorphosed into our old parakeet, Cad. But after the Brutus incident, Cad was never the same and in fact, he was much more ornery than before.

As the years rolled by, we tortured Cad less and gave him more privileges. One such privilege was putting his cage in the front yard on warm sunny days. We figured that he would be less lonely if he could communicate with the wild birds. Indeed, Cad enjoyed being outside very much and one day Karl got the brainy idea to let him fly free.

"He'll come back," Karl said confidently as he opened the cage door. Without hesitating, Cad flew into a spruce tree and refused to return (I wonder why?). Worse than not cooperating with Karl, he immediately picked a fight with a large camp robber. After the gray camp robber authoritatively pecked Cad on the head, our purple angel turned his attention to exploration rather than conflict.

Cad flew behind the house, over the sheds, and beyond the south end of Barney's property. Every time he flew deeper into the woods,

Karl, Jon, and I shouted, cussed and threw things at him in order to coax him back to us. Later that evening, Steve, our dependable hero, volunteered to aid our desperate mission.

Steve filled Dad's antique pump fire extinguisher with water and walked to the south end of the lake. He squirted Cad until he became waterlogged and could no longer fly. Steve's fire extinguisher method of immobilizing the bird was similar to, but much grander than the squirt gun method we employed inside the house. Steve's plan worked perfectly and once again we had Cad safely in our possession. Of course, Karl was very angry at the little bird and tortured him in an unprecedented manner; he gave Cad a triple dunking.

Cad experienced many more adventures throughout his life. He did battle with Karl's pet turtle, both dogs, each family member, and he even killed a large wasp that wandered into his cage. Years of relentless combat took its toll on our feathered little friend and at length, the battle-weary veteran gradually lost his sanity. In the last few days prior to his death, Cad became increasingly possessed. His eyes turned white, his head spun around backwards, and he fluttered wildly on the living room floor. In short, he should have auditioned for *The Exorcist*.

During one of Cad's episodes, he landed on my right shoulder and bit my ear with a vengeance. He got grip on my lobe so hard that I sincerely thought I was going to have to wear him to school as an earring. I reacted quickly to his assault by violently shaking my head in order to make him let go of my sensitive skin. I had no luck shaking him free so I used my hands to manually pry him from my ear. Due to the excruciating pain, I released him so that I could investigate my wounds. While wiping a drop of blood from my ear, I vowed to torture Cad as soon as I thought of a devious and appropriate method to suit his unforgivable crime.

The next morning, Dad woke up and found his little body lying on the bottom of the birdcage with his feet sticking straight up in the air. We woke up a few hours later and found the cage empty. Karl asked Dad, "Where's Cad?"

To this inquiry, Dad replied, "Cad died during the night. I threw his body in the wood stove and burned it. That way his ashes will go up the stove pipe and he'll get to heaven faster."

When Dad finished speaking, I touched the small hole in my right ear and smiled inwardly. I would have rather enjoyed killing Cad myself, but it seemed as if the Purple People Eater had had the last laugh. He not only got the best grip of his life (at my expense), but he avoided my planned torture by conveniently dying of natural causes. I could only smile at my defeat and give him the grudging respect that he deserved.

Brutus

A year after Boy died we adopted Brutus from the Glennallen state troopers. They said that a local man recently abandoned his home and two dogs. The troopers found the dogs chained to stakes outside in the snow. They were in poor health due to exposure and were nearly starved to death.

One of the dogs was a red mutt and the other was a large black Newfoundland. When we heard about the Newfoundland on the radio, Dad immediately drove to town and adopted him for free. A few hours later, Dad returned with his cargo and we were all ecstatic to have Boy's void filled.

The troopers told us that the dog's name was Buck. The family rejected this name as too "Alaskanish" or too "Jack London-esque." Whoever had owned the poor dog was probably from the Lower 48 and was

Brutus replaced the late Father Rawhide (no photo available). Although sometimes a pain in the butt, Brutus was a full-fledged and well-loved member of our family,

trying in vain to be either a mountain man, a

liver-off-the-land-man, or a great white hunter. In any case, it was painfully obvious to us that the previous owner was a cheechako who had most likely read too many stereotypical Alaskan storybooks. The name Buck did not sit well with our family.

Instead, we decided to name him Brutus. We settled on the name Brutus because it was not only masculine, but it was original. That afternoon we let Brutus run free on our property and he was excited and full of energy in no time. We tried to coax him into our home, but he refused to come in and simply cowered when the door was opened for him. Additionally, he walked with a slight limp and based on our observations we concluded that the original owner had seriously mistreated Brutus (just like Buck in Jack London's *The Call of the Wild*).

After a month, Brutus was well fed, strong and confident. He was a solid 120 pounds, had a huge head, and big lips. He loved playing lots of games, but his favorite by far was taking people for a walk. This game consisted of clamping his powerful jaws on the victim's forearm and then physically pulling the person around the yard. He never punctured our skin, but his teeth did hurt badly enough for all of us to comply with his desires. The worst damage he did to our arms consisted only of red sores, small bruises, and itchy welts. It was a small price to pay to see a big dog happy.

As the years rolled by after Fang's death, Brutus became a full-fledged member of the family. He stayed inside when he wanted and went outside at his leisure. He napped with Dad in the house and napped with Dad in the snow. He swam with us in the lake, the creek, and the river. He rode with us in the blue truck and the Maverick and thoroughly enjoyed slobbering all over us while we drove. In short, Brutus was well loved and well treated, just like one of the boys.

Sometimes Brutus was less than an angel, and he lazed around the house and yard sleeping off the better part of the day. When called or asked to move, he'd open one eyelid and sigh so deeply that it was plain that he was not going to adjust his bulk. If ever a thief had come during one of his lazy moods, Brutus would have literally been a watchdog. That is, he would have been a *dog* that *watched* the thief steal our valuables.

Brutus's overactivity and industrious character got him into more trouble than lounging. Occasionally he wandered home with an old, green caribou leg in his mouth. He often found these treats along the road where people had shot caribou and sawed their legs off as waste. Some hunters took only the caribou's rack and left the whole body, while most took the good meat and left the scraps (which included the legs).

While on his travels, Brutus occasionally stumbled onto these treasures and would be Proud Puppy upon returning home. More often than not, we let him have his treats because there was no sense in wasting good meat, and to be truthful, we could never capture him when he was snacking. We really didn't mind him eating the rancid caribou legs, but we did mind his pungent farts the entire week.

Worse than a caribou leg was human feces. About a half mile north of our home on the highway is a pull-off. Tourists and travelers stopped here and dumped their garbage, urinated and defecated in this area. There are no public restrooms or dumpsters on most of the Alaskan Highway system and many travelers are very inconsiderate to locals. Pollution and human waste products are common in and around Alaska's highways, especially in our neck of the woods.

Whereas we found the garbage and human waste disgusting, Brutus found it utterly delightful. He would sneak up to the pull-off, go through garbage, and then roll in feces. Who knows why dogs roll in crap, but they do. Perhaps it made Brutus feel more masculine and it was like an aftershave for him. Whatever the reason, he returned home Proud Puppy and we fled from him and banned him from the house.

Eventually, we built up the nerve to go outside, and he'd bound over to us as if he were saying, "Hi guys! How are you doing? Like my new, nifty odor?" We then tied him to a tree and shampooed him with cheap, cherry-scented soap. We rinsed him with lake water that was hand-pumped out of our antique red fire extinguisher. Finally, we released him and he tore around the yard in circles to clear his mind of the terrifying experience.

Brutus was always insulted after the bath ordeal and worse yet, he lamented the loss of his musky odor. He looked so dejected and depressed that we laughed and pointed at him and called him Queer Puppy because he smelled like flowers and cherry blossoms. Our teasing him was a mistake and he eventually returned to the pull-off in order to spite us and regain his manhood.

We found it ironic that Brutus enjoyed swimming, rain, and walking in the swamps, but he despised having water poured on him by humans. I even remember one occasion when the rain was coming down in sheets and he was lying outside on the path unfazed. I took a drink from the water barrel, finished half the cup, and flung the other half through the porch screen. By chance the flung water landed on Brutus and he looked up startled and insulted. He raised his nose, picked himself up and walked away. As if he wasn't already wet! I guess it was a pride thing.

Whether Brutus was Insulted Puppy, Queer Puppy, Proud Puppy, or Sad Puppy, we loved him and took good care of him. He kept the whole family company and helped me personally get through tough times such as high school, entering West Point, staying at West Point, and even leaving West Point. He listened to me intently and never judged nor mocked my decisions. He was not only a great dog, but a good listener and my best friend.

Unfortunately, Brutus was a big dog, and as is typical with big dogs, his life span was relatively short. I saw him during the summer of 1994 and he was very sick. In the fall, he disappeared into the forest and that was the last I ever saw of him. Months later, when I was at Rutgers College in New Jersey, Dad phoned me and said that he'd found Brutus hiding in the forest because he was Embarrassed Puppy. Dad discovered him just a few feet from where I had been searching earlier. Apparently, Brutus was ashamed of himself and his condition and that is why he didn't reveal his presence to me when I called for him. Dad told me that Brutus was starving and covered in his own excrement. He couldn't eat because food was tearing up his digestive system and thus he was in an inescapable downward spiral.

Mom and Dad brought Brutus home that fall and nursed him back to health. Within a month he relapsed again, but even worse. It was now October and without a vet, Dad was forced to shoot Brutus out of compassion and love for his best friend. Killing Brutus nearly killed Dad and he vowed never to have a dog again. "It hurt too much," he simply said.

Though Brutus's tragic death hurt the family, his spicy character and loyal companionship outweighed our grief ten to one. Furthermore, I believe that our family enabled him to not only recover from a tumultuous puppyhood, but also to enjoy his life to the fullest. I will never forget Brutus, and I truly believe that the wolf tracks I recently found after his death belong to him. Perhaps he was reincarnated and was just stopping by our home to say, "Hi. Thanks for everything. I'm doing well."

Sabotage!

I'm not sure exactly when it all started. I think it had something to do with a rubber snake Jon and I had. One summer day we were playing with the snake and decided to scare motorists passing by our house. With some imagination and a little ingenuity, a vision came to us and we took our two-foot long rubber snake and tied some monofilament fishing line around its neck. Then we planted it on the eastern side of the Richardson Highway while we hid in the bushes on the western side. After waiting a little over a half hour, we heard a distant car approaching from the north. Our hearts leapt with anticipation and it was nearly impossible to keep our hands from shaking.

As the vehicle approached we slowly pulled on the invisible line and the ferocious snake sprang to life. As planned, it slithered in an arthritic and awkward fashion right into the automobile's lane.

"I bet they'll slam on their brakes and really freak out! No one's ever seen a snake in Alaska!" I said to Jon. My brother didn't respond but instead just watched the scene unfold. As the car drove by, both of our expectations were dashed as it accelerated in order to run over our precious snake.

We heard the sickening bump and thud of the snake's slender body as the car rolled over it. The vehicle zipped out of sight and left Jon and me feeling like a mother who has just lost her only child. Not only did the trick fail to bring us our hoped-for entertainment, but our rubber snake now had a large split in its tail and tire treads imbedded in its head. "Dang! I guess that driver must have been from the Lower 48. No real Alaskan would have run over such a rarity," I thought to myself. We inspected the snake and declared it unserviceable. We were disgruntled and vowed to right this horrible wrong.

Jon and I mulled over several new ideas in our heads, but Ray's infamous and highly successful practical joke kept popping into our minds. No matter how hard we concentrated on an original idea, our thoughts constantly drifted back to the time when Ray put on Karl's real-looking rubber ape mask and his black leather jacket. He put a cigarette in his mouth, turned up the jacket's collar and stood beside the road late at night. As a car's headlights illuminated him, he put out his thumb as if he were hitchhiking.

Imagine what the unfortunate driver thought that night (who happened to be female). It was very late; she was on a near-deserted stretch of Alaskan highway, and the only help or humans were miles and miles away in Gakona or Paxon. The petrified woman had no time to think clearly and instinctively reacted. She attempted to avoid the leather-clad sasquatch by swerving on the icy road and careened into the snowbank right beside the ugly thing. Ray quickly ran and hid while the frightened woman dug herself out of the snow (all the while peering over her shoulder for the elusive primate). It turned out that she had had a little too much to drink that night (as we found out after the crash), but years later she still insisted that she had seen Bigfoot.

It crossed our minds that Ray's trick was cruel, but it was exactly the kind that Jon and I wanted to pull.

"Perhaps they didn't see the snake," I mentioned to Jon.

"Yeah, maybe not," he agreed. We moped around a bit more and then walked to the gravel pit down the road.

"Let's lay a board perpendicularly across a log, like a teeter-totter and place a rock on the lower end. That way, if someone drives on the gravel pit road, their tire will hit the high end of the board and launch the rock into their side window!" I suggested to Jon.

"Yeah. Maybe."

"Or how about somehow rigging up a system where a rock or log would come swinging down from a tree and hit a car?!" I shouted, confident that this idea was good.

"Yeah. Maybe," Jon said again unenthusiastically. No matter how many ideas we thought of, none of them were truly inspirational and once again we were left with saboteur's block.

As we walked home with slumped shoulders and dragging feet, I spotted something in the ditch.

"That's it!" I yelled and pointed to the top of a black spruce tree.

"What?" Jon asked, bewildered. I explained the idea to him and right away we went to work on our devilish task. We retrieved the magical fishing line, tied it to the tip of the dead spruce tree and camouflaged it in the ditch. Then we hid on the opposite side of the road and waited.

"This spruce tree is a heck of a lot bigger than the snake and it should definitely command some attention," I thought. After ten minutes a car approached and we tugged on the line in a jerky fashion. The shambling mound lurched slowly forward on unsteady limbs and was almost in the oncoming automobile's lane. We had grossly miscalculated our intended victim's speed and he came zipping by so quickly that he completely missed hitting our unidentifiable beast.

"That stupid driver didn't even notice our rare animal and he wasn't afraid of it either," I moaned in resignation.

"Dang Lower 48ers. Back to ground zero again," Jon mumbled.

Next, Ray gave us a tip. "People love to run over bags. Put some big rocks in a plastic bag and they'll run them over," he told us. We decided to see for ourselves so we put six large rocks in a black trash bag in the middle of the northbound lane. We placed the bag a half mile from our house in order to avoid linking our home with the crime. Once again we took to the bushes for safety and waited. A car approached, swerved and missed the bag entirely. Another did the same, and another and another. No luck at all, Ray must have lied to us.

At this point, due to our humiliating failure, Jon and I felt belittled and our egos were severely bruised. As a matter of fact, we were both so angry and dejected that neither one of us could rest until we discovered a foolproof way to sabotage those ignorant, smart-alecky drivers who dared to travel the highway near our dwelling.

I forget exactly how we hit on the idea, but eventually we figured that if automobiles kept swerving and ignoring our efforts, we simply would have to design a system that was entirely unavoidable. We thought for a long while and began setting up a prototype of our latest trap. We never could have guessed that this particular idea would eventually mushroom into a full-blown sabotage effort.

First, we started by finding a skinny, dead black spruce pole about ten feet high. Next we stood it on end about six inches off the asphalt. Then we dug it into the soil and stacked rocks around it so that it would stand vertically on its own. Finally, we attached the infamous fishing line to it and strung it across the road to our hiding place. As a car approached, we watched, waited and tensed. At the last possible second we gave the line a yank and the tree fell over right in front of the vehicle. That smart-aleck car had absolutely no way of avoiding the spruce tree and ran it over traveling in excess of fifty miles an hour.

It was so satisfying to see branches, bark, and spruce cones raining down from the sky! The sound of wood snapping and popping made our hearts swell with pride and joy. As these feelings flowed through our small bodies the car slowed down and stopped. "No time to gloat," I thought as I leaned and nudged Jon. We both looked at one another and took off running deep into the impenetrable forest and swamp. There was no way in the world those motorists could have caught a couple of kids (eight and nine years old) in such a desolate wilderness. We had done our wicked deed and were getting off scot-free. Dang, what a great feeling.

When we reported our success story to Karl, he became interested and demanded that we repeat the sabotage trick. Of course, he didn't have to demand anything, we willingly volunteered our services and immediately went to work setting up our trap. This time we changed our location to Rose Bud Hill (half mile north of our home) so that we didn't incriminate ourselves. Instead, Uncle Joe would take the rap.

After a few hours of solid work we set up permanent blinds made of logs, sticks, and tundra (on top of the hill). These shelters were our official hiding places and allowed us to watch the upcoming entertainment in comfort and safety. We selected a stout, twenty-five-foot, three-inch-diameter, black spruce tree that would extend across both lanes of the highway. This larger and improved spruce insured that no one, and I mean no one, would be able to avoid our neat little trick. We tied fishing line to the tree and waited patiently in our blinds. Eventually, a car came and Karl pulled the invisible line …

We spent the next few weeks merrily sabotaging whenever the mood struck us. When we were bored hanging around the house Karl would ask, "Hey guys, wanna sab?"

"OK," Jon and I would promptly reply and off to work we'd go. We must have pulled about twenty different trees in front of and on top of the same number of unsuspecting motorists. The majority of people tried to swerve out of the tree's path, but they either got nailed directly or ran over the tree's trunk. They would continue down the road dumbfounded and awestruck (What are the odds that a tree would fall over at such an inopportune moment?). Some vehicles slowed down, while others came to a grinding halt trying to figure out what in the sam-hell had just happened. Still others stopped and tried to give chase to the little miscreants who caused such impish destruction.

On one occasion, I was tying the line to a tree and a stealthy, silent car pulled up behind me. It must have been one of those non-Alaskan, newfangled cars that didn't split eardrums or backfire when it ran. The driver, a male, yelled at me, "What the hell are ya doing?"

I stood still and looked at him like a deer caught in a spotlight. I was transfixed for a full two seconds before I could get my legs working. Once properly functioning, they carried me quickly up the gray clay hill and into the forest. Technically, I was not caught (he had no idea what I was really doing), but the three of us agreed that the incident was too close for comfort. Hence, we wisely decided to modify our operation instead of eliminating it altogether (sabotaging is a very addictive habit and is considered a disease).

After brainstorming awhile and following Henry David Thoreau's advice, "Simplify, simplify, simplify," we came up with a fantastic idea.

"Laying logs all the way across the road will insure that they don't avoid our trap," I mentioned to Karl as we placed a tree in the southbound lane.

"Yup. It's also less suspicious 'cause we're not using any fishing line," he replied. Although our handiwork resembled a primitive roadblock, it successfully severed any definite connection to us and thus we would not be implicated in the crime. After all, those trees could have easily fallen off of a logging truck from Tok and landed on the road in a perfectly straight line.

Over the next couple of weeks we dragged all sorts of logs across the highway and watched with utter delight as cars slowed, stopped or ran over them at full speed. In any one of the three cases mentioned, we were never let down and we finished each day with a great sense of satisfaction and contentment. Life as a saboteur was good.

The only motorist who successfully avoided our clever trick was a motorcyclist. He simply slowed down, drove off of the road onto the gravel berm and circumnavigated the whole trap. However, no automobiles were as fortunate and a few particular instances are well worth noting.

The most memorable vehicle was the A-team van. One day the three of us dragged a huge tree (about one and one-half feet in diameter) across the road. The tree was so large that moving it required our combined strength and we thought for sure that this trick would be a real doozy. No sooner had we taken our hiding places than a big black van with red stripes and no windows came to a screeching halt. We couldn't see who or what emerged, but we heard some muttering and a loud crashing sound. The crash was followed by footsteps confidently approaching our blinds.

We didn't wait around to see who threatened us, but instead we took off in a dead sprint into the wilderness. After our adrenaline settled, we returned to the scene of the crime and beheld a ghastly sight. Somehow, whoever or whatever was in that van, be he man or beast, had picked up the huge tree and thrown it into the ditch.

"Thank God that dude didn't get us!" I thought. I could see the looks of horror on Karl's and Jon's faces and I knew that they were thinking the exact same thing. Despite our fear, we continued working diligently on our duties.

On a separate occasion, we set up a roadblock with six trees lying in random fashion (people seemed to suspect the linear nature of our previous roadblocks). As usual, we hid in our blinds and waited awhile before we heard a car. Actually, two cars approached this time, and both were going very fast. As they came around the corner we saw two convertibles (tops down and rock music pounding) quickly reducing the distance between themselves and our beautiful roadblock. Two "high school heads" (or perhaps they were college kids) wearing sunglasses were in each vehicle and didn't seem to notice the huge barricade. In fact, neither vehicle slowed down a bit, and they both ran over the logs with a loud explosion.

What was so special about this case was that their shaking and nodding heads never missed a beat of music as they ran over the roadblock. What was more curious was that their speed never varied and they continued down the road going more than seventy miles per hour.

"Holy cow! Those high school heads must've been stoned or something!" Karl yelled excitedly.

"Yeah!" Jon and I answered in unison. Then all three of us broke out laughing and we rolled in the tundra with visions of those idiots nodding their heads. Heck, we didn't even have to reset the blockade for the next victim.

We used the roadblock sabotaging method for some time because it produced such gratifying and consistent results. We enjoyed it so much that we eventually told Jim and David Dawson about our adventures.

"Man, that sounds like fun," Jim said, "Can I do it too?"

"Yeah, you oughta stay overnight this week," Karl replied.

"OK," Jim said and hence, the scene was set for something truly spectacular.

What happened the night that Jim stayed over was to be the most climactic sabotaging experience ever. I only wish that I had been there to see it. As it was, I had stayed the night at David's house and I was not physically present at the festivities. I can only chronicle what Karl, Jon, and Jim told me the day after it happened.

Apparently, for some reason or another, Karl and Jim reverted to the old method of tying line to a freestanding tree. However, instead of using a single, skinny tree, they set up two huge trees on opposite sides of the road. Karl and Jim hid in the bushes across from one another (each with fishing line in hand) and waited patiently for the proper victim.

They were soon rewarded for their efforts when an immense, seventy-five-foot-long Winnebago came rumbling down the road at a swift forty-five miles per hour. The swaying boat was so pathetically slow and huge it was almost a crime to activate the trap (a slow-moving vehicle provides little sport for the professional saboteur). But Karl and Jim didn't hesitate and on the count of three they both began reeling fishing line hand over hand as fast as possible. The two trees teetered, swayed, and fell on top of the hood of the camper. They wedged themselves into an "X" pattern in front of the windshield and on top of the engine compartment. Amazingly enough, the juggernaut did not slow and kept driving down the road dragging the trees along with it!

Eventually, the camper stopped in front of Uncle Joe's cabin and an old man dislodged the trees from his vehicle. He gazed confusedly at the nest of fishing line tangled in his windshield wipers. Karl and Jim laughed like hyenas and hid in the bushes.

"Man, that was the best! We got one of them dang Winnebago campers!" Jim wheezed and coughed.

"Yeah, I hate them things. That was the best sabotage ever!" Karl replied. It is common knowledge that Alaskans HATE slow-moving campers and tourists, especially Winnebagos. Due to their extremely good fortune, Karl, Jim, and Jon clapped each other on the back and decided to call it a day's work. It must have been a fantastic show, otherwise it would have been blasphemy to quit after doing only one job.

As the days wore on, our luck was bound to wear out. One day while we were at school, a state trooper came to our house and asked Dad if he had any knowledge of the mysterious logs strewn on the road.

"Oh, I think someone's been wood-gettin' up there," Dad said. The trooper didn't say much and left silently with his suspicions. When we returned from school Dad mentioned that a state trooper had visited our home. Dad didn't tell us why he visited and never mentioned anything else about the incident. He didn't need to; we were certainly smart enough to figure out that we had better quit while we were ahead.

I often wonder how our sabotaging pranks appeared to a tourist. Did they notice the one lone tree standing near the white line of the highway? Did they see the telltale glint of sunshine reflecting off the fishing line? Could they see my brothers and me hiding in the forest? Did they want to go "medieval" on us for the destruction that we caused? God knows, if I were one of them I would have done my best to catch the little brats who sabotaged me.

As it turned out, no one ever caught us, and that is what makes

our ignoble deeds so memorable. We never intended to hurt anyone or damage anyone's vehicles, we only wanted to alleviate our
boredom and exercise our adrenaline. We not only fulfilled both of
these desires, but we did what all young boys love to do—we flirted
with danger and avoided the consequences—time and time and
time again.

*What would you think if you rounded a curve on a lonely highway and saw
this motley-looking crew? (Sourdough Lodge shown in the background)*

Christmas a la Chmielowski

I am aware that many people believe Christmas at their house is fabulous and cannot be outdone by any other family. However, it is a simple fact that Christmas in any other household pales when compared to that of a typical Chmielowski Christmas. In other words, there is no Christmas season celebrated by anyone, anywhere, anytime (past or present) with more enthusiasm than that of the Chmielowski Clan. When a visitor entered our home during the Christmas season, he or she was thoroughly overwhelmed by our holiday spirit.

In a sense, the Christmas season started in August when the fall J.C. Penney and Sears catalogs came in the mail. From the moment the mail order catalogs arrived, my brothers and I would spend one or two hours each day repeatedly looking at them and dog-earing their pages. We drooled over all the neat toys before finally circling a few that we wanted most. Based on our catalog choices, in October Mom asked each of us to make a Christmas list of potential "prizes." We gave the lists to Dad and he threw them into the wood stove. Dad threw our Christmas lists into the stove so that their ashes would fly up the stovepipe, into the air, and travel quickly on the wind to the North Pole. Santa Claus would receive our airmailed lists in plenty of time for Christmas (those elves had a lot of prizes to make for the five Chmielowski brothers).

The day after Thanksgiving we started the Christmas season proper. Mom spearheaded the holiday preparations by first making a Christmas chain from construction paper. The chain was composed of twenty-five alternating red and green links and we hung it vertically alongside the curtains in the living room. Each night, prior to the family going to sleep, Mom selected one brother (depending on whose turn it was that night; otherwise fights might break out) to cut the link. Cutting the link symbolized that Christmas had inched closer by one day and that it was just around the corner. Mom successfully employed the Christmas chain in order to hype the holiday season and build anticipation to the point of explosion.

Once the Christmas chain was finished and hung, Mom began preparing the cookie factory. In this case, I do not use the word factory lightly. I purposefully use "factory" to relate the methodical and industrial nature of Mom's cookie work.

Mom began her enormous operation by making double batches of cookie batter. With minimal breaks, from 10 a.m. to 4 p.m., Mom made as many double batches as possible. She would spend the

Months before Christmas, the five brothers cluster their shaved heads around the Fall Sears catalog (Dad in background). Note the shear marks on our scalps, compliments of Mom's skillful haircutting techniques.

entire afternoon (not just the morning or a couple hours after lunch) in the kitchen, making only cookie batter. At the end of the day she cleaned up all her baking implements so that Dad could use the kitchen to prepare dinner. She put the whole day's batter supply in ziplock bags on the porch to freeze (the temperature is between forty below and thirty above this time of the year).

The next morning, Mom would wake up and the whole process began anew. On some days she made chocolate chips, and on others she made peanut butter, gingersnap, or sugar cookies. The batter-making phase usually took Mom about two weeks of solid work to complete and it ended with dozens of bags of frozen cookie batter dotting our porch.

After Mom had worked every day, all day, for two weeks straight, building batter (good cookie batter is built, not made), it was now time to start baking the cookies. For the next two weeks we constantly used our propane oven to bake cookies. Except when we were at school, Karl, Jon, and I were employed nearly full-time to make balls. We rolled the cookie dough into little balls slightly smaller than golf balls and put them onto cookie sheets to be baked. Each of us manned the oven for about two hours until another brother took over the baking operation.

Rolling balls was a time-consuming and labor-intensive process but well worth the effort. A ball roller could easily sneak a fingerful of raw batter or even an entire ball without getting caught. Better yet, when letting the cookies cool it was possible to consume a few and blame the loss on Fang. Often we were able to link Fang with the disappearing cookies because we put the hot cookie sheets onto our porch floor to cool. We did so because our snowy porch floor and the sub-zero air temperature helped cool the cookies very quickly.

Our porch cooling process was expedient, but it was not without risk. Occasionally, Fang opened the porch door from the outside and found twenty-four neatly arranged treats resting on a silver platter. Fang may have been a little crazy, but he wasn't stupid and he never hesitated to eat our homemade cookies.

On other occasions, Dad forgot about the temporary cookie-cooling area. He'd come into the porch from working on the generator or truck and step smack-dab in the middle of the cookies. The unfortunate baker in the kitchen heard Dad stumble, curse and then say something such as, "Well, they got stepped on so I guess I'll have to eat the dang things." In situations such as these, the baker counted the missing cookies as a business loss and the factory continued to churn out products without missing a beat or losing its momentum.

The end result of all our labor was that each Christmas Mom produced approximately one thousand chocolate chips, one thousand peanut butters, one thousand sugar cookies and five hundred ginger snaps (not as popular as the other cookies). She stored the cookies in 2-gallon, empty mayonnaise containers and put a couple of jugs behind the couch (for quick access), a few in the middle and back bedrooms, some on the porch, and the remainder in the meat shed (deep-freeze for long-term storage). We would spend the Christmas holidays and the following month (sometimes well into February if Ray didn't do too much damage) eating the fruits of our labor.

Mom didn't just make cookies. After and between batches of cookies she made fudge, gingerbread men, lollypops, various hard candies, and pies, and imported enormous quantities of Christmas candy from Anchorage (via The Zoo Wagon or sometimes with the aid of Uncle Ray and Josie). Needless to say, due to overconsumption of sweets throughout the Christmas season, we were often queasy and on the verge of hurling.

On December 1, while Mom's cookie factory was at peak production, my brothers and I set up the Christmas tree. In most households, setting up and decorating a tree is a pleasant task and not of unusual proportions. This was definitely not the case in the Chmielowski household and setting up our Christmas tree was a monumental task. Any sane person would have gleefully chosen suicide as an alternative to helping my family erect our overdecorated tree.

In order to set up the Christmas tree we had to brave the subzero arctic temperatures. We went into the garage (not heated or even attached to the house) and rooted around under piles of junk until we located and extracted the tree's platform. Dad made the four-by-four-foot plywood platform to set the tree on and keep it stable. Next, we again braved the frigid temperatures in order to retrieve the stem and all the branches of our fake Christmas tree.

Our family chose to have a fake tree because it looked nicer than the skinny, sickly black spruce poles common to our area. Additionally, Dad chose a fake tree out of practicality. He didn't want to be tromping around the frozen Alaskan forests this time of year looking for a nice tree and my brothers and I sure didn't want to either. Finally, a live spruce tree adorned with electric lights and real candles is a disaster waiting to happen. Dad did not want to add yet another fire hazard to our already long list of possible hazards, including the wood stove, oil stove, propane stove, propane lights, each and every kerosene lamp, and five rambunctious kids.

When the whole tree was assembled it was more than five feet in diameter at the base and scraped the ceiling at the top. Our tree was more appropriate for an office building than a Thoreau-like cabin in the woods. The colossal tree seemed to take up about one third of the living room (keep in mind that our house is about the size of a single-wide trailer) and was quite an odd picture.

The entire time my brothers and I were assembling the tree, Dad complained incessantly and often pointed out that we were putting branches in the wrong holes. Sometimes we were, but that was not our fault. The dang tree was more than thirty years old and all the color-coordinating paint on the inside tips of the branches had worn off ages ago. Year after year, Dad cussed and complained and we set up the tree without ever considering repainting the branches. We figured that if we could just get the tree set up this year we would not have to worry about it for another whole year; as a result, the cycle continued.

Once the tree was properly assembled (or improperly, as the case might be), we began the real work. "Wait! Ah, crap. We forgot the lights and glittery stuff!" someone inevitably said.

"Aah-ha," Dad would reply sagely to no one in particular. "I told you guys not to rush, dang it. See what happens when you rush?" We then took all the branches out of the holes and started from scratch. This time we wrapped five full lengths of lights around the tree's stem with two strands of shimmery stuff in order to give the tree a distinct "core". We repeated the entire branch ordeal (including Dad's frustrated comments and cussing) until the tree was re-set up. In the end, we wrapped more than ten strands of lights around the middle and outside of the tree and voilà! It was ready to be decorated (in very distinct and precise stages).

The first phase, hanging little balls, was much dreaded and feared by all. This phase would have easily frayed the nerves of even the calmest Tibetan Monk. Hanging little balls consisted of hanging five full boxes' worth of tiny balls (one to two inches in diameter) around the core, and only the core, of the Christmas tree. The object was to hang all the little balls as close as possible to the inside of the tree in order to accentuate the core. During this inglorious phase of decorating, Dad often reclined in the rocking chair, munched on candy and gave us his expert advice. He also yelled and howled and listened to KCAM at ear-breaking volumes. In short, he worked us boys into a very crabby state.

Our only relief from Dad's verbal barrage came one Christmas when he bit into a frozen chocolate chip cookie and broke his false teeth. The cookie had been chilled to 30 below zero on the porch and when Dad bit into it his false teeth snapped.

"Dang teeth," he whistled. "Dang chocolate chip cookies. I hate 'em!" he murmured under his breath as he proceeded to eat the rapidly thawing devil-cookie.

To make a long story short, hanging little balls was hell on earth and we shunned this remedial task. Karl and I often bequeathed the painful chore to Jon because we considered him the workhorse of the family. When given a chore, he complained halfheartedly while working incessantly. Jon was perfect for hanging little balls and often did so until they were completely finished. Karl and I provided moral support by buzzing around the work area so that he did not feel lonely. Additionally, while munching on cookies, we made ourselves look busy so that thoughts of mutiny did not enter Jon's mind.

We almost always let Jon shoulder the brunt of the little balls. I think that hanging the little balls year after year taxed his soul and drained the essence of his person. I cannot stress enough the agony, misery, and sheer torture of hanging little balls and it is with intense pleasure that I move on to other, more pleasant topics.

The moment that Jon announced, "Little balls are all done, dang it," brothers and parental units came streaming from hitherto unknown recesses of the house. Everyone came rushing to the living room to sincerely help decorate the Christmas tree. The cause of all the commotion and enthusiasm was phase two of the decorating process, hanging big balls.

Every member of the household considered hanging big balls a fun activity because they were effortless to hang and a person could readily say, "Yup. I helped set up the tree. See there? I hung that ball, and that ball too!" But no one could ever point inside the tree and say, "I hung up that pathetic little ball. No wait, that's not the one. Maybe it was that one. Nope. Let me see …" Furthermore, no one cared about the inside of the tree because it was only for backdrop effect and shed absolutely no glory upon the decorator. The outside of the tree was a chance to artistically express oneself and each member of the family eagerly jumped at this glamorous opportunity.

The big balls went fast, especially the fancy German balls, which were costly and irreplaceable. We placed these rare balls high on the tree to avoid Fang's infamous whip-tail. We lost more balls to Fang's destructive tail every year than we did to human error. When Fang came out of the cold he would vigorously prance around the living room smiling and trying to warm his numb body. While performing his gymnastic routine he constantly swung his whip-like tail dangerously close to the Christmas tree. Each Christmas season he inevitably knocked a few balls onto the platform where they shattered.

Sometimes Fang smashed a ball without knocking it to the floor. His tail was so wiry and hard that it was capable of breaking the delicate glass balls while they hung freely on the branches. As a matter of fact, Fang's tail even hurt us when he innocently wagged it against our cold legs. Needless to say, during Christmas, Fang's presence was unwelcome and the old jailbird spent most of the holiday season locked in the back bedroom. Poor Fang, I am sure that each time we locked him up he was probably thinking "What the hell? I display a little Christmas spirit and now they're all pissed off? Bah-humbug."

When we completed hanging all the big balls, we started phase three of the decoration operation, hanging beads. Hanging beads consisted of draping many strands of hollow glass beads on the tips of the branches. Mom procured these beads via a mail order catalog in 1965 and they were painted red, blue, green, silver and yellow. The strands of beads varied in length, but we strung them in such a way that they formed a continuous spiral on the outside of the tree. The beads were beautiful and added a distinctly old-fashioned touch to our Christmas tree.

The fourth phase of decorating was hanging ornaments. We had two mandarin orange cardboard boxes full of random ornaments including: little birds, insects, owls, mice, Santas, soldiers, gingerbread men and a large elf. Steve (the tallest brother), always took the honor of placing the elf (aptly named Patrick) on the tippy-top of the tree. Although the word Christmas is indicative of Christianity, our innocent pagan ornaments fit our home in the woods better than strict religious symbols.

Setting up the rest of the ornaments took some time because little balls, big balls, and beads already occupied most available spaces. Additionally, we were drained of energy and frustrated because, at this point, we had been working on the tree for more than eight hours. My brothers and I looked forward to completing the goddang tree and we threw artistic balance to the wind as we carelessly hung the ornaments.

Before completely finishing and abandoning the tree, each of us boys took great care in hanging our one personal ornament in a place of prominence (even if this meant shifting a couple big balls). Steve had a train, Ray had a car, Karl had a car, Jon had an angel ball, and I had a bear with glittery shorts. This final task being accomplished, most of my brothers fled.

The fifth stage, for those who remained, consisted of fastening candles to the tips of the tree branches, hanging candy canes, and draping tinsel over the whole tree. By now there was absolutely no room left for any of these final touches, but they were nonetheless crowded onto the tree. When the last string of tinsel fell onto a branch, the Christmas tree was declared officially complete. We then spent an additional couple of hours cleaning up the empty boxes, fallen tinsel, broken glass and decorating wreckage. Once the living room was orderly, we all would stand back proudly and say such things as: "Yup. It's the best tree in the whole valley, maybe even in the whole country. Better than last year. Yup, I hung up that ball right there, and that ornament over there! I basically did the whole tree myself."

Our Christmas tree was truly spectacular. Granted, it was a bit overdone, but it was nonetheless spectacular and intriguing. Not a single visitor or even one of us could strip our gaze from the tree. When we cranked up the generator, and all fifteen strands of lights were shining and blinking brilliantly, no human was immune to a tree-induced trance. My brothers and I would often place a pillow on the platform and look up into the tree for hours. We would pick out certain balls, reflections, ornaments, or light patterns and daydream about the big day. From the comfort of their chairs, Dad and Mom would stare at the tree for hours each morning and evening. The Chmielowski Christmas tree was huge, overdecorated, and the best dang tree in the valley.

As previously mentioned, Mom was the main thrust behind Christmas. She not only baked the cookies and helped with the tree, she decorated our whole house. Due to the sheer magnitude of the self-imposed project, Mom decorated in distinct stages.

Mom's first stage was decorating what we called "the divider." The divider resembled a tall bookcase with three large shelves at the top (see Appendix A). Mom used it to store knickknacks, antique china and other interesting items. During the holidays she would remove all the normal knickknacks and decorate each of the three shelves with a different Christmas diorama.

On the lower shelf Mom set up a scene depicting Hansel and Gretel and the evil gingerbread house. The scene depicted two children walking through a snowy forest heading towards their doom (a candy-encrusted house). Mom told us boys never to touch the small house because if we did, the wicked witch who dwelled within would come and eat us. We believed her wholeheartedly and until we were much older we never attempted to invoke the wrath of the tiny unseen witch. I am not sure what witchcraft and potential cannibalism had to do with fanning the flames of our Christmas spirit, but I think it had something to do with Mom's old-fashioned German upbringing.

On the second shelf, Mom set up a detailed Santa Claus diorama. This scene consisted of a huge, one-foot long Santa (a very old doll handcrafted in Germany) riding in a sled through a snowy forest of cotton. Mom created the forest by painting old gnarled willow branches silver and draping them with white angel hair tinsel. The tinsel was so fine that it resembled cobwebs. For contrast, she hung round loop-like gumdrops from the tree's branches. The Santa Claus scene was somewhat Gothic as the ancient doll wore a grim expression and the trees were twisted and black beneath the silver paint. Although a bit disturbing, the scene was nonetheless intriguing.

Mom decorated the top shelf with a nondescript, but realistic nativity scene. Dad built the stable out of small logs and scrap wood, and it looked authentically rustic. Even though Christmas for the

Chmielowski brothers had little religious meaning, year after year, Mom set up this scene. Perhaps it was because Mom and Dad were born and raised Catholics (both went to Catholic school as well) and could never shake their upbringing. At any rate, the scene was pleasant, if somewhat out of place in our home.

Mom's second decorating phase was hanging the stars. Many years ago Mom and Dad were fortunate enough to acquire some antique handmade Christmas stars from the Copper Valley Mission School. The stars were made of wire and twisted in very complex shapes resembling intricate snowflakes more than stars. Around the stiff wire frames were threaded the same multi-colored glass beads that we strung on our Christmas tree. The glass beads were various hues of blue, green, red, silver, and gold. We had approximately eighteen of these stars ranging in size from six inches to more than a foot in diameter. Mom hung these very beautiful and eccentric ornaments from the living room and kitchen ceilings.

The light from the tree, propane lights and each kerosene lamp reflected from the gently swaying and rotating stars. The overall effect was mesmerizing, as the stars not only tied the wall decorations and tree together, but created a sense of continuity throughout our home.

Mom's third task was preparing the piñata. True, there was a severe shortage of ceiling space due to the stars, but Mom nonetheless hung a papier-mâché piñata in the living room. The misshapen snowman wore a black top hat and was empty for weeks until the eve of Christmas. On this day, two red ribbons with glass bells attached would mysteriously descend from the bottom hatch door of the snowman. This was Patrick's signal that he had filled the piñata with candy and prizes and it was ready to be emptied in the grand ceremony.

During the Patrick/piñata ceremony, each family member held a corner of a tablecloth, which was centered directly under the piñata. Either Karl, Jon, or I, depending on whose turn it was, would pull on the ribbons so that the insides of the snowman cascaded into the tablecloth. Our booty consisted of loads of candy and many small prizes with each of our names clearly written on them. We loved the piñata and it helped relieve, or sometimes heighten, our Christmas Eve tensions.

The fourth phase of Mom's operation was decorating the general living area. She draped shimmery stuff around each window and set up Santa Claus dolls riding in sleds on the windowsills. Mom also decorated our red barn clock with the "hickory dickory dock" mice. She set up a scene depicting the nursery rhyme about three mice running up a clock. The mice were in little Christmas outfits with tiny holly bunches on their uniforms.

Mom put up more Santa scenes on top of the antique telephone and potbellied stove. She put shimmery stuff around the kitchen door frame, and windows, and she hung bells on the back of the front door so that they rang every single time the door was opened or closed. She set out multitudes of candy, cookies, and junk food in artistic ways so that they tied all of her decorations together. Mom worked very hard to make each Christmas better than the last and she never failed in her endeavor.

Once the living room and kitchen were completely decorated and incapable of being maneuvered through, the decorations were still not complete. After all, we boys had to have our own Christmas decorations. In our small bedroom, we somehow managed to erect a three-foot tall fake tree. We decorated it with tiny balls and leftover ornaments and placed another nativity scene beside it (whatever Mom and Dad had, we wanted too). Sometimes we set up the little tree outside in the snow. We did this so that when we looked out our living room window we saw more decorations, but primarily, we wanted the wild animals to have an opportunity to enjoy Christmas.

Once we completely decorated our home and finished baking, there were typically only a few days left until Christmas. My brothers and I spent this downtime in nervous anticipation of the big day, while Mom and Dad took this opportunity to rest. Dad walked around the house singing, whistling, and listening to KCAM Christmas carols. By the time Christmas actually rolled around, we were all sick of the repetitive songs and desperately tried to persuade Dad not to whistle or hum them anymore. We never succeeded in stopping him and Dad continued to exude the Christmas spirit as if he himself was Santa.

On Christmas Eve Mom made us go to sleep early so that the morning would arrive more quickly for us. Santa would come in the night and leave our presents and prizes in the living room. We knew that Santa was coming because on the Alaska news reporters would track his sled on radar and announce it over the radio and television. We also knew that he didn't come down our stovepipe, but that Patrick let him in the front door. Also, because our rooftop was too small to accommodate his sled, he landed on the lake. We believed that he used our lake as a runway because in the past we had observed reindeer hoof prints on the snow-capped ice. The prints looked remarkably similar to caribou tracks, but we were convinced that they were Santa's reindeer tracks.

Karl, Jon, and I never waited until morning to find the presents. One of us inevitably woke up around one in the morning and whispered gently to another, "Pssst, wanna see if Santa came?" We then crept out of bed to see if the toys had been deposited. It was pitch-black as we attempted to sneak into the living room and feel our way around the piles of treasure. After locating the gifts we turned on our flashlights (which were close at hand during the Christmas season) and determined which pile was which. Whoever had the smallest pile would cuss and whoever had the largest would gloat. Santa was pretty good at keeping the piles almost the exact same size. He seemed to perceive that fights might break out if the piles' volumes varied significantly. After assuring ourselves that he had visited our home, we sneaked back to bed and impatiently waited out the rest of the night.

In our minds, the night, which began at 11 p.m., lasted five full days. In reality, it lasted only five hours because at 4 a.m., Jon and I would wake up and spring into action. "Santa came!" we shouted as we ran into the living room. Dad cussed happily and tried to locate his false teeth while Mom chain-smoked and chain-drank coffee. We had boundless energy and enthusiasm, whereas Mom and Dad were completely whooped from their late-night clandestine Santa operations. They just sat in their chairs and drank cup after cup of coffee and watched the zoo.

We yelled, ripped, played, compared, and opened presents for over an hour. The whole time we did so, Dad cussed and repeatedly stated, "Dang it, don't throw all of the paper away. You're gonna lose something."

Mom coughed and replied, "Oh, Bubz. Let them go, they're having fun."

"I'm telling ya, every year they lose something. Slow down boys. Don't throw anything away. You're not listening to your old man." Dad was right, and each year he found some small part or set of directions that was carelessly thrown in the garbage. It was imperative that he fish these items out of the trash because every day at noon he burned the garbage in a 55-gallon barrel drum.

By eight in the morning our excitement died down and serious playing and comparing ensued. We carefully scrutinized toys with critical eyes and Santa was either praised or reproached. Mom and Dad did their best to try and help explain Santa's reasoning when he was in trouble. Sometimes my parents' efforts were successful and sometimes they were not.

I remember one year in particular Karl received an elegant box of skinny coloring crayons. The box contained 250 different crayons including rare colors such as gold, silver, copper, and white. Jon and I each received a box containing eight large fat crayons. I cried and asked Mom, "Why did Santa give us those goddang fat crayons? How come Karl got the good ones?"

Mom answered, "Well, Santa probably thought that because you were little you should have big ones." Jon and I considered Mom's response illogical because, in our opinions, little kids have little fingers and should color with little crayons. We could not properly grip the fat crayons in order to do the detailed artwork we had in mind. Santa had put a serious damper on Christmas and we moped around the house for a couple of hours.

We soon forgot about the crayon debacle when Jon began launching his Godzilla's fist around the house. Jon's Godzilla toy was two feet tall and had a cardboard tongue with flames painted on it. The toy's finest feature was a spring-loaded fist that launched well over ten feet. Jon took advantage of his toy's supernatural powers and launched its green fist into the Christmas tree. Mom put Jon on restriction for taking out a few balls, but Godzilla helped us vent our anger and in time we forgot about Santa Claus's poor judgment.

Ninety-nine percent of the time, Santa did very well and he brought me memorable presents, including a black electronic robot with machine guns that popped out of his chest, an electronic silver robot, Lone Ranger dolls and horses, a "Pots and Pans and Things in Cans" cowboy set, original GI Joe stuff, plastic army men, a Noah's Ark boat with animals, an army tank with wire remote, a battery-operated missile game, a baseball game, playdough equipment, and a Sergeant Rock uniform complete with plastic helmet. I remember the Sergeant Rock helmet most vividly thanks to Karl and his brand-new gift, the Stretch Monster.

Karl's Stretch Monster was a ten-pound rubber toy filled with a gelatinous, gluey substance that allowed the monster to stretch to incredible lengths and slowly retract. Upon opening his gift, Karl stretched and watched the monster retract several times before growing bored with the toy.

He turned to me and said, "Hey Joe, let's see if your new helmet really works. Let me hit you over the head with this Stretch Monster." It didn't sound like the best idea, but I was five years old and Karl convinced me that the high quality Sergeant Rock helmet would shield me from the force of the blow. If not, he reasoned, the helmet was a useless piece of crap and best not worn in combat. I readily agreed with his logic and donned my thin plastic helmet.

The cheap OD helmet had no liner to speak of, but instead, rested directly on my scalp via four small plastic pegs. Karl was true to his word and delivered a fantastically crushing blow. He clubbed me squarely on my helmeted head so hard that he brought me to my knees. Not only did I have a concussion, but worse than that, the four plastic pegs were now imbedded in my skull. I was dizzy and confused for some time and spent the next few hours crying and whimpering. I was pissed at Karl, but worse than that, I was sad because my substandard Sergeant Rock helmet was clearly unfit for use in the Chmielowski combat zone.

As we grew older, Santa quit bringing prizes. Instead, Mom and Dad gave us some very interesting gifts (at our requests of course). Over the years I received throwing knives (small three-inch ones as well as six- and twelve-inch ones), a hand crossbow, a six-foot collapsible blowgun and various other knives. Karl often received a gun or large quantities of ammunition. Each Christmas Dad would get either a gun, a small working cannon, gunpowder, or reloading equipment. To make a long story short, Christmas for the Chmielowskis

I received a Sergeant Rock uniform complete with plastic helmet. I remember the Sergeant Rock helmet most vividly thanks to Karl and his brand-new gift, the Stretch Monster.

was a chance to increase each person's arsenal of deadly weapons. The rest of Christmas day was then spent stabbing, shooting, and blowing up things in a benign manner.

As Christmas day wore on and our energy wore out, thoughts of food entered our minds. We prepared the table by inserting an extra plank in its center and placing a huge white tablecloth over it. We placed lit candles on the table and Dad served our Christmas meal, which he himself cooked. It consisted of a large turkey, eight pounds of mashed potatoes, two cans cranberry sauce, two cans whole corn, and Dad's special stuffing. The seven of us gathered around the table and ate until we could not move. Eventually, we gained enough mobility to unseat ourselves and raid the cookies and candy.

At the end of the very long day, the Chmielowski Christmas was complete and all our anxieties were put to rest. Mom and Dad relaxed, the brothers slept soundly and life returned to normal. Other than cleaning up wrapping paper, disassembling the tree, and removing large quantities of decorations, the household was again quiet.

Puff Goes the Dragon

"What the hell is he doing?" I thought to myself. I squinted hard but I couldn't see from the angle I was at. I shortened the distance between Karl and me, and took another look. "Is he smoking?" I pondered.

I stood still and held my breath. "Nope. What is he doing?" I thought for the third time in two minutes. I could not take the suspense any longer and decided to emerge from my hiding place. Upon hearing my footsteps, Karl hurriedly looked up and began coughing and laughing at the same time.

My eyes locked on his face and on the brown smoke that was billowing from his nostrils and mouth. He seemed to be sincerely struggling for air and was snorting and coughing without relief. No, he wasn't smoking cigarettes (we had tried that a year or two before and nearly killed ourselves from lack of oxygen), but he was doing something that smelled a lot like trouble. It also smelled a lot like chocolate.

"Cough, cough, snort, ha, ha, cough, snort, ha … hey Joe, snort," he finally managed to say, "wanna try some?" When he made the offer he smiled a big politician smile and handed me a package of dried hot cocoa. As I leaned forward to take the cocoa I knew where he had gotten it. Dad kept all the dried foods in the meat shed and he had a couple of cases of instant hot cocoa stored there in a barrel. Karl must have stolen the packs from the shed and that meant that he was in BIG trouble. I was looking forward to seeing him getting his butt whipped and he could plainly see the anticipation on my face.

"C'mon Joe, it's good!" he implored while forcing the small package of cocoa into my hands.

"I don't know …"

"Oh, you'll like it," he continued, "just pour it in your mouth and eat." He had me hooked before I knew what had happened. I ripped open the packet, tilted my head back and opened my mouth. I poured the whole packet in at once and began to slowly chew. Granted, it was like eating sand, but it did have an excellent chocolate flavor.

The second after the dust was in my mouth, Karl intentionally cracked a joke and I started to laugh. The dry cocoa issued forth from my mouth like a steam vent. I tried to inhale, but a big dose of the stuff got caught in my throat and then I started to cough. Hot cocoa shot out of my nostrils and I resembled an angry dragon. Karl just laughed harder and took a hit himself. We spent the next half hour doing cocoa, making jokes and having the time of our lives. When we were finally finished we hid the evidence by tossing the empty packages under the hobby shop.

Karl and I would do raw cocoa ("raw" was our secret word meaning without water or uncooked) from a few times a week to a couple times a day. We were definitely addicted to it and had no hope or desire of quitting. The supply ran out rather quickly and Dad found the empty packages (no thanks to Draggy who dug under the hobby shop and routinely turned up evidence).

Yeah, we got in trouble for eating cocoa, but we were quick to improvise. We found that Saltine crackers produced an ecstasy that was a close substitute to that of dry hot chocolate. Karl and I would often steal a package of crackers and hide behind the garage. We would cram our mouths full of Saltines and eat them while blowing crumbs at one another. Mostly the crumbs were dry, and posed no threat, but occasionally a big wet ball of cracker and saliva stuck to one of us and a bitter cracker blowing war ensued.

The Saltine crackers were a blessing and eased us out of the cocoa addiction, but nothing could ever replace the thrill of dry cocoa spewing simultaneously from my nasal cavity and mouth. As a matter of fact, the addiction proved so strong that even though I quit cocoa during high school, several years later I relapsed while attending West Point. On long difficult marches I would forget my physical pain and psychological anguish by eating the raw cocoa from my MREs (meals ready to eat).

Fire A-1

On a dark October night (one week after Draggy died), Mom, Dad, Karl, Jon, and I were watching the television when, suddenly, it blinked a few times and went completely blank.

"What's wrong with that generator? I know I fueled it up," Dad muttered as he put on his bunny boots and thin work jacket. He turned his head and asked, "What's that noise, engines?" Of course, Dad's hearing was never the best and consequently he *always* heard engines. Nonetheless, as he walked out the front door I curiously trailed behind him.

As Dad approached the generator shed I watched him stand casually behind the door when he opened it. A half second later, a huge tongue of flame burst through the open doorway and shot more than fifty feet into the sky.

"Fire, fire, fire!" Dad yelled. Apparently, the generator had started a small fire inside the shed, but without sufficient oxygen, it had been slowly smoldering. When Dad opened the shed's front door, the smoldering fire drew in plenty of fresh air and exploded into life.

"Oh my God," was my only thought as my heart sank into my jockey shorts. Jon and Karl arrived on the scene rather quickly and their faces were etched with panic and fear.

"No. No. No ..." Karl murmured. No one said a word as we stared at the flames that were beginning to consume our livelihood.

Karl was the most emotional of us and he eventually reacted to the terrible event by jumping up and down and clenching his balls. He ranted, raved and screamed, "Oh, no! The guns! I have to get the guns, Dad!"

Dad yelled back, "No way! You'll burn up and die! Don't do it!"

Karl insisted, "But I can go through the back window and just throw them out before the fire gets them! Please!"

186

"No! They're not worth it! Let 'em go."

Karl acknowledged Dad's final order and watched in horror as the generator shed and hobby shop were consumed in flames.

At length, we managed to break the fire's spell and we chopped open an icehole in the frozen lake. We began filling bucket after bucket of water and throwing them uselessly onto the inferno. When we realized that our efforts were in vain, we decided to try and control the fire's perimeter in order to keep it from spreading. Hence, we periodically doused the side of the ice shed, the meat shed, and some of the nearby spruce trees. More than once we extinguished small fires that ignited some distance from the main blaze.

Despite our efforts, the fire kept growing and all the oils, paints, gasoline, and diesel stored in the shop burned hotter and hotter. Worse than the burning combustibles was Dad's exploding rifle ammunition. It sounded like World War II with bullets going off by the dozens. The propane tanks standing next to the burning shed began to get extremely hot and started to hiss.

"Oh God! They're gonna blow!" someone yelled. We ran a short distance away and waited, but the tanks did not explode. Instead, the safety valve on them allowed the propane to escape in a steady and controlled manner. The propane ignited and produced a marvelous flame-thrower. The gout of flame was about three inches in diameter and spewed forth horizontally more than fifteen feet (right on the ice and meat sheds). After the tank expended its fuel, we immediately began dousing the two smaller buildings.

To top off the nightmare, a 55-gallon diesel drum (standing behind the generator shed) got too hot and exploded. Luckily, only its bottom blew out and as a result, the force of the blast was harmlessly directed into the ground and launched the metal drum high into the night sky. Although I cannot say for sure, I estimated that the projectile's maximum height was between two and three hundred feet. It was intriguing to watch the rocket's trajectory until I realized that what goes up, must come down.

As the drum came rushing towards the ground, I ran for cover and thought that it was going to punch a hole in the roof of the house. Fortunately, it crashed through the trees and landed safely between the meat shed and outhouse.

With the hellish inferno blazing before our eyes, a most peculiar thing transpired. No, an angel did not descend upon the scene, and no, a giant did not appear and conveniently extinguish the fire by urinating on it. What actually transpired was even more bizarre. A complete stranger walked up the path to the shed, casually stood next to Dad, and inquired in a pleasant voice, "Hi. I was just driving down the road and someone hit a moose about a mile up. Do you have a saw I can borrow so that I can get the racks?"

My Dad stood dumbfounded for two seconds before he pointed into the depths of the satanic blaze and yelled, "Yup. It's right in there!"

"Oh. You don't happen to have another ..." the idiot began to ask before he was cut short by a hissing propane tank. At that moment, the tank did its spiffy flame-thrower thing and a huge fifteen-foot flame erupted close to his chest.

"Oh man! I'm getting out of here!" he shouted as he hastily departed (as if realizing for the first time that we were preoccupied with an emergency). For the life of us, we could never figure out who that guy was, or how he could be so amazingly stupid (he must have been a Lower 48er). But we did not have time to ponder riddles such as this; instead, we had to start evacuating our home because it looked like the whole forest was going to burn.

Dad, Karl, and Jon kept fighting the fire while I ran inside the house to check on Mom. She was a wreck but had been packing cold-weather clothes and other essentials into the car.

"Joe, help me get stuff out!" she yelled hoarsely. I grabbed the parakeet's cage and Fang and put both of them in the back seat of the Maverick.

I took the television and Atari out the door and Mom yelled at me, "No! Get the important things!"

"We can sell these if we need to!" I answered.

I went back inside the house and Mom said in a shaky voice, "Get clothes!" I followed Mom's orders and went into her closet and collected armfuls of clothes (a day later we discovered that they were actually table cloths and nightgowns). I also grabbed food and anything else that my addled brain could think of. The entire time I was gathering random things, red and orange flames, explosions and discharging bullets constantly distracted me.

"I have to get back! Dad might be dead!" I yelled as I left Mom with the car and our meager belongings.

The situation was grim when I returned to the generator shed. Dad, Karl, and Jon were still pouring buckets of water on the infernal blaze that was obviously way out of control. Dad told us to move the cars away from the house because it was "all going to go."

Karl, Jon, and I ran back to the house, collected one last load of stuff and hopped in the cars. I was with Mom in the Chevette and Karl and Jon were in the Maverick. Mom and I backed out of the driveway first and went up the road a couple of hundred feet in order to let Jon and Karl pull out.

"Damn it! There's an orange under the gas pedal!" Mom screamed.

Apparently the fruit basket I threw in the car was not such a good idea, as one of the oranges had rolled out of the basket and was now wedged under the accelerator.

"We can't go anywhere!" Mom yelled in frustration. Our situation was entirely unbelievable and reminded me of a stereotypical scene in a cheap horror flick. After more than a minute of spazzing out, Mom unwedged the orange and we drove twenty feet down the road.

"What about Dad?" I yelled. "We can't leave him. He might die!" The whole time I was yelling I was also crying (high-stress situations tend to have this effect on people). Mom carefully considered my words and we pulled back up the driveway and parked in front of our doomed home. Thirty seconds later, Karl and Jon pulled up behind our vehicle with similar concerns (after driving all the way to the gravel pit and turning around).

My brothers and I scrambled out of our cars and ran back to the shed. By this time the roof had collapsed and Dad was patiently watching our belongings burn. He had soot on his face, burns up and down his arms and he looked nearly dead. With renewed energy, the three of us boys began throwing water onto the adjacent sheds and trees and we kept everything under control. The propane tanks were drained, the diesel drum had played its wicked trick, and even the bullets were nearly spent. The worst of the fire was over and we could finally relax a little; just enough to let the cruel reality of the situation sink into our numb minds.

I have no idea how long we fought the fire, but at some point in the morning, Dad told us boys to go in the house and rest. We argued halfheartedly, but at length, we did as he asked. We went inside and Mom warmed our nearly frostbitten hands and feet under her armpits and in her hands. Our adrenaline was pumping furiously and we had no hope of resting while flickering lights continued to reflect off the living room walls (not to mention the occasional explosion or discharging bullet). Our worst fear was that the fire would spread, and as a result, my brothers and I lay down on the floor fully clothed and ready to work.

When the sun eventually rose above the Wrangell Mountains, we returned to the smoldering shed complex and found it obscured by thick smoke and still emitting audible pops and crackles. Our lungs hurt, we were scarred from burns, and each of us was deathly sick to his stomach from the smell of burnt peat moss. I expected the whole ordeal to be some kind of twisted nightmare, but it was not. Fully half of all our belongings had disappeared in just a few hours.

We lost the ice shed, screen shed (antique "handsome prince" chair, skis, and snowshoes), generator shed (the generator powered the freezer, television, and warmed our cars in the winter), hoards of tools, fishing equipment, antiques, washer and dryer, heaps of clothing, more than fifteen guns, Ray's war relics, Steve's trains, Jon's remote-controlled planes, and all our childhood toys (including the original twelve-inch tall GI Joe dolls, antique glass dolls, a metal farm set, numerous cast-iron toys, and on and on). The fire destroyed so many things that I cannot even begin to recall a small portion of them (see Appendix B). I do, however, remember that our belongings were worth a lot of money, and more importantly, they were priceless with regard to their sentimental value. To make a long story short, the shed complex was gone and we had to start from scratch.

We never did find out exactly what started the fire, but we guessed that the generator shorted out and threw a spark onto the oil-soaked floor. It didn't really matter what the cause was, because the result was still the same and as Dad said, "There's no use worrying about it. What's done is done."

The next day we cleaned up the ashes with heavy hearts and removed the garbage from the site. Everything was completely burned, and even metal items were useless (the fire removed all of the metals' temper). There was absolutely nothing salvageable. Fire A-1* was very thorough in relieving us of our already meager possessions.

*We named the fire that destroyed the generator shed complex, Fire A-1, because over the next two years, our family experienced two more fires. Fire B-2 happened in the middle of the winter when Barney's abandoned trailer burned to the ground. Fire C-3 occurred in late summer when the new shed (see property map, Appendix B) caught on fire, which Dad and I successfully extinguished. The causes of the two latter fires were unknown, but due to circumstantial evidence we strongly suspected arson in each case.

The Mother of all Battles

After graduating from high school, I entered the United States Military Academy at West Point, New York (see timeline, Appendix C). During my third summer of military training, I took leave and returned home for a much-needed two-week vacation.

Living in New York for more than two years had drained away a lot of my childhood memories, but upon arriving at my old homestead most came flooding back to me. Furthermore, my brothers' idle conversation around the living room table brought back even more memories and we firmly resolved to do something fun, just like the good old days.

Ray, Karl, Jon, and I unanimously agreed that, because my vacation was short, we *had* to do something memorable. In addition, because jobs, families, and finances often kept us from gathering, we felt a keen pressure to make our reunion historical. We rejected several ideas, took four votes, and made a decision. We then pooled our money, drove thirty-six miles to Glennallen and purchased a large quantity of fireworks. Finally, we returned home and divided the cache into two equal portions.

Next, we picked teams. This task was easy because we simply reverted to our childhood teams. Jon and I were on one side, and Karl and Ray were on the other (Steve was in Anchorage during this particular adventure).

Once we decided who was on what team, we argued about which group should get which boat. Just like the good old days, Karl and Ray took the sleek aluminum boat and left Jon and me with the "Lone Star" (a twelve-foot steel battleship). "Old habits die hard," I thought wryly as Karl and Ray made the final decision.

"OK. Everyone collect supplies and we'll start in ten minutes," Ray announced. Immediately, Karl and Ray ran to the garage and grabbed two iron pipes. They returned to the dock smiling and gloating over their treasures. In the meantime, Jon and I scoured Dad's old metal pile and found a large iron pipe with threaded ends. We searched a bit more and found the top of a 55-gallon barrel drum with a large threaded hole in it.

I picked up the metal disc and thought to myself, "I wonder if this pipe will actually fit?" I set the rusty pipe in the disc's hole and it screwed in perfectly.

We took our pipe/disc combination and a small L-shaped piece of chrome tubing and deposited them inside our floating fortress. Next, I collected a pair of chemistry goggles, two pairs of "Monkey Face" gloves, an umbrella and a lighter. Jon and I secretly placed these items, as well as our share of the fireworks, in the bow of our boat. We climbed into our sturdy craft and I declared in a loud voice, "We're ready for war!"

Ray and Karl had been prepared for some time and they rowed their agile dinghy into the middle of the lake. Jon and I strained with our massive ship because it was so large and we had only one oar. At length, we paddled to the middle of the lake and turned to face Karl and Ray, situated one hundred feet from us. Each crew member shifted nervously, a gentle breeze blew and a loon cried forlornly. The stage was set and each combatant sat on the edge of his seat in eager anticipation of the upcoming action.

"Jon, man the shield!" I yelled. Jon reacted quickly and picked up the disc-pipe combination. He rested the hollow iron pipe on his right shoulder like a bazooka and pointed the apparatus at the opposing team. The large metal plate protected his neck and torso but left his line of sight completely unobstructed.

"You cheaters! We'll kick your butts anyway!" Karl yelled across the water. Karl lit a bottle rocket and shoved it backwards down the pipe Ray was holding. Two seconds later the missile came screaming out of Ray's pipe and zipped by our boat harmlessly.

Jon pointed our bazooka-shield device at their boat and I loaded a lit rocket from behind. Our projectile flew horizontally for fifteen feet, careened downward and traveled in the water like a torpedo. A muffled explosion and a few bubbles were the only result of our efforts.

Both teams launched numerous bottle rockets at one another without any direct hits. Ray and Karl could easily outmaneuver us, but Jon and I could fire missile after missile while safely concealed behind our shield. After twenty minutes, the battle became a deadlock and neither team was able to get the upper hand.

With no end to the stalemate in sight, Karl and Ray paddled closer and closer to us. Jon and I were nervous but we did not dare to move.

We knew that if we attempted to shift our position or escape we would expose our unprotected flanks. With these thoughts in my mind, I grimly donned my goggles and gloves and we both hunkered down behind the shield.

Ray and Karl came at us head-on. As Ray vigorously paddled, Karl continuously shot rockets in our direction. Jon and I retaliated as best we could, but our ammunition was in short supply. We decided that our best battle plan was to maximize our defenses and wait for them to waste their fireworks.

As their boat approached, I could see Karl grinning wickedly and pointing his little pipe at us like a pistol. He shot at us with one eye open and the other closed; he looked just like a pirate with a flint-lock pistol. Karl was a dang good aim and he forced Jon and me to dodge and duck his relentless barrage. Fortunately, though under heavy fire, I had enough presence of mind to grab the umbrella and open it.

When I produced this unexpected toy, I felt like the Penguin in Batman. I cackled loudly for dramatic effect as Jon and I crouched behind our new larger shield.

"You goddang cheaters! Where did you get a Marlboro Lights' umbrella?" Karl yelled over the noise of exploding fireworks.

"From Mom!" I yelled back laughing.

Karl fired another shot and it flew directly at Jon and me. If it had not been for the umbrella, without a doubt, we would have been doomed. Instead, luck was on our side and the rocket bounced harmlessly off the umbrella. It then deflected directly towards Karl and flew perfectly straight at his chest. Karl was not expecting this unfortunate change of events and could not dodge the screaming missile. The rocket burrowed into his brand-new plaid shirt, exploded and caught him on fire. Little flames licked his ribs and burned holes in his shirt before he could extinguish them.

"Damn that umbrella!" he raved.

"Thank you, umbrella," I murmured under my breath.

A second later, one of Jon's rockets finally flew true and nailed Ray in the crotch region. The tide of the battle had turned and we managed to press our attack for a few minutes. Karl and Ray were in a bind and knew that in order to overcome our metal shield and impregnable umbrella defense, they would have to do an all-out frontal assault.

They mounted a fresh and vigorous attack which we had no hope of stopping. Even when I nailed Karl in his "Morrissey" hair-do (Morrissey is a big-haired alternative rock star), they forged onward with grit and determination. When our foes were within twenty feet of us, they began lobbing firecrackers and smoke bombs into our boat. They were attempting to catch our ammo cache on fire and make us jump ship.

Jon and I courageously held our ground, or water, as the case was, and flung firecrackers and smoke bombs into their boat. In a last-ditch effort to repel their attack, we launched roman candles, bumble-bees, jumping jacks and a couple of big plastic-tipped rockets at them. None of our weapons slowed their momentum and they closed in for the killing blow.

When Karl and Ray were within mere inches of our boat, we all noticed random missiles strafing the combat zone. Each team accused the other of foul play, but quickly realized that the source of the mystery missiles was on land.

Apparently, after viewing our ferocious battle from the house, Dad decided to join in the fun. He set up a small arsenal of bottle rockets on the dock and took his time launching them indiscriminately at both of our boats. He was thoroughly enjoying the war without participating in any of its risks.

Without shields or proper protection, Dad's devious attack halted Karl and Ray's progress. This new distraction gave Jon and me enough time to organize a fresh offensive and press our advantage. I grabbed a box of fifty continuous missiles and launched them at our enemies. One rocket per second flew at our opponents and they were quickly forced to retreat.

Instead of paddling home, they headed to the west side of the lake and docked in the grass. They did some mysterious things in the woods (we later found out that they hid their fireworks on the bank to keep them from getting wet) and climbed back into their boat.

Karl and Ray quickly rowed towards us, successfully dodged our missiles and grabbed our boat. They attempted to sink our mighty vessel by leaning over and rocking it back and forth. But our boat was so large and their boat was so tiny, they took in more water than us and actually sank themselves.

Being quite embarrassed and without a boat, they swam after us and clutched the side of our ship desperately. Ray hung on one end of the boat rocking it hard while Karl beached himself like a whale on the back. Water poured into our boat and though we tried to pry our enemies from the craft, their assault was relentless. The Lone Star went down like the Bismarck.

All four of us swam ashore, shook hands, and took off our wet clothes. Then we went back into the lake and raised both boats and retrieved their oars. We tried to salvage our equipment, but the fireworks were wet and the metal shield, pipes, and infamous umbrella were lost in the weeds.

"It'll give the archaeologists something to find in a hundred million grillion jillion years," Karl stated. We concurred wholeheartedly and left the historical relics on the bottom of the lake.

As we hung our wet jeans on Mom's clothesline, there were no doubts in our minds that we had just survived an experience reminiscent of the good old days. And like the good old days, we bickered about who cheated (we had shields but they jumped ship) and who won. Finally, after an incredibly heated debate, the four of us agreed that as in all great wars, there were no victors in the Mother of all Battles, just survivors.

A view toward the north end of our lake. The summer sun typically sets around 11 p.m.. On nights like this, scores of frogs along the shoreline often raised their voices and lulled us to sleep.

Epilogue

According to Cervantes, "All human things are not eternal, and even their beginnings are but steps to their end." And so, although I have just begun to pen some of my family's strange tales, I must end this work so that I may partake in new adventures.

Given enough time, I would have really enjoyed writing about the following events: trick-or-treating on Halloween (we had two stops, Sourdough Lodge and Uncle Joe's cabin), the afternoon a Cessna airplane pulled into our driveway, Mom's illustrious Easter tree, playing at the north end of the lake in a place we called "summertime" (the first patch of ground within miles to be snow-free in the spring), and finally, shaking hands with Muhammad Ali and graciously declining his offer to fight. However, if I was to write about the situations listed above and all the others that continually pop into my head, I would be selling a bible, not a book.

All dressed up and nowhere to go! Actually, we had two trick-or-treat stops: Sourdough Lodge and Uncle Joe's cabin. Left to right: Karl, Jon, and Joe.

Without writing umpteen more twisted tales, I think that the best way a reader can grasp my family's spirit and that of rural life, is to thoroughly tour or preferably inhabit the Alaska bush. I am aware that such an undertaking may not always be convenient or financially feasible, in which case I strongly recommend becoming intimately familiar with Henry David Thoreau's writings, especially *Walden Pond*. Keep in mind that Thoreau practiced his philosophy of life for only two years in a quaint community (Concord, Massachusetts), while our family actively lived his philosophy for thirty-six years in the isolated Alaskan wilderness. Other valuable references include all Jeff Foxworthy's, *You Know You're a Redneck If ...* joke books, which provide uncanny insight into living in rural Alaska.

Perhaps Foxworthy would classify my family and me as rednecks, but the odds are, any family in a similar situation (oldest permanent residents of Sourdough, Alaska) would have found it very difficult *not* to be eccentric. But, I believe that our quirks were our strengths

Holy cow! Are we in Alabama or Alaska? Jeff Foxworthy would be downright proud of the Chmielowski Clan. Left to right: Ray, Steve, and Karl.

and odd or not, we were always kindhearted and eager to lend a helping hand to anyone in need. More importantly, though my brothers and I did not attend church, Mom and Dad taught us respect, responsibility, honesty, and love, and anything they forgot, nature taught us. Our lifestyle in the wilderness forged strong individuals who were each essential members of a tight-knit family.

Oh, I almost forgot to answer those exasperating questions about Alaska. First, it is *not* dark all the time. We have much more sunlight than the Lower 48 from March 21 to September 21 and around six hours of light on the shortest day of the year (winter solstice). Second, it is *not* always cold here. True, I have seen temperatures dip as low as minus sixty-three without wind-chill (even at this temperature, I never have been able to toss water out of a glass and watch it freeze before falling to the ground), I have also seen them soar to plus ninety-six. Third, I am *not* an Alaskan Native, I do *not* own a dogsled, and I have *never* laid eyes upon a walrus, polar bear, or whale. Furthermore, I do *not* hunt or trap animals, and I have *never* even caught a salmon. Fourth, Alaska is *not* flat and barren; there are beautiful mountains, rushing rivers, blue lakes, and even rain forests. Fifth, Alaska is *not* backwards (although my book does tend to undermine this claim), and we have cars, malls, roads, schools, TV, and so forth. Finally, penguins do *not*, I repeat, do *not* live in Alaska; they live near the South Pole for God's sake!

Perhaps it is best that the majority of the Lower 48 still regard Alaska as a frozen wasteland inhabited only by mosquitoes. As Dad used to say, "Those Lower 48ers don't know a lick about Alaska, otherwise they'd all be up here. Let them think whatever they want, it'll keep 'em from invading us. Especially those dang Californians!" I suppose Dad was correct, and it is just as well that most people remain ignorant of Alaska's truths and breathtaking beauty; otherwise, it might end up too crowded (like Colorado or Montana).

As true Alaskans, my family enjoys being alone and we would shrivel up and die if our state became overpopulated. We believe that real beauty is always accompanied by solitude and that Thoreau was right when he said, "As the truest society approaches nearer to solitude, so the most excellent speech finally falls into silence."

Appendix A

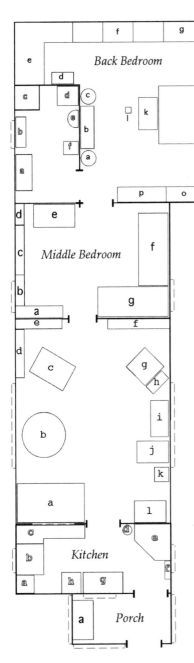

Chmielowski Household
(circa 1980)

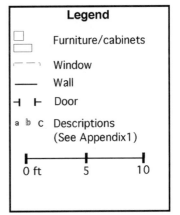

Legend	
⬜	Furniture/cabinets
⬜	
- - -	Window
——	Wall
⊣ ⊢	Door
a b c	Descriptions (See Appendix1)

0 ft   5   10

Back Bedroom Ceiling 7.33 ft
Middle Bedroom Ceiling 7.83 ft
Living Room Ceiling 7.75 ft
Kitchen Ceiling 7.75 ft
Porch Ceiling 7.25 ft

Note: Our house was approximately 800 square feet (about the size of an one bedroom apartment). For the seven people living here, it amounted to about 100 square foot per person.

Back Bedroom

a) Flour Barrel: This large wooden barrel was held together by iron bands and stood near the entrance of the back bedroom. Its wood portions were faded gray with age while its bands were painted white. Mom and Dad originally stored flour in the barrel, but years later they put in our entire supply of Milkman powdered milk.

b) Green Cabinet: Dad acquired this homemade cabinet from Sourdough Lodge and later refurbished it. The green cabinet was waist-high and its doors were shutters from the windows of an old house. We stored butter, jarred salmon, and canned goods in it. Mom kept her small white mirror, jewelry tin, and some makeup (for school) on top of the cabinet.

c) Clothes Barrel: A large green plastic trash can stood in this space. It contained hand-me-down hats and gloves that were mismatched, out of style, ripped, or altogether useless. My brothers and I dreaded the green barrel because finding a needed article of winter clothing in its depths was a time-consuming and futile effort.

Jon and I particularly feared the green barrel because Karl used to smother us with it. He would trap us under the inverted barrel and sit on it to keep us from escaping. Our cries for help as we asphyxiated never weighed upon Karl's conscience and he would not let us go until *he* was tired of lounging.

d) Secretary's Desk: Mom purchased this antique desk from the Copper Valley Mission School and it was made of a dark oak. The desk intrigued me and I would often rummage through Mom's paperwork, envelopes, tape, and pencils (stored in the main compartment and drawer) searching for unknown sorts of treasures.

e) Hanging Clothes Closet: Mom rightfully claimed the "hanging clothes closet" because she was the only one in the family with clothes that required hanging. Furthermore, the closet was especially valuable to her after she became a teacher's aide at the elementary school and had to wear nice slacks and blouses. The closet was divided into a bottom, middle, and top portion. Mom stored her shoes and random accessories in the lower level of the closet (which was one and a half feet high and smelled moldy). She hung her shirts and pants in the middle portion (which extended from knee to head level) and stored extra blankets on a high shelf near the ceiling.

f) Closets: Five brown-stained wood closets occupied this portion of the back bedroom. Each closet extended from the floor to the ceiling and resembled a large army or prison locker rather than a clothes closet. There were no walls separating the closets so we could easily reach into our neighbor's territory and borrow a shirt or pair of socks. The closets were divided among family members from left to right as follows: Mom had the closet adjacent to the hanging clothes closet, Steve and Ray shared the next one, Karl and I shared the next, and Dad and Jon shared the last closet that was closest to the typing desk. When I was very young, for a brief period of time I shared my closet with the canned goods in the TV cabinet, then with the groceries in the tall grocery cabinet and eventually with Karl in the closet conglomerate just described.

My brothers and I stored our folded clothes on the five shelves that divided each closet at regular intervals. We had identical layouts that included one shelf for our pants, one for our shirts, and one for our socks and underwear. Due to our space constraints and in order to avoid wrinkling, Mom always folded our clothes according to army regulations. She even rolled our socks into little balls (once again, army style) and put them in sock boxes. Our sock boxes were either a sturdy cardboard or wood box that kept the spherical bundles from rolling around the closet.

g) Typing Desk: Mom named this piece of furniture the "typing desk," not because she did that much typing, but because she stored an old manual typewriter on top of it. The ancient metallic device weighed over thirty pounds and its stiff keys made Mom's fingers sore after only a page of typing. Mom occasionally used her typewriter for paperwork and to help Steve and Ray type their high school reports. Dad and Mom stored all their important papers, such as property deeds, birth certificates, water rights, and trapping rights, in a metal box to the right of the desk.

h) Window Box: This triangular box was made of unfinished half-inch plywood. Mom and Dad stored food in it, while my brothers and I used it as a chair or a nice flat space to play with our toys.

i) Dough Box: Dad built this small bedside table out of Sitka spruce and stained it dark brown. He referred to this piece of furniture as the "dough box," and hid a pistol inside of it in case a burglar or hitchhiker intruded our home (we equated hitchhikers with criminals because in our area of Alaska, most hitchhikers *were* criminals and most criminals hitchhiked). Also, Dad stored batteries, electrical tape, and household tools in the dough box.

On top of the dough box was a white doily, on which rested a single kerosene lamp. To the right of the lamp was a small, white plastic box that contained Clorox. Prior to going to bed, Dad submerged his false teeth in the bleach in order to clean them. Years before I was born, when he was in his mid-thirties, Dad had all his teeth removed because they were bothering him and there were no dentists in the valley. "Just pull 'em all!" he told Doc Huffman (Lafayette Huffman was a World War I pilot who later became a dentist in Fairbanks. In 1934 he had had enough of society and civilization and headed to a remote place called Paxon Lake. He brought with him some of his basic handheld dentistry tools including a few picks, pullers, and needles). Old Doc unhesitatingly followed Dad's orders and pulled out each and every one of his teeth with a pair of pliers. He gave Dad a shot of whiskey and that was that.

j) Bed: Mom and Dad's modern queen-sized bed took up most of the back bedroom's floor space. When my brothers and I wanted to sit, lie, or play in the back bedroom, we usually did so on my parents' bed (due to our cramped living conditions, our family never quite grasped the concept of privacy).

k) Trunk: Mom stored clean towels, wash cloths, and sheets in her antique trunk. It had a round top, was made out of steel, and was bound with wood. The trunk was in mint condition and always rested at the foot of the bed.

l) Brown Beam: A four-by-four-inch wooden beam extended vertically from the floor to the ceiling where it supported a horizontal beam that extended across the width of the back bedroom's sagging ceiling. Before going to sleep, Dad hung his shirt and pants on two pegs that protruded from the middle of the brown beam. Jon and I liked to swing on the pegs but Mom, Dad, and the older brothers would always yell at us, "No swingin' on the pegs, goddang it! You're gonna break 'em!"

m) Brown Chest: Mom and Dad acquired this chest of drawers from Sourdough Lodge. Carved in the bottom of each of the five drawers were circular indentations that were used to store old-time glass record cylinders in an upright position. This was an exclusive, single-purpose chest since the cylinders were the forerunners of glass records. We used the brown chest to store miscellaneous things such as shoe-shining equipment, sewing thread, candles, tape, hair clippers and assorted odds and ends.

n) Window Box: Originally designed for food storage, my brothers and I used this particular window box as a place to daydream. Sun often filtered through the back bedroom's two corner windows, making it an ideal chair for relaxation and meditation.

o) Tall Grocery Cabinet: This closet extended from the floor to the ceiling and was similar in shape and layout to our clothes closets except for the tan, water-stained paper that lined its rear wall. Mom and Dad stored groceries on its four shelves and hence referred to it as the "tall grocery cabinet." We had to purchase large quantities of food because we could only drive to Anchorage once a year for shopping (we avoided shopping in Glennallen's small store because merchandise was unaffordable). The cabinet's doors were brown and nondescript except where an inscription in black magic marker read: "Karl and Joe wrote this." Jon scrawled these words on the cabinet door in a pathetic attempt to frame Karl and me so that we would get a butt blistering. Even though we would have gotten a good one for writing on the cabinet, I think that Mom saw through Jon's thinly disguised ploy and we never received the anticipated spanking.

p) TV Cabinet: Mom and Dad placed their first television set on top of this short cabinet and therefore, we called it the "TV cabinet." Inside the cabinet were three shelves on which we stored many canned goods (and also my clothes for a brief period). In the bottom right hand corner, Dad kept a large yellow vat filled with grease for cooking. For years, an ancient black and white TV stood on top of the cabinet like a monolith. It was enormous, weighed sixty pounds and was nearly useless. The television was impractical for two reasons. First, we could only watch it when we cranked up the generator (a few times a week for three or four hours). Second, we received only one channel and it was always foggy. After Steve and Ray graduated from high school, they purchased a brand-new color TV for Mom and Dad. This improved our situation somewhat, but we were still at the mercy of the generator (which drank a lot of expensive diesel fuel) and even then, we received only two channels (Detroit came in perfectly, but the Alaska channel was snowy). At some point, Dad placed the color TV on a board that he hung (via chrome chains) from the ceiling. The television's new setup not only gave everyone a really stiff neck, but also freed up the top of the TV cabinet for a big gun rack.

Floor O' Splinters: For many years the back bedroom's floor was bare wood and countless splinters found their way into the soft bottoms of our feet. Eventually, Dad and Mom covered the plywood floor with the yellow indoor/outdoor rug from the living room. The thin worn rug offered little relief from the hard wood floor, but it did curb our splinter situation.

Walls: All the back bedroom's walls were constructed from packyboard (small wood chips glued and pressed together in the shape of plywood). The imitation plywood was painted white and it sagged considerably due to dampness and age.

Ceiling: The ceiling was constructed from packyboard and strongly resembled a sagging circus tent. As an added bonus, water periodically stained portions of the ceiling rust-brown, with an artistic effect in some cases. A double-paned propane light hung in the middle of the ceiling and emitted more heat than light. The lamp also produced an audible noise like that of someone slowly and continuously exhaling, "Pwwaaaaahhhhh."

Bathroom

a) Washstand: This antique, marble-topped washstand contained most of our toiletry articles and was a gift from Steve and Ray to Mom. A large white bowl and pitcher, Mom's brush, and a small white mirror sat atop this stand. To the left of it, all our toothbrushes and random bathroom supplies rested on a narrow wooden shelf. Directly above the washstand, but beneath the propane light, Steve and Ray glued flat, square mirrors to the wall.

b) Shoe Box: Dad made this large plywood chest as a storage area for our extra and unused shoes. Whenever we required the services of outdated sneakers, old combat boots, and leaky rubber boots, we investigated this container.

c) Vacuum Closet: As the name implies, this small closet housed our ancient and nearly useless electric vacuum cleaner. We used this horrific contraption only when we garnered sufficient courage *and* the generator was running. As an alternative to the vacuum, Mom made us boys nitpick the entire house. Nitpicking consisted of crawling on our hands and knees and picking up pine needles, fuzzes, and small specks of dirt out of the carpet. Our tedious chore made us careful not to track dirt inside the house.

Shelves: Five consecutive shelves were attached to the right side of the vacuum closet. We used the shelves as a place to store our winter clothes and boots. The shelves not only kept our winter clothes organized and out of the way, but they allowed our wet gear to dry by the nearby oil stove.

d) Oil Stove: A small brown oil stove stood in this corner. We used it only occasionally because it caused condensation in the roof and oil was expensive.

e) Tin Tub: This dandy of a bathtub was made of galvanized steel and when unoccupied, stood on end against the wall. During use, the victim would place it flat on the bathroom floor and fill it with one to two inches of heated lake water. Much to Mom's chagrin, Ray discovered that the tub was more useful as a small boat than as a bathroom appliance. He rowed around the lake in it for some time before hitting a submerged and pointed beaver stump (which punctured the hull). Dad fixed the tub with some rough solder and thus, bathing in our bathtub made for an unforgettable experience and unusually irritated and sore buttocks.

f) Commode: When Mom deemed that outside conditions were inhospitable (colder than twenty below), she urinated in this small, plastic, portable toilet. She used the toilet only for urination and very sparingly because it filled up quickly and was unpleasant to empty. On pain of death, Mom forbade all male members of the household to use this luxury item. Above the commode was our frequently used medicine cabinet. The cabinet consisted of three narrow shelves built into the wall and hidden from view by two miniature barn doors. The family often raided the medicine cabinet in order to doctor anything from scrapes, cuts and bruises to major head injuries and sucking chest wounds. Injuries and pain are part of everyday life for the independent and isolated Alaskan.

Doors: A cast-iron beetle, used to help remove boots, held open one of the double doors to the bathroom. The "hobo plunger" propped open the opposite door. Mom told us that the plunger was an antique device used to agitate water in an old washtub. My brothers and I were not so easily convinced and we thought that it was some sort of cleaning device for a fancy ceramic toilet. It not only resembled the toilet plungers we had seen in "normal homes" (despite the fact that it had a metal head and wooden handle), but its close proximity to the commode practically proved that it was somehow associated with cleaning toilets. We never played with or touched the hobo plunger and we learned to respect, if not despise it.

Floor and Ceiling: The white, sagging, packyboard ceiling was identical to that of the back bedroom. The floor was covered with a blue-spotted, indoor-outdoor carpet that rarely encountered foot traffic. Our visits to the bathroom were rare because without a working sink, shower, toilet, running water, or electricity, it was not really a bathroom.

Middle Room

a) Dinosaur Cabinet: Dad built this four-feet-tall cabinet out of pine and stained it brown. We referred to this piece of furniture as the "dinosaur cabinet" because Jon hung his dinosaur display case (filled with painted porcelain dinosaurs) on the wall directly above it. Furthermore, he stored all his plastic dinosaurs in a bin inside the cabinet. The plastic dinosaurs in Jon's original set were colored gray and brown, and in our opinions, looked very realistic. Over the years, Jon collected many more plastic dinosaurs, but unfortunately, they were every color of the rainbow (the toy manufacturers no longer made gray and brown figures) and he despised them because they looked like "kid's toys." Jon also kept his "Colossal-Fossil-Fight" (a game where each opponent controlled a dinosaur and whose object was to eat as many bones from the center pit as possible) as well as two 3-feet-tall T-Rexes (one colored red and the other green) near the bottom of the cabinet.

In addition to Jon's dinosaur collection, I stored my green plastic army men in a bucket on the middle shelf. I also put my Lone Ranger dolls and "Pots and Pans and Things in Cans" cowboy set on the top shelf. Karl stored his gray plastic German soldiers, blue and white plastic civil war soldiers ("blue guy, white guy" as we used to say), and Star Wars figures near my army men. Finally, we stored our large toys, such as the Peggar castle, Star Wars spaceships and large white castle (with knights and Roman soldiers) on the floor of the cabinet.

On the wall, to the left of the dinosaur cabinet, hung four plaques from the Glennallen wrestling tournament (while in elementary school, Steve, Ray, Karl, and I each placed in the tournament). Above the cabinet, and above Jon's dinosaur display case, was a wide plywood shelf, on which we stacked all our games (Stratego, chess and checkers, Erector sets, Monopoly, Battleship, Stop Thief, Lost Treasure, and race cars).

b) Window Cabinet: Directly above this chest-high cabinet was a window that faced our sandboxes in the front yard. We placed all sorts of junk on the windowsill and even more junk and toys inside the cabinet itself (including Steve's and Ray's motorized purple hippopotamus and white rhinoceros).

c) Tall Bedroom Closet: This wood cabinet extended all the way from the floor to the ceiling and was approximately five feet wide. It had shelves spaced at one-foot intervals, on which my brothers and I stored our main supply of toys. Steve and Ray had the upper shelves, Karl had the middle shelves, and Jon and I had the lower ones. On the top three shelves were intricate metal tanks, King Size construction toys and Matchbox cars. On the middle shelves were Karl's toys and two large boxes of wooden popsicle sticks. Jon purchased the sticks at the Glennallen Radio Shack and gave them to Karl as a Christmas present. The instructions indicated that the sticks could be used to build a birdcage, a doll's house, or any number of imaginative things. The moment Karl opened his gift on Christmas morning he yelled, "What on God's green earth am I suppose to do with these things? Throw them in the wood stove and burn 'em?" Yeah, Karl's remark was malicious, but I must admit that I hated those dang popsicle sticks because they spilled off the shelf every time we opened the tall cabinet. On the bottom two shelves, we stored our Legos (not including Jon's special Legos that were called "Tontis") in several 2-gallon mayonnaise jars.

By far the most impressive facet of the tall bedroom closet was the "town board." The town board was a gigantic sheet of plywood that folded down from the ceiling (and acted as the cabinet's doors when stored in the upright position). The retractable table had legs on hinges that swung down and out to support the far end of the board. Dad designed the town board in this retractable manner because our room was so small that we could not afford to have a four-by-four-foot table in our walking area. The top of the table was painted green (to represent grass) with white lines and boxes (representing streets and buildings respectively). The town board was akin to viewing a small town from a low-flying airplane. My brothers and I played with Matchbox cars, King Size trucks, and metal tanks on the town board. We also used it as a place to set up army soldiers, dinosaurs, and any other balancing toys that required a nice flat surface (as all boys know, balancing army men on the carpet is a frustrating task). Our town board was the envy of every child that visited our home.

d) Corner Closet: This wood closet extended from the floor to the ceiling, and was three feet wide and seven inches deep. Among many other toys, I stored my "smash-up derby" cars on the lower shelves. Karl put his World War II trivia cards and metal tanks on the upper shelves.

e) Desk: Ray and Karl's large wooden desk (with a smooth yellow top) occupied this portion of the middle room. They used the desk as an area to make crafts and assemble or paint models. The desk was truly an eyesore, since its entire surface was covered with a myriad of paint smudges. Directly above the desk, Karl stored his military book collection on three shelves that were bracketed to the wall.

Karl lounging on Ray's top left bunk bed. Karl's bed is the lower left, Steve's the upper right, Jon the lower right, and mine is the trundle bed beneath Jon's.

Before we acquired the desk, when my brothers and I were young we put our toy box, train box and dice box in this area of the room. The toy box was a large rectangular box made out of plywood and painted brown. It rolled on wheels and had a lid that we locked with a huge brass lock (inscribed with the single word: *Best*). Karl stored a good number of his toys in the toy box including his Weeble village structures, a large wooden zoo cart, and miscellaneous Weeble and Peggar supplies. I remember one occasion when we were playing Blind Man's Bluff with Karl's friend, Danny Lausen. When it was Danny's turn to be blindfolded, he decided that searching for victims would be much easier crawling on the floor. Thus, when he heard one of us walking, he lowered his head and charged on all fours like an angry muskox. Danny's forehead did not smash into a soft human thigh—instead, it found the brass *Best* lock on the front of the toy box. Danny went home with a gash between his eyes and one heck of a headache.

Adjacent to the toy box, Steve had a four-foot-long, plastic train caboose. We stored numerous toys inside of the red and brown caboose including the Puffin' Toot train set.

Next to Steve's caboose was the dice box (a red plywood box on wheels with large white dots). Jon and I not only used the dice box to store our toys (Lincoln Log collection and my wire-remote-controlled tank), but we also used it as a place of concealment during hide-and-go-seek.

f) Bunk Beds #1: Dad modeled our bunk beds after a standard U.S. army sleeping cot to economize valuable floor space. They were exactly six feet long and twenty-seven and one-half inches wide. Originally, Dad had painted all of the beds puke green, but in later years, he painted them fire-engine red.

In this particular set of beds, Ray slept on the top bunk (with his leopard print bedspread that Mom made) and Karl occupied the middle bunk (he had a zebra bedspread). Directly underneath Karl was a short trundle bed (about as long as the bunk beds) that contained all, or nearly all, of our winter hats and gloves. Often, we heedlessly threw our arctic gear in the trundle bed and as a result, finding a matching pair of gloves or wool socks was nearly impossible. Sometimes, for fun Jon and I would burrow in the clothes and roll the trundle bed under the bunks (we enjoyed entombing ourselves).

To the right of the trundle bed, but still under Karl's middle bed, was a gray plastic box and a wooden Blazo box (at one time, fuel oil was sold in wood boxes with the brand name, "Blazo" stamped on their sides). Jon and I stored toys in both of these boxes, including a couple of yellow and orange metal planes. These two large boxes were not only used as toy boxes, but they played a key role in creating a private playing area. That is, when the two sets of bunk beds were arranged end to end in an "L" shape, they formed a three-by-three-foot square in the corner of the middle room. Then, by shifting either the gray box or the Blazo box, Jon and I had access to the small cubicle formed by the beds.

On one occasion, we hid from Dad in our makeshift fort in order to avoid a whippin'. I distinctly remember that the wooden spoon was confused and angry as it searched and sought, clacked and cracked and flailed around the inside of our cubicle. Dad was on the other end of the spoon yelling, "Come out of that hole, so I can give you a good whippin'!" But on this occasion, and only this occasion, we deliberately disobeyed Dad and refused to leave the safety of our cubbyhole. I guess if Dad really wanted to "get us," he could have easily moved the bed and exposed our pathetic forms; apparently, he was not as angry as we thought.

Shelves: To the right of the back bedroom door were two shelves. Steve kept his blue-painted, plastic Germans and military models on the bottom shelf. He put his clear V-8 engine model (that actually worked) and a see-through plastic model of the human body and anatomy on the top shelf. After Steve and Ray graduated from high school, we replaced the shelves with a homemade display case. Its edges were made out of oak and its center was covered by green velvet, on which we hung three black powder pistols (Ray gave a pistol to Karl, Jon, and me for Christmas).

g) Bunk Beds #2: This set of bunk beds was identical in size and shape to the first set. Steve had the top bunk (he had a tiger bedspread), Jon had the middle bunk (snow leopard bedspread), and I had the full-sized trundle bed (much to my chagrin, I did not have an animal bedspread). The trundle bed was directly beneath Jon's bunk bed and it was analogous to a huge dresser drawer that rolled on wheels. I rarely rolled my bed out from under the bunk beds because I preferred sleeping in a claustrophobic area. Furthermore, the lakeside wall sealed off the foot of my bed and my only means of ingress or egress was through the small portal near my pillow. On some occasions, I stacked stuffed animals in this opening in order to keep the monsters out of my sleeping area.

The trundle bed was private, perpetually dark, and silent (very much like sleeping in a snug coffin). In my opinion, it was a perfect bed except on the days when I was startled awake (I would jerk my head upwards and smack it on the underside of Jon's bunk). Occasionally I would get too hot within the confines of my chamber. On nights such as this, I would pull my bed out from under the bunks. I avoided rolling out my bed at all costs because I did not like to be exposed to the monsters or to my brothers (kicking me in the morning or in Karl's case, puking on me one night).

Besides the heat factor and a minor bruise every now and again, the trundle bed treated me well except for the one night that I did *not* sleep inside of it. For one reason or another, I had rolled out my bed, but instead of sleeping in it, I ended up in Steve's bunk. In the middle of the night, I dreamt that I was Superman flying through the air. In reality, I jumped off the top bunk and cracked my jaw on the corner of the dang trundle bed (I could not talk or eat Cocoa Puffs for a week).

Ceiling: The ceiling was made of packyboard and drooped just like the back bedroom. In the ceiling, near the doorway to the living room, was the attic hatch. Karl, Jon, and I always eyed it curiously because we knew that Patrick lived in the attic and we wanted a peek at him. Except for the attic hatch, the ceiling was cluttered with all sorts of hanging models. We hung so many airplanes, helicopters, Star Trek and Star Wars models from the ceiling that it was like walking into an Anchorage hobby shop.

Walls: The walls were constructed of light brown packyboard. Sometimes during a cold snap, frost would build up on the walls and windowsills. When the weather warmed up, the frost would melt and water would soak into the wood. I suspect that it was this freeze and thaw cycle that caused the walls to sag and warp so badly.

Floor: A gray indoor/outdoor carpet with black spots covered the floor. After many years of use, Mom and Dad replaced it with a brown shaggy carpet.

Living Room

a) Sofa: When I was very young we had a brown, upholstered, 1960s-style sofa. When I turned five, Mom and Dad purchased a modern hardwood couch with brown and white cushions. It was fairly luxurious by Chmielowski standards until the unfortunate day Marie flopped on it and broke its springs (Marie was our rotund cousin from Anchorage). Dad fixed the couch in a halfhearted manner (i.e., he jury-rigged it) by permanently installing a piece of plywood under the cushions.

An old crank telephone from the Native village hung on the wall directly above the couch. When Mom originally purchased the phone, it was in working order. However, because there were no telephone lines within twenty-five miles of our home, we had little opportunity to use the nifty device and instead, we used its main compartment as storage for our extra car keys. Mom's red barn-shaped clock hung on the wall above the eastern end of the couch. According to Uncle Barney, the "dang clock sounded like a time bomb," and indeed, it was the loudest clock I have ever heard. On the right side of the clock hung a solitary brass skeleton key from my Mom's grandfather.

b) Round Table: Four antique chairs and my red stool stood around this oak table that Mom acquired from the Copper Valley Mission School. On special occasions, we made the table into a long oval shape by sliding it apart and inserting planks into its middle. On a day to day basis, our living room was too small to accommodate the enlarged table so we usually left it compact. As such, our table was not large enough for the whole family to eat together so a couple of us boys ate on the sofa or queen's chair.

c) Rocking Chair: Mom's dark-stained pine rocking chair had brown and white cushions that matched those of the sofa. It was strategically located near the stove and was always cozy. The rocking chair occupied this particular spot in the living room for so long that it "grew roots" to the floor. Analogously, Mom occupied the rocking chair for so many years that we considered it an extension of her person.

d) The Divider: "The divider" resembled a large bookcase that was as high as the living room ceiling and about a foot deep. Its lower half had no shelves, but instead, was adorned with red, orange and brown plastic bricks. Its top half had three shelves evenly separated about two feet apart. Mom and Dad built the divider out of narrow redwood planks and named it such because originally, it divided the stove's area from the rest of the living room.

In later years, Dad moved the divider up against the eastern living room wall and Mom used it to display her delicate knickknacks. On the lowest shelf she placed her ornate antique bottles (some of which Dad found at the abandoned gold-mining town of Coldfoot near the Arctic Circle), a few small plates, an old "Log Cabin" syrup tin, a cigarette tin, and a woman's coin purse. On the middle shelf sat a complete and perfectly intact set of Depression glassware that had belonged to my Mom's parents. Finally, a "flying phoenix" chocolate set (also from my Mom's parents), sat on the top shelf. Mom treasured the two sets of glassware as she received very few keepsakes from her parents in Pennsylvania. As a matter of fact, my grandparents were so angry that Mom married a poor Polak in Alaska, they disowned her and until the mid-eighties, gave her very little. In 1986 my grandmother passed away and her lawyers sent Mom a check for exactly $1.00 (the rest of the sizeable estate was willed exclusively to Mom's siblings).

e) Sliding Door Closet #1: This eight-inch deep closet extended from the floor to the ceiling. We stored our spices, baking ingredients, and snacks on its five shelves. Occasionally, the sliding door would slide off its track and hang uselessly from the ceiling.

f) Sliding Door Closet #2: We kept spaghetti, pasta, Kool-Aid, popcorn and other food items in this closet.

g) Wood Stove: We originally had an oil stove in the 1960s, but a decade later, Dad purchased a wood stove from the Montgomery Ward's store in order to save money. Every summer, Dad would selectively cut dead trees in the forest and stack them in order to let them dry. In the winter, he would haul them home on the snowmachine and we would help cut them into small lengths to be burned in the stove. On top of the stove sat an antique copper boiler (from Sourdough Lodge) and two old kettles. All three of these containers were always filled with water and thus we had a makeshift water heater. We stacked our shoes, inserts, felt liners, mittens, gloves, hats, scarves, and boots on top of the boiler. Additionally, when other items such as pants, long johns, underwear, and socks were wet, we placed them on the boiler too. We also used the boiler and stove to heat food and defrost meat.

My brothers and I often hovered near the wood stove (a virtual demigod) to stay warm or rid a stubborn chill from our backs. The area in front of the stove was not only warm, but also a very convenient place to stand and socialize; it was seldom free of loiterers. Behind the stove, protruding from the wall, were several large pegs on which we hung our coats and shirts to dry. Above the pegs was a shelf where we placed yet more shoes, gloves, socks, and felts.

h) Wood Box: We stored our logs (about two feet long) and kindling in this box (composed of one-foot planking) that was adjacent to the wood stove. Dad put our logs in this box because the heat from the stove warmed and dried them. It was also much more pleasant to fill up the wood box once a day rather than going outside in the snow to retrieve logs each time we needed to stoke the stove.

i) Sewing Machine: This antique treadle Singer sewing machine was in perfect working order and Mom used it for all her sewing needs. Dad traded a .22 rifle to Pettijohn (living at Sourdough Lodge) for this invaluable piece of equipment. An antique kerosene lamp with a painted shade stood in the middle of the sewing machine. To the left of the sewing machine was an old basket from Mom's Aunt Mettie that held all our mail order catalogs.

j) Handsome Prince Chair: Mom named this piece of furniture the "handsome prince chair" because she said that when Karl lounged on it (a full-length, red velvet, antique chair), he resembled a "handsome prince." The chair came from the Gurtlers who were from the village of Ruby and of Alaska Native and Russian blood. Unfortunately, this beautiful chair was burned in Fire A-1. In later years we replaced the handsome prince chair with the "queen's chair." Mom purchased this antique chair from a store in Anchorage and she called it the queen's chair because of its Queen Anne leg design. Its frame was hardwood while its sides and back were wicker. Mom upholstered its cushion with red velvet reminiscent of our previous chair.

k) Potbellied Stove: We had two cast-iron, coal/wood stoves from a railroad caboose. Mom and Dad found one of the stoves in a pond near Sourdough Lodge and traded a crank telephone to Bud Lausen (the owner of Sourdough Lodge at the time) for the other. Mom painted both stoves black and used them as end tables.

l) Record Player: This antique mahogany and walnut crank record player was four feet high, three feet wide and two feet deep. Mom and Dad traded five lynx pelts to Oscar Ewan (an old Native) for it. Originally, the record player came from Gakona Lodge, but it was most likely brought up during or just after the Gold Rush. It worked perfectly well and we would often listen to Dad's glass records on it. My brothers and I particularly liked the song "Here Comes Peter Cotton Tail," which Dad played every Easter.

A kerosene lamp and Mom's ornately carved jewelry box stood on top of the record player. Behind the lamp hung an antique mirror (two feet wide by three and a half feet high) which Mom and Dad purchased from Pettijohn. It was salvaged from a Valdez hotel that was destroyed in the 1964 earthquake and tsunami. Also hanging on the wall was an ancient faded piece of cloth with a poem written on it. A person named Josephine wrote the poem in 1841 while residing in Philadelphia. It was given to Mom by her Aunt Mettie Spring (who lived in Cape May, New Jersey).

Floor: A puke yellow indoor/outdoor rug with brown spots covered our living room floor. It was similar to a leopard print bedspread that is commonly associated with red-light districts. In the 1980s, Mom replaced this atrocity with a brand-new brown carpet (much to the whole family's pleasure).

Ceiling: Dad originally painted the ceiling white but leaking water stained patches of it rust-brown. The ceiling was seven feet, ten inches above the floor (low ceilings are common in Alaska to keep houses warm) and had four brown beams perpendicular to its length. In the center of the ceiling was a three-paned propane light, which shed much more heat than light.

The only other feature of interest was a small two-by-four-inch pock mark or water bulge near the north end of the living room. Karl, Jon, and I referred to this outline as the "Beamer." We emphatically believed that if we walked beneath or sat on the sofa under the Beamer, it would beam us up like a Star Trek spaceship. I do not have the slightest clue where we got this far-fetched idea (perhaps older brothers or twisted parents suggested it), but after Karl played a cruel trick on me, I firmly believed in the Beamer. When I was four years old Karl hid cunningly behind the drapes and screamed in a distant voice, "Joe! The Beamer got me! Save yourself!" I vividly remember Karl's disembodied voice and the lump of fear that wedged in my throat. For months after the trick I gave the Beamer an especially wide berth and regarded the thing with a mixture of awe and respect.

Miscellaneous: The doors separating the living room and the middle room looked like old stereotypical barn doors (a big letter "Z" was formed by the intersection of three wooden braces). The living room windows measured three and a half-by-six-foot and the plate glass came from the Paxon Roadhouse. Finally, on the north side of the living room, there was a four-by-four-foot opening which not only allowed heat to flow in and out of the kitchen, but also permitted the cook to converse with inhabitants of the living room (or in Jon's case, to fling food at the inhabitants seated at the living room table).

Kitchen

a) Water Bin: Dad originally pumped our drinking water directly from the lake into a plastic, 15-gallon garbage can that rested on the floor. But, in 1974 he made a tall wood box (with a hinged lid) in order to house the plastic water barrel. Below the box's main compartment, Dad built a secret cubbyhole, which he named the "Kutch." We stored dairy products in the Kutch to keep them cool (the cold water above and the drafts on the floor kept the small compartment cool) and to hide them from Jon, who, as a toddler, scavenged and consumed butter in large quantities. We kept the water bin in the kitchen during the winter to keep it from freezing and put it on the porch during the summer to keep it cool.

Above the water cooler was a hardwood cabinet suspended in the corner. Steve made the cabinet in high school woodshop and it had a door with six panels of glass, three of which were stained yellow, green, and blue, respec-

An east view of our small (one person) kitchen. Left is the copper-lined dry sink with bowl and pitcher. Front is our propane stove heating kettles of water for bathing. Right is the counter top and coffee grinder.

tively. Inside the cabinet Mom kept her cookbooks, measuring cups, and other odds and ends. We hung our coffee and hot chocolate mugs from the bottom of Steve's cabinet.

b) Kitchen Stove: Mom and Dad replaced their original secondhand, white propane stove with this somewhat modern yellow propane stove. An old coffee-pot painted with colorful farm pictures always stood on the near right burner; the pot was never empty and rarely cold. Due to a lack of kitchen space, we stored all our cast-iron pots and pans inside the stove's oven. On the windowsill above the stove, Mom displayed her spices in seven multi-colored antique bottles.

c) Counter: A two-and-a-half-by-five-foot wood kitchen counter with an inset oak cutting board occupied this corner. Beneath the counter was a small food cabinet, a high antique bar stool (acquired from the Wonder Bar in Fairbanks shortly after the great 1967 flood), and a second cabinet where we stored mixing bowls. On top of the kitchen counter we put our flour, salt and sugar jugs. Additionally, on the right-hand side of the counter we kept our utensil jug. This large black crock held Dad's wooden spoons, which doubled as cooking utensils and spanking implements. Mounted on the wall directly above the counter was a homemade cutlery case and two kerosene lamps (acquired from Doc Huffman at Sourdough Lodge).

d) Potato Barrel: This antique wood barrel was bound with iron straps and may have originally been used to transport nails. Dad found it on the West Fork of the Gulkana River while trapping and used it in our house as a potato bin. As a lid for the makeshift bin, Mom placed a white antique chamber pot on top of the barrel. In turn, we used the ceramic pot as a container for our onions. Directly above the potato barrel hung a rolling pin, and above that was a kerosene lamp mounted on the wall.

e) Corner Cabinet: We stored our plates, bowls, and miscellaneous dinnerware in this large corner cabinet (we had matching white dishes with blue trim). On top of the cabinet sat our wooden utensil bin, behind which Dad hid a loaded pistol in case of emergencies. A huge gray crock filled with sugar, a small brown crock filled with popcorn seeds, and a tiny crystal cup (used for toothpicks) rested on the cabinet. Additionally, three wood shelves were mounted on top of the cabinet. On the lowest shelf there was a pewter pitcher, pewter candleholders, matching pewter salt and pepper shakers and a large white platter. On the middle shelf, Mom and Dad kept the candy jar, medicine tin and a huge platter with a New England fisherman's face on it. A large ceramic bowl and a big platter with a turkey painted on it (used on Thanksgiving Day) adorned the very top shelf.

f) Small Cabinet: Dad made this small wood cabinet to store perishable food during the winter months. It was strategically located by the front door to capitalize on the bursts of cold air that poured into the house every time the door was opened. Additionally, the tiny bit of cold air that continuously trickled beneath the front door also helped keep the cabinet and its contents cool. In the summer, we moved our perishables into the icebox on the porch.

Front Door: Dad constructed our medieval-style door from thick spruce planks and reinforced it with tongue and groove cedar. The door was easily four inches thick and made entirely of solid wood. In fact, the door was so thick that Dad could not install a conventional doorknob. Instead, he installed a huge black iron barn latch. Thus, to open our massive front door, we had to press a heavy iron catch with our thumb which lifted an even larger iron bar above a second catch inside the house. Though the door technically did not have a lock, Dad's idea of a doorknob would have discouraged even the most determined thief.

g) Kitchen Sink: Dad built this two-by-four-foot sink out of Sitka spruce in 1969. He waterproofed its square basin with thin copper sheets from Tony Sipary at the Copper Valley Mission School. Mom put a lot of wear and tear on this stout sink by washing countless cast-iron dishes and bathing all of us children in it. The sink's antique construction style and well-worn nature caused many visitors to confuse it with an authentic pioneer's sink.

An antique bowl was placed within the sink's basin, while the matching pitcher stood on the shelf to the right of the basin. We used the area under the sink as a place to stack our dirty plates, store our dirty utensils (in an old Folgers' coffee can) and keep a 5-gallon plastic bucket. We used the bucket as a container to store used dishwater. After dishes were done, we removed a small cork from the copper drain and the dirty water flowed into the bucket below. Once full, we emptied the dishwater at the end of the pissing path. To the left of the kitchen sink was our plastic garbage can whose contents were emptied into the trash barrel and burned daily.

h) Cabinet: In this three-and-a-half-foot-high cabinet we stored our non-cast-iron pots and a few small mixing bowls. Our cookie jar, Premium cracker tin, antique Lipton Tea tin, hot pads, and bread were kept conveniently on top of the cabinet. Two shelves, similar to a short bookcase, rested directly on the cabinet. Mom displayed seven pottery pitchers and three metal milk cans on these shelves. Finally, Dad kept a small pine step stool to the right of this cabinet. Traditionally, we used this little stool to access high places, but it is of historical significance because Dad broke it over Ray's head during a heated argument.

Porch

a) Icebox: An old icebox stood against the eastern wall of the porch. The large metal box was approximately four feet tall and contained three separate compartments. The door on the left opened into its main compartment in which we stored meats, perishables, and leftovers. On the right side of the icebox were two small compartments, one above the other. We kept our bread in the top compartment and a block of ice in the bottom compartment. The ice was a source of coolness for the entire icebox and it kept our food from spoiling. In the winter, nature converted the icebox from a refrigerator to a freezer. Each year, as fall approached and our food began to freeze, we moved it from the icebox to the small kitchen cabinet (see Kitchen, item **f**).

Miscellaneous: The only other item on the porch (accept for the water bin in the summer) was a three-piece, metal mesh basket hanging from the ceiling. During the summer months we stored our fruit and eggs in these connected concentric baskets.

Floor and Ceiling: The wood floor was partly covered by a small piece of indoor-outdoor carpet placed in front of the main door. The ceiling was simply a piece of green, corrugated plastic, similar to that of a greenhouse. The white walls were made of plywood and the windows and door were covered with fine screen. Both the plywood and screen portions of the porch were dotted with hundreds of smashed mosquito carcasses and dried blood spots. The screen was perforated with many holes that were bored by voles, squirrels, dogs and the worst culprits of all, the brothers. Although the porch never impeded insects or animals, it was still functional. In the summer, we left our muddy shoes on the porch and in the winter, it was here that we kicked excess snow off our boots.

214

Appendix B

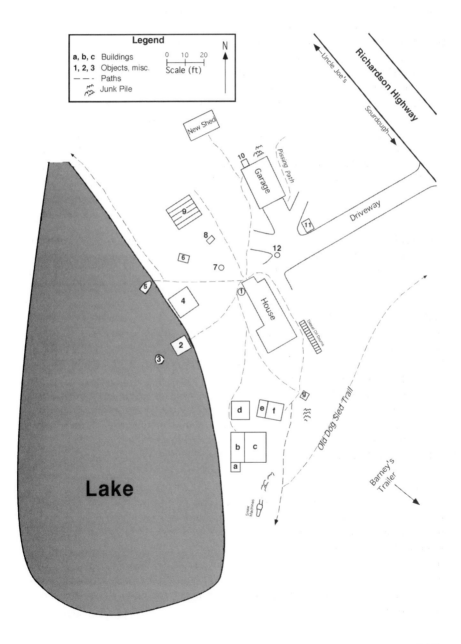

Sheds

Note: In order to qualify as a real Alaskan, a person must have sheds on his property. I am not referring to one or two structures, but instead, numerous sheds dotting the landscape. In addition, the outbuildings cannot be constructed with any forethought or skill; they must be hastily assembled with deficient materials in random locations.

It is an easy task to accurately judge an Alaskan's character by noting the number and conditions of his sheds. For instance, if he has a lot of them, he is a good man and has probably been "up in the country" for a long time (a real sourdough). If he is shedless, or possesses only one or two, or if the sheds look too nice, then this man is most likely a city person (a know-it-all), a suburbanite, or a cheechako (a newcomer to Alaska). The motto Dad lived by was, "The more sheds, the merrier."

My brothers and I would often joke that our family did not own just a house, but an entire village. I cannot remember exactly how many sheds/outbuildings/shacks we had, but I will list them in order and attempt to describe their purpose and function.

a) Kupper's Shed: Mom and Dad named this outbuilding "Kupper's shed" because when Karl was young he demanded that a shed be named after him (Kupper was one of Karl's many nicknames). This particular shed was covered in black tarpaper and was missing a couple of glass windows (due to Steve and Ray smashing them). We stored our winter clothes, ice-skates and old clothes in the small five-by-five-foot shed.

b) Generator Shed: This red-stained eight-by-fifteen-foot building housed the old "Lister" generator, the ringer washer, the propane dryer, and the bulk of our tool collection. Inside, there was a workbench and several shelves, on which Dad stored all his paints, oils and combustibles. Attached to the outside of the generator shed, nearest the lake and Kupper's shed, were several large shelves. Dad stored nails and aluminum sheeting on the shelves and protected them from the elements with a gray tarp.

c) Hobby Shop: Dad constructed this twelve-by-fifteen-foot shed as an area for us to play and store some of our toys. Originally, it was solely intended for Steve and Ray because they were older and required more space and privacy. Steve stored his model trains and Ray kept all his war relics in the hobby shop. When Karl entered junior high school, he demanded a whole corner, but was given a pathetic little desk. He made the best use of his small space by setting up a whiskey still, and thus, his career as a professional alcoholic began at an early age.

d) Screen Shed: This shed was simply a frame (constructed from two-by-fours) enclosed by a screen. Dad intended it to be used as an insect-free environment for hanging and drying moose meat. However, as far back as I can remember, we only used the screen shed as a place to store our extra junk.

There was "the handsome prince" chair, some old wooden army skis, a potbellied stove, snowshoes and several other items that occupied the gravel floor.

e) Ice Shed: This low, squat shed was covered with corrugated steel siding and had a door that opened upwards. The door weighed well over fifty pounds and would occasionally slam down on our heads, backs, or legs. Dad constructed the small building as a place to store ice, which we would cut out of the lake during the winter. The ice shed's floor was completely covered in sawdust to provide insulation from the summer heat (additionally, we separated each block of ice with a layer of sawdust). I only remember one year when we actually cut and stored ice in this shed; all the other years we stored junk inside of it (i.e., the dice box, Jon's broken homemade kites, loads of sawdust, and tons of squirrel debris).

Note: Fire A-1 destroyed all of the above structures.

f) Freezer Shed: This eight-by-nine-foot shed was stained red and sported two windows (one had Plexiglas in it while the opposite window was simply empty). Dad originally built it as a place to store clothes, household goods and as a fort for Steve and Ray. As long as I can remember, I never saw this structure used for anything but as a place to keep the freezer and store all of our meats, breads, and dried foods. The freezer shed (also called "the meat shed") was a squirrel haven and we often found dried mushrooms, grass, and pinecones mixed in with our belongings. The freezer/meat shed was the first outbuilding that Dad constructed, and luckily, it was not harmed during Fire A-1. This historical monument survives not only as a rare example of early Chmielowski architecture, but as a symbol of "the good old days."

g) Outhouse: Dad procured this well-constructed outhouse from the Paxon campground in 1964 and brought it thirty miles down the highway in an upright position in the back of his 1950 Chevy (what an eye-opener for the tourists passing him on the road). This red-stained outhouse was a real beauty compared to the old black one (which stood approximately twenty feet behind the new red outhouse).

The old "bathroom" was completely covered in ripped black tarpaper and was crooked as a snake. Furthermore, the door was barely hanging on its hinges and it smelled horrible. Though none of us kids ever went near the old outhouse, I told some of my visiting friends that the nice red outhouse was a storage shed and the black outhouse was the real bathroom. David Dawson fell for my practical joke and actually used the black death trap and survived. Unfortunately, neither outhouse was harmed by Fire A-1.

Garage: Our red-stained garage was not insulated or heated. Its roof sagged considerably and the squirrels used it as a playground. Potentially, it would have been a decent one-car garage had the floor ever been cleared of junk and tools. Attached to the outside of the garage (nearest the Pissing Path), was a big green wooden chest that contained various useless and obscure tools.

New Shed: After Fire A-1 destroyed our little village of sheds, the teachers in Glennallen collected money and constructed us a new shed (intended as a laundry/generator room). The new ten-by-sixteen-foot shed was very well built, wired for electricity and fireproof. Unfortunately, they delivered the shed months after Dad and I had constructed new and separate laundry and generator sheds (occupying the former generator shed's area and the screen shed's area respectively). As a result, Karl, Jon, and I took over the new shed and spent our entire high school years living in it (both in the summer and winter). Technically, the new shed was fireproof, but somehow it caught on fire (Fire C-3). We extinguished it thanks to the sheetrock paneling.

Barney's Trailer: Barney covered a single-wide trailer with wood shingles and called it a home. Furthermore, he built a medium-sized shed and covered it with black tarpaper. He stored excess clothing and other useless belongings inside of it. He also had an outhouse south of his home and a tool shed behind his house. These eyesores were located directly behind our house and added to the entire village effect. The mysterious Fire B-2 destroyed the house and tool shed, while I personally tore down the black shack.

Final Note: Though Fire A-1 destroyed many of our original sheds, Dad diligently rebuilt a separate generator shed, a laundry shed, a small storage shed (out of the old Polak shower), repaired the meat shed and the teachers in Glennallen built us a new shed. Hence, we maintained our village status.

Dad was proud of his sheds, but I think that he was even more proud of his junk. That is right, the only thing that an old sourdough would consider on a par with large numbers of sheds, is massive heaps of junk. It is a second and equally reliable method by which to judge a true Alaskan's worth; the more junk he has the better man he is.

Things in the Yard

1) Spool Table: A five-foot-diameter wooden spool (from industrial cable or wire) occupied the area on the west side of the porch. We put our dirty pots and pans on it so that the birds, animals, and rain would pre-clean our dishes prior to dishwashing day.

2) Dock: We used the dock as a place to get water, go swimming and as a moor for our small boats. Additionally, when we were very bored, my brothers and I would lie on the dock on our stomachs with our heads hanging over the water. In this manner, we would pass away many summer hours studying the pond life (shrimp, larvae, "wrigglies," "kohlers," mini-clams, beetles, and other types of bugs).

3) Icehole: In the winter, we would chop an icehole a few feet in front of the dock. Typically, the hole was two feet in diameter (big enough for a 5-gallon bucket to fit through) and penetrated anywhere from one to three feet of ice (depending on the month of winter).

4) Platform: Steve constructed this large wood platform to be used as the floor for our eight-man tent. Mom wanted the tent so that she could sit outside and enjoy the lake without having to deal with all the mosquitoes. The tent lasted one season; after that, us boys used the platform as a flat area on which to aim cannons, launch fireworks, and fire rifles.

5) Boats: We stored the twelve-foot-long "Lone Star" steel boat and the eight-foot-long aluminum dinghy on this portion of the lake's embankment. Additionally, we spent many afternoons catching frogs in the deep grass near the boats.

6) Dog House: Dad constructed this deluxe doghouse solely for Brutus. It was well insulated, comfortable and almost fit for a human. As a result, he never used it (except when a bear cornered him inside of it) and preferred Fang's old doghouse (located in the niche between the porch and the kitchen). I think that Brutus liked the ancient doghouse because it was well seasoned and historical (it was passed down through many generations of dogs).

7) Pump: Our antique cast-iron hand pump was mounted on a small, two-foot-diameter spool table. We only used the pump in summer (it drew water out of the lake via a black plastic hose connected to a floating Clorox bottle) because it would quickly freeze in the winter.

8) Fireplace: Mom, Steve, and Ray constructed this fire pit out of rocks from Hogan's Hill which were cemented together by glacier mud from our lake. We had many cookouts in the fireplace and it was here that Jon began his career as a high-speed cook by charring his hot dogs.

9) Log Piles: Rows and rows of two-foot-long logs (from three to fourteen inches in diameter) occupied this area of our front yard. Dad would go wood gettin' in the summer and haul the felled trees to our home in the winter. After drying out over a cold winter, we would then cut the trees into small lengths the following summer and stack them in neat rows. We always had a large supply of wood on hand for our ever hungry wood stove.

10) Tire Shed: Behind the garage was a small four-by-four-foot shed. Dad stored all our tires (studded tires in summer; all-weather tires in winter) in this small shack and so we called it the "tire shed."

11) Gas and Diesel Tanks: Two large cylindrical fuel tanks (each with a 300-gallon capacity) occupied this area of our yard. Dad set them on wood frames about five feet off of the ground so that they were high enough to flow into our gas tanks without a pump. We kept these tanks filled with fuel because it was convenient, economical, and mandatory for our rural lifestyle.

12) Trash Barrels: Two rusty soot-covered 55-gallon steel drums stood next to the driveway. Each day we would burn our kitchen trash in the drums and when they both became full we would haul them into the forest and empty their contents.

Miscellaneous: Numerous other oddities, apparatuses, and items inundated different portions of our yard. To name just a few, we had: a basketball hoop, strawberry patch, tire swing, trapeze, porch swing, bird houses, governmental weather bureau equipment, picnic table, saw horses, two sand boxes, numerous 55-gallon diesel drums, wood and metal piles and random heaps of useless junk (a typical yard in the Alaskan bush).

Appendix C
Time Line

1930   Dad is born on October 5 in Mahanoy City, Pennsylvania.

1939   Mom is born on November 27 in Philadelphia, Pennsylvania.

1942   Dad moves to Philadelphia, Pennsylvania.

1947   Dad leaves Ben Franklin High School after tenth grade and works for a year.

1948   Dad enters the army (by forging his mother's signature) and is stationed at Ft. Dix, New Jersey, and later at Ft. Warren, Boston.

1950   Dad is stationed at Ft. Greely in the Alaskan Territory. Participates in the army's arctic research program.

1951   A large buffalo rams Dad's army truck.

1952   After serving a four-year term, Dad is honorably discharged from the army. Dad leaves Ft. Greely and goes home to Philadelphia.

1953   Dad meets Mom for the first time.

1954   Dad rejoins the army and is stationed at the DMZ (demilitarized zone) in Korea.

1956   After seventeen months in Korea, Dad is stationed in Little Ferry, New Jersey.

1957   Dad is honorably discharged from the army. Mom graduates from Notre Dame High School and attends St. Joe's evening division college in Philly.

1959   Mom works in payroll for WCAU-CBS in Philly. Mom and Dad go on a couple of dates in Cape May, New Jersey. Alaska becomes a state.

1960   Dad, Uncle Joe, and Uncle Lenny drive from Philadelphia to Alaska in a one-ton truck. Upon arriving they homestead five acres of land on the Richardson Highway. The three brothers build a small log cabin and live a subsistence lifestyle. Mom still lives in Philly and is now working for Botany 500.

1961   Dad's mother, Nana, visits Alaska for the first time.

1962   On March 18, Mom and her brother, Barney, arrive in Alaska. A month later Mom marries Dad (April 28). They tear down and rebuild a two-room construction shed for their home. This edifice was from Greene's Construction, which was left after the paving of the old Richardson trail.

1963   Barney joins the army and leaves Alaska. On January 20, Steve is born in the Glennallen hospital. President Kennedy is assassinated but no one cares; Alaska is isolated and the Lower 48 forgotten.

1964   Ray is born on March 20. One week later the Great Alaskan Earthquake (9.2 magnitude, and four minutes' duration) completely destroys the towns of Valdez and Seward. The Chmielowski family and home weather the disaster just fine.

1965   Hunting and trapping barely provide adequate income for the family. Nana visits Alaska for the second time.

1967   The historical Fairbanks flood occurs. Dad joins the laborers' union for steady employment. The family moves into the "Bingedy-Bangedy" hippie school bus (named after an old children's book from Golden Press: *The Bingedy-Bangedy School Bus*) in order to accompany Dad during his work season.

1968   In August, Mom (with Steve and Ray) flies to Philadelphia to attend her father's funeral. Karl is born on November 17.

1969   Steve and Ray start home school.

1970   Uncle Lenny marries Cathy, leaves the original cabin and moves to Fairbanks. Construction on the trans-Alaska pipeline begins at Livengood near the Arctic Circle. Dad is employed as a well-paid laborer on the pipeline until 1976.

1971   Steve and Ray board at Gakona Lodge in order to attend elementary school. Later in the year, they board with the Sipary family to attend Glennallen Elementary School.

1972   Jon is born on January 4.

1973   The Watergate scandal occurs in Washington, D.C., and President Nixon resigns. I am born on September 30.

1974   Aunt Josie moves from Philadelphia to Alaska.

1975   Cousin Richie moves from Philadelphia to Alaska in order to work on the pipeline.

1976   Uncle Ray retires from the air force and moves to Alaska. Dad purchases a brand-new wood stove, freezer, and generator prior to the large pipeline lay-offs.

1977   Steve, Ray, and Karl leave the state and visit our relatives in Philadelphia.

1978   I start kindergarten and begin my wrestling career at Gakona Elementary School. Jon starts first grade.

1979   Uncle Joe marries Ruth and moves to Fairbanks. The original cabin is now empty and used only occasionally as a weekend getaway.

1980   Cousin George moves from Philadelphia to Southeast Alaska. Money is scarce; Mom begins working as a bilingual teacher's aide for Native students at Gakona Elementary School. Steve and Ray join the army reserves. The first State Permanent Fund dividend checks for $1000 are distributed to each Alaskan resident.

1982   Steve and Ray graduate from Glennallen High School, move to Anchorage and work while remaining active in the reserves.

1983   Mom, Karl, Jon, and I transfer from Gakona School to Glennallen School. We spend the next nine years commuting forty miles one way to Glennallen School.

1984   Dad retires from the laborers' union. Steve joins the air force (becomes
-1985   a bomb disposal person) and marries Corry. Ray also joins the air force (becomes an MP) and marries Tammy. I leave Alaska for the first time and visit my best friend David Dawson in southern Missouri.

1986   During the summer I attend the University of Denver's summer science program. The space shuttle Challenger explodes.

1987   Karl graduates from Glennallen High School and goes to California for work. I graduate from junior high.

1988   While wrestling my freshman year of high school, I wrestle two female athletes in the regional tournament. In the summer, I attend the University of Pennsylvania's summer science program.

1989   I spend the summer studying calculus and biology at the University of Alaska, Anchorage (UAA).

1990   Jon graduates from Glennallen High School with honors and attends UAA. I teach myself Calculus II and attend UAA in the summer.

1991   My senior year of high school I take third place in state championship wrestling, complete my second term as school president, take geology through the community college, and graduate valedictorian. Though accepted and offered scholarships at Princeton, University of Pennsylvania, Brandeis, Harvey Mudd, and Annapolis, due to finances, I half-heartedly choose to attend West Point. I leave for the academy in June.

1991   I am a plebe in the United States Military Academy at West Point, New York. I continue to date my high school sweetheart who lives in Alaska.

1992   To the chagrin of many West Point cadets, Clinton becomes our Commander in Chief. Over the Christmas holidays, Sourdough Lodge (built in 1903 and at this time the oldest operating lodge in Alaska) burns to the ground. The business that gave name to our hamlet disappears. The Chmielowski brothers' original cabin and our home are now the first- and second-oldest establishments in the Sourdough area.

1993   In September, I leave West Point and work laying tile in Philadelphia with my cousin Tony. Mom leaves Alaska for the first time in twenty-five years in order to visit Philadelphia.

1994   I attend Rutgers College in New Brunswick, New Jersey. I graduate as
-1996   a double major in physics and geology.

1996   Dad leaves Alaska for the first time in thirty-six years. He flies on a jet airplane for the first time in his life, and tours Las Vegas ("a city of sinners") and Death Valley, California ("a really neat place") with Steve and Karl. I attend the University of Arizona in Tucson as a research assistant in global geophysics.

1997   I work in the Bolivian Andes studying earthquakes and climb three
-1998   separate mountains, each approximately 20,000 feet high.

1998   I continue to rock-climb in Arizona, qualify for my scuba-diving license,
-2001   learn to surf in California, experience Mardi Gras in New Orleans, vacation in Jamaica during spring break, receive my MS in Geophysics, move to Houston to visit Jessie, earn my skydiving license, travel to Europe for three months, take up snowboarding, and begin working as a geophysicist for a large international corporation in Anchorage, Alaska.

Where are They Now?

Mom & Dad: In 1996, after living in the bush for thirty-six years, Mom and Dad moved to Wasilla for medical purposes. Hunting, trapping, fishing, and working in a harsh environment for extended amounts of time tends to wear down a human body. Mom and Dad are happy with the constant electricity, showers (sometimes Dad takes two per day just because he can) and mild winters. "Hell, we only had to plug in the car one time last winter. The coldest it ever got was twenty-five below." Thus, Mom and Dad are living it up in their first normal house since leaving Philadelphia nearly four decades ago.

1997: The Chmielowski brothers suburbanized for one night at Steve's wedding. This was the first, last, and only time the brothers wore a tux. Left to right: Karl, Ray, Steve, Jon, and Joe.

Steve: Steve is happily married to Katrina Church (a local from Copper Center) and has a newborn son, Gerek. He owns a nice home in Copper Center and is a heavy equipment operator for the state's Department of Transportation. I guess all those days playing with Tonka and King Size trucks in the gravel pit finally paid off for old Revo.

Ray: Military service in Guam and Utah launched Ray's career as a police officer for the city of Wasilla. Additionally, he is the police force's firearms instructor and is highly qualified for SCUBA diving recovery missions. Ray enjoys working on his home, firing his civil war cannon and playing with his dog. I am pleased to say that he rarely has migraine headaches, is extremely generous and is a very pleasant person. Ray has two daughters, Jennifer and Dana.

Karl: Currently a foreman of the drilling and blasting team for the Whittier tunnel project, Karl resides in Anchorage and is doing very well. After graduating from high school he lived in California for a number of years before returning to Alaska. Once back in the state, he joined the laborers' union as an apprentice rock driller and eventually became certified in demolition. Karl always loved fire and explosions and thus, he enjoys his work like none other. Contrary to his laziness as a child, Karl works harder than anyone I know (seven-day work weeks and sixty to eighty hours per week are the norm). Additionally, Karl is no longer overweight, angry, bossy, or evil (otherwise he wouldn't be married to his wife, Laquita). It just goes to show that sometimes, just sometimes, people really do change.

Jon: Jonny-Cakes worked for nearly eight years as an airplane engine mechanic but recently joined the laborer's union for financial gain and medical benefits. He is happily married to Heidi Pedersen (a local who grew up five miles south of Sourdough Lodge) and has a daughter, Emily, and a son, Steven. Jon owns a lovely home in Anchorage but frequently spends weekends at Sourdough with his family. The lonesome polecat is not only still "in his own world," but just as good-hearted as always.

Joe: After attending the United States Military Academy at West Point for two and a half years, I graduated from Rutgers University, New Jersey with a BA in physics and a BS in geology. I then attended graduate school at the University of Arizona, Tucson where I received an MS in geophysics. I am currently a geophysicist for a large corporation in Anchorage, Alaska. My head is no longer shaved like a cue ball and my ribs do not visibly protrude. Finally, I am the least finicky eater out of all the boys (including Dad), but unfortunately, I have lost my superhuman pissing ability.

The Uncles: After leaving the original cabin, Uncle Joe and Uncle Lenny both moved to Fairbanks and joined the laborers' union. Uncle Joe married Ruth, eventually retired from the union and is currently living in Wasilla. Uncle Lenny married Cathy, retired from the union and currently lives in Juneau where he operates a charter fishing boat and bed and breakfast. After retiring from the air force, Uncle Ray worked for the laborer's union for a number of years, retired from it and lived with Kathleen in Anchorage until his death in 1997. After being discharged from the army, Uncle Barney settled in Fairbanks, raised a family and is currently self-employed.

1996: Left to right, Uncle Joe, Uncle Ray, Dad, and Uncle Lenny.